The Sermon on the Mount: Its Old Testament Roots

Roland H. Worth, Jr.

PAULIST PRESS
New York / Mahwah, N.J.

Scripture verses used in this book came from both the *New King James Version* as well as the *New Revised Standard Version* of the Bible.

Cover design by Cindy Dunne

Library of Congress Cataloging-in-Publication Data

Worth, Roland H., 1943–
    The Sermon on the mount : its Old Testament roots / by Roland H. Worth.
        p. cm.
    Includes bibliographical references and index.
    ISBN 0-8091-3746-1 (alk. paper)
    1. Sermon on the mount—Criticism, interpretation, etc. 2. Bible. N.T. Matthew V–VII—Relation to the Old Testament. 3. Bible. O.T.—Relation to Matthew V–VII. I. Title.
BT380.2.W67   1997
226.9′06—dc21   97-30842
                                                                       CIP

Published by Paulist Press
997 Macarthur Boulevard
Mahwah, New Jersey 07430

Printed and bound in the United States of America

Contents

SECTION TWO:
RELATIVELY OBVIOUS OLD
TESTAMENT PARALLELS

SECTION THREE:
OLD TESTAMENT ROOTS OF
JESUS' MORE "RADICAL" TEACHING

dedicated to
MICHAEL ALEXANDER WORTH
(age 9 months)
May God protect you through this strange
and mysterious thing we call life

INTRODUCTORY MATTERS

1

The Linguistic Setting of Jesus and His Teaching

In Jesus' day at least four languages were spoken in Jewish Palestine: Latin, Hebrew, Greek, and Aramaic.[1] Of these Jesus spoke at least two and possibly three. We read of his reading the Hebrew Isaiah scroll in the synagogue service on the Sabbath day (Lk. 4:17–21).[2] The Dead Sea Scrolls have far more Hebrew language documents than Aramaic, which argues that however less popular Hebrew may have been as a spoken tongue, it certainly retained a key role as the language of *written religious discourse.*[3] Jesus' ability to read Hebrew (and presumably write it) is in accord with this evidence.[4]

Jesus was raised in Nazareth, an area where the Gentile influence was so great that it was called "Galilee of the Gentiles" (Mt. 4:15). Although one would anticipate the presence of the Greek language throughout the land, one was more likely to have a knowledge of it in Galilee than elsewhere—certainly not less likely.[5] Although Greek was clearly winning over Aramaic in popularity from A.D. 200 on,[6] it must be remembered that this was

1

after the catastrophic defeat of the Jews in two massive rebellions against Rome. After each of these (especially the second) Rome was grimly determined to maximize its culture and influence in the region. Jesus spoke, without translators stated or implied, with both Pilate (Mk. 15:1–5; Jn. 18:33–37) and a centurion (Mt. 8:5–13). Since the natural language of both was probably Greek, it may well be that he spoke with them in that tongue.

Aramaic was the dominant language in first-century Palestine,[7] and this by itself would make us expect that it was the tongue most preferred by Jesus. Certainly he used it in at least some private conversation, for his words to Jairus' little girl whom he raised from the dead are preserved in Aramaic (Mk. 5:41). More relevant is his use of Aramaic on the cross (Mk. 15:34) and in his agony in the Garden of Gethsemane prior to his betrayal (Mk. 14:36). During such high-intensity moments, one is most likely to revert to the language in which one is most comfortable.[8]

Hence it is most likely that Jesus spoke the Sermon on the Mount in Aramaic and that what has been preserved is a translation of it. Of course, the possibility is not excluded that in a multi-language society he spoke elements of the Sermon in both Aramaic and Greek, though if he did so, one would expect it to have grown out of the circumstances under which the Sermon was delivered. When we run together the verses leading into the Sermon (Mt. 4:25–5:2), the appropriateness of a Greek language component is enhanced: "And *great multitudes* followed Him—from Galilee, and from *Decapolis,* Jerusalem, Judea, and beyond the Jordan. And seeing the *multitudes,* He went up on a mountain, and when He was seated His disciples came to Him"(our emphasis). Not only were the crowds large (cf. after the end of the Sermon, 8:1), but it included components from the Greek cities of the Decapolis. In such a context, providing a sermon in both languages would have been highly appropriate though not necessarily a requirement.[9]

Be that as it may, we do not have an early Aramaic Matthew that would provide us with possible additional illumination of Christ's teaching above and beyond that provided by the Greek text itself.[10] Essentially, one must work from an assumption of the exact nature of the Aramaic wording,[11] but even so, several theories of the likely Aramaic original are of interest and will be introduced where appropriate.

Various theories of contemporary criticism have an impact on the exegesis of the existing scriptural text as well. For example, textual criticism raises the question of whether "without a cause" in Jesus' rebuke of anger (Mt. 5:22) is sufficiently documented to deserve a place within the accepted text. Whichever way one decides, the question has an obvious impact on how one interprets the thrust of Jesus' teaching.

Much of modern biblical criticism attempts to "get behind" the text and determine whether it matches what Jesus "really" said or whether he said it at all. In the case of the Antitheses, a substantial reworking of a historical core is assumed by such individuals. The conflict between church and synagogue certainly intensified the gap between the two groups. Hence, if the early church (or, more correctly, the early writers and redactors of the text) did modify the Antitheses, the fervor of the conflict would surely have magnified the differences rather than minimized them. Hence, if we find in the "completed" Matthew the firm roots in the Torah and the Prophets that we hypothesize, then a similar identity certainly existed in the teachings of the "historical Jesus" as well. Hence, whether we affirm the accuracy of the Matthean version or are skeptical of its account, we come to much the same conclusion regarding the attitude of Jesus toward the Old Testament.

However one may evaluate these intellectual efforts at "reconstruction" (and the present author confesses to major skepticism), we are primarily concerned here with the meaning of the text in the form that we have it today. With that task before us, such matters need only be considered when a direct impact on the fundamental meaning is involved, as in the case of the questioned genuineness of the exception clause in Jesus' discussion of divorce (Mt. 5:32).[12]

Another source of information that will be used to determine whether Jesus' teaching was compatible with the Prophets and the Torah will be whether similar opinions existed in contemporary and later Jewish writers and rabbis. Throughout this volume we will be introducing such cases of possible and probable parallelism. In the cases of Josephus and Philo, we find educated and well-versed Jewish individuals who lived in the same century as the Lord, as we do in the case of a few of the rabbis we cite. The rabbinical writers have been preserved through the Talmud. Overall, though, the contents of the Talmud were compiled over a period of centuries, and caution must therefore be taken in interpreting its contents as reflective of first century conditions.[13]

Furthermore, Jesus speaks in the Antitheses in terms of personal authority ("but I say to you"), whereas the Talmud discuss matters in terms of prior rabbinic precedents for one's exegesis.[14] In some of the longer extracts of rabbis in this volume, this trait will be obvious; in cases where the quotation is of only the most parallel thought, one will often be unaware of this normal broader setting.[15]

A further complication arises in regard to the relationship between rabbinical and Pharisaic opinion: to what degree does the *rabbinic* opinion of the following centuries reflect the *Pharisaic* opinion of the first century? The traditional assumption has been that one evolved into the other and that there is a close relationship between the two. The degree to which this was actually the case has only begun to be analyzed in recent decades.[16]

Hence, though we may vindicate from the Talmud the congeniality of certain of the antitheses with Jesus' teaching, we can not be certain whether these are cases of his walking in a popular (or, at least, minority) stream of interpretation. Anthony J. Saldarini points out that after the destruction of the temple, considerable divergencies existed within Judaism. Indeed, it took a century or two "before talmudic Judaism became normative for all diaspora Jewish communities."[17] It seems both reasonable in itself and compatible with the conflicting interpretations known to have existed between the Essenes, Pharisees, and Sadducees to argue that similar disagreements existed even in Jesus' lifetime as well.

Hence, like later Talmudic writers, Jesus' contemporaries would have found areas of both agreement and disagreement. The degree to which Jesus himself created or encouraged others to adopt these viewpoints further complicates the picture. Certainly many who found agreement on a number of points never left orthodox Judaism behind, and Jesus may well have had a significant role in creating the very ways of thinking later generations have cited as parallelisms. Either way, the point of interest is the compatibility of Jesus' contrasts with what was conceived of as non-Christian, even anti-Christian Judaism of the early centuries.

Nor should we fall into the mistake of overstating the *amount* of compatibility. As fascinating as the *fact* of similarity, is the reality that particular rabbis or noncanonical sources will embrace one particular teaching but not a *general* concurrence with them. They embrace this or that interpretation of Torah that Jesus advocated, but not the general, overall pattern. Hence we typically find sporadic espousal rather than a general embracing of his assertions. This may be the result of the way the Talmud was compiled by later generations, or it may reflect that many Jews would have found isolated points of agreement rather than an overall agreement.

Finally, as interesting as the subject of rabbinic/Jewish-Jesus parallels is, in one very real sense this begs the question: Even where there are parallels, that does not necessarily prove that either side faithfully represented Torah teaching. Hence the need for careful analysis of the Old Testament texts as well, which will represent the central thrust of this study.

NOTES

[1]For a survey of the evidence see Joseph A. Fitzmyer, "The Languages of Palestine in the First Century A.D.," in Joseph A. Fitzmyer, *A Wandering Aramean: Collected Aramaic Essays* (Missoula, Mont.: Scholars Press, 1979), 29–56.

[2]The custom, in its known form, was to read the Hebrew first and then read or spontaneously render the Aramaic targum (translation/paraphrase). "The Aramaic version was declaimed after each individual verse of the Penteuchal reading, and after every three verses of the Prophetic reading, reflecting the greater juridical and religious import attached

to the former" (Etan Levine, *The Aramaic Version of the Bible: Contents and Context* [Berlin: Walter de Gruyter, 1983], 11). The lack of such a practice being referred to in this text would suggest that either this custom was so taken for granted that elaboration was not required or that in certain synagogues of this period such an Aramaic rendering was not yet considered essential.

[3]Cf. Matthew Black, *An Aramacic Approach to the Gospels and Acts,* 3rd ed. (Oxford: Clarendon, 1967), 47.

[4]Max Wilcox summarizes some of the evidence that Hebrew-language teaching may underlie certain teaching and phrases found in the gospel accounts ("The Aramaic Background of the New Testament," in *The Aramaic Bible: Targums in Their Historical Context,* ed. D. R. G. Beattie and M. J. McNamara [Sheffield, England: JSOT Press, 1994], 365).

[5]For a discussion of the probability that Jesus spoke Greek—but with a necessary cautionary note—see Fitzmyer, "The Languages of Palestine," 37–38. On the possible impact of Greek thought, culture, and language not so much on Palestine in general, but on Galilee in particular, see Bernard J. Lee, *The Galilean Jewishness of Jesus: Retrieving the Jewish Origins of Christianity* (New York: A Stimulus Book/Paulist Press, 1988), 58–66. On the everyday impact of Galilean Gentile society on Jewry, see also Sean Freyne, *Galilee, Jesus and the Gospels: Literary Approaches and Historical Investigations* (Philadelphia: Fortress, 1988), 167–75.

[6]Fitzmyer, "Languages of Palestine," 38.

[7]Black, 47, and Joseph A. Fitzmyer, "The Study of the Aramaic Background of the New Testament" in Joseph A. Fitzmyer, *A Wandering Aramean: Collected Essays* (Missoula, Mont.: Scholars Press, 1979), 7. On the use of Aramaic among the Jews of Palestine also see Martin McNamara, *Targum and Testament: Aramaic Paraphrases of the Hebrew Bible—A Light on the New Testament* (Grand Rapids: Eerdmans, 1972), 54–62.

[8]On the theme of reverting to one's preferred language when under stress, see Wilcox, 364.

[9]On the scenario of Jesus giving certain of his teachings in Greek and others in Aramaic, see John Drane, *Son of Man: A New Life of Christ* (Grand Rapids: Eerdmans, 1993), 120.

[10]Most assume an Aramaic original of none of the gospel accounts, others of Matthew alone, yet others of all four. In the latter category was C. C. Torrey, who demonstrated his zeal for the theory by translating all four accounts into their presumed original Aramaic form. The ability to do this, of course, "is in reality no proof of the Aramaic substratum itself" (Fitzmyer, "Aramaic Background," 10). Torrey died in 1956. For a more recent presentation of this approach see Frank Zimmermann, *The Aramaic Origin of the Four Gospels* (New York: KTAV, 1979). Of course, if one is convinced that much or most of Jesus' teaching was in Aramaic, there is the very real question of whether it was rendered into Greek directly by the authors of the four gospel accounts or by the composers of whatever earlier sources these authors may have used.

[11]A good example of the need for caution can be found in the discussion concerning the original language reading of Jesus' surprising admonition to a would-be follower to "let the dead bury their own dead" (Lk. 9:60). F. Perles, in the late teens of the twentieth century, argued that this was a mistranslation of an Aramaic original, that read, "Leave the dead to their dead-burier." Decades later, Matthew Black concurred in the mistranslation hypothesis but argued for a substantially different Aramaic, which actually read, "Let the waverers bury their dead." For a discussion of these and other interpretations, see Joseph A. Fitzmyer, *Luke,* in the *Anchor Bible* series (Garden City, N.Y.: Doubleday, 1981; 1982 printing), 835–836.

[12]Unfortunately much of modern "critical" analysis of the text is fundamentally antithetical to exegesis. The more extreme critics seem to spend their careers seeking reasons to deny the historical Jesus a varying (but always substantial, often overwhelming) amount of the gospel text. Indeed, by the time they are through, precious little is usually left to work

with. In contrast, exegesis, by and large, requires the existence of an established and reliable text from which to work: If there is nothing genuine left to examine, there is nothing historical left to interpret.

[13]Because its contents come from a multicentury period, Bruce D. Chilton argues, "[W]hat justification is there for reading the Talmud's picture of devotion to Torah back into the efforts of Jews in the first century to maintain their faith in the face of national dissolution? No historian can lightly assume that the attitudes and movements of a period are to be understood by referring to documents which postdate that period by some five centuries" (*A Galilean Rabbi and His Bible: Jesus' Use of the Interpreted Scripture of His Time* [Wilmington, Del.: Michael Glazier, 1984], 23). On the need for caution in using the Talmud to illustrate first-century Jewish opinion, see also Calvin J. Roetzel, *The World That Shaped the New Testament* (Atlanta: John Knox, 1985), 27–28.

[14]Not that Jesus was unwilling to use Scripture to vindicate his positions. The narratives of the days of wilderness temptation and the discussion of divorce in Matthew 19 exhibit his clear willingness to do battle on this ground. But in the context of the Antithesis, Jesus is making it a matter of his own authority versus that of others. When we contrast this with his willingness in other contexts to pivot his argument on Scripture, we find additional evidence that Jesus' target in the Antithesis is not the Old Testament itself, but the interpretation of it.

[15]On this matter of the nature of rabbinic deduction versus Jesus' presenting his interpretation as standing on its own inherent authority, see Richard E. Menninger, *Israel and the Church in the Gospel of Matthew* (New York: Peter Lang, 1994), p. 131, n. 73. The rabbis also cited Scripture, but often their fanciful pleading finds them falling into the same pit endangering modern "proof-texting." Needing a passage to prove a point, one may stretch its point beyond its reasonable contextual meaning. Perhaps in a narrative setting this tendency would not be

as noticeable, but when the citations are run together as tightly as they are in the Talmud, the defect is extremely conspicuous.

[16]Daniel J. Harrington, "The Jewishness of Jesus: Facing Some Problems," in *Jesus' Jewishness: Exploring the Place of Jesus Within Early Judaism,* ed. James H. Charlesworth (New York: American Interfaith Institute, 1991), 129.

[17]Anthony J. Saldarini, "The Gospel of Matthew and Jewish-Christian Conflict," in *Social History of the Matthean Community: Cross-Disciplinary Approaches,* ed. David L. Balch (Minneapolis: Fortress, 1991), 49.

2

Pattern of Interpreting
the Antitheses

Relationship of the Antitheses to the Old Testament

Since we will be examining the Antitheses in detail, an appropriate beginning point would be to present the text in full so that the reader can grasp the overall flow of Jesus' argumentation. The text is divided into sections labeled with the same headings as the chapter titles in this book. The two divisions discussing non-retaliation and related issues actually constitute a single antithesis but, for purposes of analysis, it was more convenient to separate it into two sections, utilizing (as throughout this volume) the rendition of the New King James Version. For comparison purposes we have also included a second translation, in brackets—that of the New Revised Standard Version.

Luke (6:17-49) includes an account of the Sermon on the Mount—or of a sermon whose contents were very similar. These are presented under the heading *Lucan*

Sermon. Under the label *Lucan Parallel* we have presented those texts where similar teaching is found but within a different context.

Interpreting the Antitheses in Context
(Matthew 5:17–20)

Do not think that I came to destroy the Law or the Prophets. I did not come to destroy but to fulfill.

For assuredly, I say to you, till heaven and earth pass away, one jot or one tittle will by no means pass from the law till all is fulfilled.

Whoever therefore breaks one of the least of these commandments, and teaches men so, shall be called least in the kingdom of heaven; but whoever does and teaches them, he shall be called great in the kingdom of heaven.

For I say to you, that unless your righteousness exceeds the righteousness of the scribes and Pharisees, you will by no means enter the kingdom of heaven. (NKJV)

[Do not think that I have come to abolish the law or the prophets; I have come not to abolish but to fulfill.

For truly I tell you, until heaven and earth pass away, not one letter, not one stroke of a letter, will pass from the law until all is accomplished.

Therefore, whoever breaks one of the least of these commandments, and teaches others to do the same, will be called least in the kingdom of heaven; but whoever does them and teaches them will be called great in the kingdom of of heaven.

For I tell you, unless your righteousness exceeds that of the scribes and Pharisees, you will never enter the kingdom of heaven. (NRSV)]

Lucan Parallel (Luke 16:17)

And it is easier for heaven and earth to pass away than for one tittle of the law to fail. (NKJV)

[But it is easier for heaven and earth to pass away, than for one stroke of a letter in the law to be dropped. (NRSV)]

Murder and Anger (Matthew 5:21–26)

You have heard that it was said to those of old, "You shall not murder," and whoever murders will be in danger of the judgment.

But I say to you that whoever is angry with his brother without a cause shall be in danger of the judgment. And whoever says to his brother, "Raca!" shall be in danger of the council. But whoever says, "You fool!" shall be in danger of hell fire.

Therefore if you bring your gift to the altar, and there remember that your brother has something against you,

leave your gift there before the altar, and go your way. First be reconciled to your brother, and then come and offer your gift.

Agree with your adversary quickly, while you are on the way with him, lest your adversary deliver you to the judge, the judge hand you over to the officer, and you be thrown into prison.

Assuredly, I say to you, you will by no means get out of there till you have paid the last penny. (NKJV)

[You have heard that it was said to those of ancient times, "You shall not murder"; and "whoever murders shall be liable to judgment."

But I say to you that if you are angry with a brother or sister, you will be liable to judgment; and if you insult a brother or sister, you will be liable to the council; and if you say, "You fool," you will be liable to the hell of fire.

So when you are offering your gift at the altar, if you remember that your brother or sister has something against you,

leave your gift there before the altar and go; first be reconciled to your brother or sister, and then come and offer your gift.

Come to terms quickly with your accuser while you are on the way to court with him, or your accuser may hand you over to the judge, and the judge to the guard, and you will be thrown into prison.

Truly I tell you, you will never get out until you have paid the last penny. (NRSV)]

Lucan Parallel (Luke 12:57–59)

Yes, and why, even of yourselves, do you not judge what is right?

When you go with your adversary to the magistrate, make every effort along the way to settle with him, lest he drag you to the judge, the judge deliver you to the officer, and the officer throw you into prison.

I tell you, you shall not depart from there till you have paid the very last mite. (NKJV)

[And why do you not judge for yourselves what is right?

Thus, when you go with your accuser before a magistrate, on the way make an effort to settle the case, or you may be dragged before the judge, and the judge hand you over to the officer, and the officer throw you in prison.

I tell you, you will never get out until you have paid the very last penny. (NRSV)]

Adultery and Lust (Matthew 5:27–30)

You have heard that it was said to those of old, "You shall not commit adultery."

But I say to you that whoever looks at a woman to lust for her has already committed adultery with her in his heart.

And if your right eye causes you to sin, pluck it out and cast it from you; for it is more profitable for you that one of your members perish, than for your whole body to be cast into hell.

And if your right hand causes you to sin, cut it off and cast it from you; for it is more profitable for you that one of your members perish, than for your whole body to be cast into hell. (NKJV)

[You have heard that it was said, "You shall not commit adultery."

But I say to you that everyone who looks at a woman with lust has already committed adultery with her in his heart.

If your right eye causes you to sin, tear it out and throw it away; it is better for you to lose one of your members than for your whole body to be thrown into hell.

And if your right hand causes you to sin, cut it off and throw it away; it is better for you to lose one of your members than for your whole body to go into hell. (NRSV)]

Divorce (Matthew 5:31–32)

Furthermore it has been said, "Whoever divorces his wife let him give her a certificate of divorce."

But I say to you that whoever divorces his wife for any reason except sexual immorality causes her to commit adultery; and whoever marries a woman who is divorced commits adultery.

[It was also said, "Whoever divorces his wife, let him give her a certificate of divorce."

But I say to you that anyone who divorces his wife, except on the ground of unchastity, causes her to commit adultery; and whoever married a divorced woman committed adultery. (NRSV)]

Lucan Parallel (Luke 16:18)

Whoever divorces his wife and marries another commits adultery; and whoever marries her who is divorced from her husband commits adultery. (NKJV)

[Anyone who divorces his wife and marries another commits adultery; and whoever marries a woman divorced from her husband commits adultery. (NRSV)]

Oaths and Swearing (Matthew 5:33–37)

Again you have heard that it was said to those of old, "You shall not swear falsely, but shall perform your oaths to the Lord."

But I say to you, do not swear at all: neither by heaven, for it is God's throne;

nor by the earth, for it is His footstool; nor by Jerusalem, for it is the city of the great King.

nor shall you swear by your head, because you cannot make one hair white or black.

But let your "Yes" be "Yes," and your "No," "No." For whatever is more than these is from the evil one. (NKJV)

[Again, you have heard that it was said to those of ancient times, "You shall not swear falsely, but carry out the vows you have made to the Lord."

But I say to you, Do not swear at all, either by heaven, for it is the throne of God.

Or by the earth, for it is his footstool, or by Jerusalem, for it is the city of the great King.

And do not swear by your head, for you cannot make one hair white or black.

Let your word be "Yes, Yes" or "No, No"; anything more than this comes from the evil one. (NRSV)]

Nonviolence (Matthew 5:38–39)

You have heard that it was said, "An eye for an eye and a tooth for a tooth."

But I tell you not to resist an evil person. But whoever slaps you on your right cheek, turn the other to him also. (NKJV)

[You have heard that it was said, "An eye for an eye and a tooth for a tooth."

But I say to you, Do not resist an evildoer. But if anyone strikes you on the right cheek, turn the other also. (NRSV)]

Lucan Sermon (Luke 6:29a)

To him who strikes you on the one cheek, offer the other also…. (NKJV)

[If anyone strikes you on the cheek, offer the other also…. (NRSV)]

Loaning, Compulsion, and Unfair Law Courts (Matthew 5:40–42)

If anyone wants to sue you and take away your tunic, let him have your cloak also.

And whoever compels you to go one mile, go with him two.

Give to him who asks you, and from him who wants to borrow from you do not turn away. (NKJV)

[And if anyone wants to sue you and take your coat, give your cloak as well;

And if anyone forces you to go one mile, go also the second mile.

Give to everyone who begs from you, and do not refuse anyone who wants to borrow from you. (NRSV)]

Lucan Sermon (Luke 6:29b–30)

…And from him who takes away your cloak, do not withhold your tunic either.

Give to everyone who asks of you. And from him who takes away your goods do not ask them back. (NKJV)

[…And from anyone who takes away your coat do not withhold even your shirt.

Give to everyone who begs from you; and if anyone takes away your goods, do not ask for them again. (NRSV)]

Love and Hate (Matthew 5:43–48)

You have heard that it was said, You shall love your neighbor and hate your enemy.

But I say to you, love your enemies, bless those who curse you, do good to those who hate you, and pray for those who spitefully use you and persecute you,

That you may be sons of your Father in heaven; for He makes His sun rise on the evil and on the good, and sends rain on the just and on the unjust.

For if you love those who love you, what reward have you? Do not even the tax collectors do the same?

And if you greet your brethren only, what do you more than others? Do not even the tax collectors do so?

Therefore you shall be perfect, just as your Father in heaven is perfect. (NKJV)

[You have heard that it was said, "You shall love your neighbor and hate your enemy."

But I say to you, Love your enemies and pray for those who persecute you,

so that you may be children of your Father in heaven; for he makes his sun rise on the evil and on the good, and sends rain on the righteous and on the unrighteous.

For if you love those who love you, what reward do you have? Do not even the tax collectors do the same?

And if you greet only your brothers and sisters, what more are you doing than others? Do not even the Gentiles do the same?

Be perfect, therefore, as your heavenly Father is perfect. (NRSV).]

Lucan Sermon (Luke 6:27–28, 31–36).

But I say to you who hear: Love your enemies, do good to those who hate you.

Bless those who curse you, and pray for those who spitefully use you.

And just as you want men to do to you, you also do to them likewise.

But if you love those who love you, what credit is that to you? For even sinners love those who love them.

And if you do good to those who do good to you, what credit is that to you? For even sinners do the same.

And if you lend to those from whom you hope to receive back, what credit is that to you? For even sinners lend to sinners to receive as much back.

But love your enemies, do good, and lend, hoping for nothing in return; and your reward will be great, and you will be sons of the Highest. For He is kind to the unthankful and evil.

Therefore be merciful, just as your Father also is merciful. (NKJV)

[But I say to you that listen, Love your enemies, do good to those who hate you.

Bless those who curse you, pray for those who abuse you.

Do to others as you would have them do to you.

If you love those who love you, what credit is that to you? For even sinners love those who love them.

If you do good to those who do good to you, what credit is that to you? For even sinners do the same.

If you lend to those from whom you hope to receive, what credit is that to you? Even sinners lend to sinners, to receive as much again.

But love your enemies, do good, and lend, expecting nothing in return. Your reward will be great, and you will be children of the Most High; for he is kind to the ungrateful and the wicked.

Be merciful, just as your Father is merciful. (NRSV)]

Although Jesus discusses several different themes in the Sermon on the Mount, the doctrinal heart of the discourse lies in the six antitheses found in verses 2–48 of Matthew 5. In each of these cases, Jesus cites a statement and promptly repudiates or modifies it (or its interpretation) by insisting, "but I say," thereby placing his own teaching on record in clear contrast. Is Jesus functioning here as the Old Testament prophets did and calling his countrymen to a faithful living out of the demands of the Mosaic Torah, or is he throwing down a gauntlet and relentlessly contrasting the instructions of Moses with his own demands? Is he challenging the popular or clerical misinterpretation of the Old Testament, or is he challenging the adequacy of the texts themselves? Inevitably one's answer must involve the broader question of Jesus' attitude toward the Mosaic Law, not only in general, but specifically in light of his strong remarks reaffirming its authority immediately before presenting his antithesis (v. 17–20).

We could attempt to avoid the entire question of whether Jesus is dealing with Old Testament Law or scribal interpretation by dismissing it as, essentially, an irrelevancy. As the Messiah and final revealer of God's will to the human race, we would expect there to be such a profound intermingling of *both* contrary and continuing elements that to come down on one side or the other would be inappropriate and misleading.[1] Richard B. Gardner offers another way to avoid the question when he writes, "[T]he church does not simply take over the law as given to those of ancient times. The radical part of Matthew's stance is that the law remains valid *as redefined by Jesus*" (his emphasis).[2]

Although there is certainly an element of truth in these approaches as theoretical constructions, in real life Jesus' listeners (both friendly and hostile) would have had to distinguish which of the two basic options represented the essence of the Lord's doctrine. If one opted for essential unity between Jesus and Torah, then one could easily embrace him as a disciple; if one perceived them as essentially contradictory, then one could hardly select discipleship!

Yet others ignore the question of compatibility or contradiction by insisting that Jesus never intended for the specifics of his teaching to be taken very seriously.[3] If so, agreement or disagreement again becomes an irrelevancy. This is the least reasonable approach one is likely to encounter. There is a profound difference between individuals putting a "spin" on the meaning of Jesus' words above and beyond what he intended, and claiming that the words were never intended to be taken as guidelines for conduct in the first place.

Others seem guilty of "fudging" the issue, of trying to have it, simultaneously, both ways. One scholar, for example, speaks of how "*nothing* (our emphasis) Jesus says here contradicts the Torah," but in a footnote he shifts the ground a bit: "But not all he says is contradictory; some is supplementary, some is intensification, some is interpretation of older statements" (again our emphasis).[4]

Others define the question in such a way that any more restrictive approach than the Old Testament teaches is both compatible and noncontradictory. Although several commentators on the subject seem to have such an attitude underlying their remarks, the most explicit is that of Frederick J. Murphy. Of divorce he writes, "Although Moses allowed divorce, Jesus did not negate Torah by His prohibition of divorce. *It is not a negation of Torah to be stricter than Torah itself.*"[5] If Jesus had said you shall not offer sacrifice except once in your lifetime, would not that be a clear contradiction of the Torah's implicit demand for continuing sacrifices? Would the mere fact that it was "stricter" than the Torah change the fact? Although there is an element of truth that greater strictness is not *necessarily* contradictory, surely at *some* point a sufficient degree of variance produces a contradiction.

Laying aside these intentional or unintentional efforts to avoid the question, there are two basic approaches to the question of Jesus' intent in the Antitheses:

1. Jesus and the Torah are in complete harmony when both are properly understood and interpreted.

W. D. Davies contends that "the so-called 'antitheses' are to be regarded more accurately as exegesis than as strict antitheses...." When Jesus offers his contrasts, he is not contradicting the Law but "offering His own interpretation" of it.[6] Along the same line, Pinchas Lapide speaks of the comparisons, not as antitheses, but as "'supertheses,' which deepen, intensify, and radicalize the biblical commandments—guiding us back to their roots and original intention."[7]

Those who assume a oneness between Torah and Jesus' teaching fall into two broad (but overlapping) categories:

a. *Those who assume that Jesus rooted his commands in the Torah and the Prophets but who do little or nothing to establish their assumption.* It is a given, but an assumed rather than verified given. Commentaries are prime offenders on this score. They are as likely as not to assert that Jesus was amplifying on the Old Testament but then fail to provide any textual citations to establish it. In more general works, some have elaborated at length on rabbinical parallels, but they commonly fail to provide any documentation that either the rabbis or Jesus had specific Torah texts to back up their assertions. Others deal at length with alleged *violations* of the Law by Jesus and do an effective job in vindicating that his life was in conformity with the existing body of supreme religious law found in the Old Testament, yet even here the Antitheses easily play a secondary (or lesser!) role in the analysis. Even when only one specific antithesis is the subject of discussion, Old Testament texts that might be relevant as precedent for Jesus' teaching are generally barely touched on. The rule of thumb seems to be: "His advocacy was based on the Old Covenant." Oddly, even books written with the intent of proving that Jesus' teaching was in strict conformity with the Mosaic system can omit a discussion of the Antitheses![8]

b. *Those who assume that Jesus intended his six contrasts to be reaffirmations of the Jewish law—and denials of popular or clerical glosses on the Law—but who retreat from that blanket statement when analyzing specific texts.* Instead of representing a consistent pattern for other contrasts Jesus gives in the same exposition of the Old Testament, the "but I say" becomes different and contradictory to what had already been revealed. Such expository reversals may involve only one or two antitheses, but their very existence is especially interesting because the writers do not seem to recognize that they have reversed the basis of their underlying theory of analysis. Such writers are quoted time and time again in the remainder of this book as dissenting from an Old Testament basis for specific antitheses. Yet they were sometimes the same individuals who provided a thought-provoking analysis of the Old Testament text on a different topic.

Assuming that Jesus is affirming the doctrines of the Old Testament leaves unanswered the question of what are the targets of Jesus' antitheses. If Jesus is teaching consistent with the Mosaic and prophetic revelation of old and yet is also teaching *against* something, the process of elimination leaves as his target the rabbinical, scribal, or popular interpretations of his day.

Among the minority who do not overlook this implication is Kari Syreeni, who writes that "one of Matthew's concerns was to juxtapose Jesus' teaching with the piety taught by the contemporary Jewish authorities."[9] Consistency is hard to maintain. Robert E. Obach and Albert

Kirk, for example, speak of how "[o]ur Lord is not contrasting an old Law with a new one. He is contrasting a Jewish *interpretation* of the Law with His own" (our emphasis).[10] Yet he proceeds to tell us that Jesus was repudiating the teaching of the Law in regard to oath taking.[11]

2. *Those who effectively ignore or deny Jesus' role as faithful expositor of the Mosaic Law and work from the assumption that the contrasts often involve new and contradictory teaching.* Jesus, in this scenario, is laying aside the teaching of the old covenant and substituting for it his own revelation. It becomes distinctly an issue of Jesus *versus* the Old Testament.

John P. Meier argues that in some cases, Jesus "dares to contrast his word with God's word. What is more startling still, in three cases (antitheses three, four, and five, on divorce, oaths and vows, and retaliation), Jesus revokes the letter of the Law and replaces it with his own diametrically opposed command. Despite the permissions and commands of the Law, there is to be no divorce, no oaths or vows, no legal retaliation."[12] In another work Meier speaks of how in these three cases "the letter of the Torah...is revoked....When there is a conflict over what is the genuine will of God, the words of Torah must cede to the word of Jesus."[13]

Eduard Schweizer contends that in the Antitheses "there are even places where Jesus annuls not only the Jewish interpretation but the Old Testament law itself." In the latter category he puts at least two of the antitheses (divorce and an eye for an eye) and considers a third as possibly belonging on the list (loving one's enemies).[14]

The same result is produced by Francis J. Moloney, who does not speak of contradiction. Instead he speaks of how Jesus is intent upon "establish[ing] a new law" on each of these three points (he individually cites each of the six sets of verse references for the Antitheses). Indeed, the circumstances of law giving are even more dramatic than in the case of Moses. "While Moses received the law from Jahweh, Jesus gives the new law."[15]

R. T. France removes love of enemies from the list of three contradictions but adds the prohibition of oaths.[16] Having noticed several commentators and scholars who consider half of the Antitheses as being targeted at the Law of Moses, we notice yet others who suggest a larger number.[17]

Implicitly, Pinchas Lapide seems to be doing this when he argues that the formulation "it is said" is used of "*biblical* traditions" and notes that this is parallel to the usage of the expression in "rabbinical writings."[18] Since Jesus clearly quotes or summarizes Old Testament teaching in at least several of these antitheses, he is largely correct in this, though it would not necessarily follow that Jesus is opposing the text rather than scribal or popular *glosses* upon the text. That is a separate and distinct question.

Lapide's possible implicit conviction that the text represents a broad-scale repudiation of Mosaic teaching is explicit in the writings of others. The widely respected William Barclay writes that in five of the six contrasts "Jesus quotes the Law, only to contradict it, and to substitute a teaching of his own. He claimed the right to point out the inadequacies of the most sacred writings in the world, and to correct them out of his own wisdom."[19] He could do this with propriety because he was uniquely the Son of God with the right to teach and bind upon all humankind.[20]

In a college-level textbook on the life of Jesus, C. Milo Connick works from the assumption that

The six contrasting statements in Matthew are directed against the Old Testament. Although the teachings about murder, adultery, and oath-taking provide only for an internalization and intensification of the prohibitions, this is not the case with the teachings about divorce and retaliation. If the saying about divorce does not annul the Old Testament injunction, it considerably restricts it; and the teaching on retaliation actually overthrows the Old Testament teaching on "an eye for an eye." The teaching about love expands and deepens certain Old Testament commands and grounds them in the character of God.[21]

Drawing a drastic contrast between Torah and Jesus' teaching can be accomplished without being quite as crude or blunt as to say that Jesus "contradicted" the Law. Herschel H. Hobbs accomplishes the same result by using terminology more acceptable to the religious conservative. He notes that Jesus "selects six pertinent points in the Law. And with each, instead of lowering the standard prescribed in the *letter,* He lifts it to the higher standards of the *spirit.* Thus more is expected of one under *grace* than of one under law" (his emphasis).[22]

When one reaches the ministry of the apostle Paul, one does find explicit contradictions with the Old Testament (though there is more in common than one sometimes thinks). If one accepts that the apostles were recipients of genuine, external revelation from the Godhead, it follows that ultimately Christianity was foreordained to walk a very different path from Judaism. On the other hand, individuals such as myself date this contradictory stance much earlier, in the Lord's own earthly ministry and teaching. Many years ago, in a series of class lessons for new converts, I appealed to the Antitheses as proof of Jesus' laying down a sterner and far more demanding moral code than the Torah ever did. I spoke of how the Old Testament prohibited only the act of adultery, whereas Jesus prohibited the uncontrolled desire that would lead to adultery. I spoke of how Moses only forbade murder, whereas Jesus forbade the hate that led to murder.

A few years ago a short book on divorce and remarriage compelled me to reconsider my long-standing assumption.[23] I knew full well, of course, that my Jesus-versus-Old Testament approach was diametrically opposed to the consensus of commentators. On the other hand, to the limited degree that I had pursued the topic at all, little scriptural substantiation was ever provided to back up the assertion that the teaching of Jesus' antitheses and the Old Testament were identical. In this compact treatment of the antithesis on divorce, I discovered for the first time that there were a number of texts that seemed to be either identical or amazingly similar to that "new" teaching the Lord was giving in his contrasts in Matthew 5.

When one's fundamental working assumptions are convincingly challenged (whether or not one yet accepts a revised viewpoint), that always comes as quite a shock. With a heavy burden of time commitments on my hands, it was a little over a year later that I returned to the question once again. I re-examined each of the texts that was introduced and expanded the list by carefully running down cross reference after cross reference and then "codifying" it all together into an initial study of all biblical texts related to Jesus' antitheses. Now there was no doubt in my mind—though a few difficult points remained, the central assertion was inescapable: The Antitheses were firmly rooted in Old Testament teaching. Therefore, when Jesus insisted "but I say to you," he was not denying the teaching of Moses but was taking pointed issue with the popular (or clerical) distortions of his own day. It was not a case of Jesus versus Moses, but of Jesus versus traditional interpretation, something profoundly different.

One more step was required to make my study complete: a careful analysis of what others (especially commentators) had to say about the Antitheses and the general question of how faithful Jesus was to the Law of Moses in his own lifetime. After I had done this and produced what I regarded as a reasonably thorough analysis, a friendly editor suggested it might be wise to go back and cast my factual net even further. This I proceeded to do, and the current volume is the result.

In blending all of this material together with my own initial study, a great many questions of application have had to be omitted. The question of how these teachings are meant to apply to the daily life of the believer is too wide-ranging to more than touch on in the pages of this book. Indeed, if we were to investigate all of these issues, we would only do what others have done perhaps far better. What we have done in these passages is to fill in the gap others have left wide open, to clearly vindicate, by a close examination of the relevant Old Testament texts, that Jesus' antitheses were faithful applications of what the Law of Moses already taught. Others have assumed it; in the following pages we hope to prove it.

*   *   *

Although much of modern scholarship has challenged the traditional authorship and time of origin of the various Old Testament books, these questions are beyond the scope of the present work. Unquestionably the completed works of the Old Testament as we now have them were in existence in the first century, and to cite them in terms of their "completed" forms is appropriate and proper. Indeed, those of Jesus' own day would have framed the terms of debate within such terminology, speaking of "the Law of Moses" and "Isaiah" and so forth even if two millennia later many scholars break these down into allegedly preceding subcomponents. We have retained this usage not only because of our own skepticism of much of modern theory, but also as most faithful to the fact that both Jesus and early Christians were analyzing the relevance of Old Testament precedent within terms of such presumptions of authenticity and supernatural origin. Whether there was only one Isaiah or two—or even three—whether "he" was a sole individual or an Isaian movement, if Jesus grounds his teaching in principles and precepts rooted in this "Isaiah," it remains true that those principles and texts already existed as precedent, which is our central point. The same is true of the Pentateuch, whether attributed to Moses (substantially alone) or as the result of multiple documents ultimately codified into one. *There was precedent* for Jesus' teaching—and if there was, then he must be viewed in the Antitheses, not as a religious revolutionary, but as a reformer, bringing the people back to the original intents of their ancient sacred works.

NOTES

[1]Cf. the implication of the remarks of Menninger, 117.

[2]Richard B. Gardner, *Matthew* (Scottdale, Pa.: Herald Press, 1991), 111. For a similar argument also see Augustine

Stock, *The Method and Message of Matthew* (Collegeville, Minn.: Liturgical Press, 1994), 80.

[3]Writing of Matthew 5:39-41 in particular, Edwin Cox contends, "This can be used as lesson material provided we realise that these passages are slightly humorous and exaggerated illustrations and not precepts to be followed…Jesus was illustrating His teaching by examples, and pushing them to their over-logical conclusions so that they became slightly humourous. Hearers would smile at this, but they would remember" (*This Elusive Jesus* [London: Marshall's Educational, 1975], 37).

[4]R. David Kaylor, *Jesus the Prophet: His Vision of the Kingdom on Earth* (Louisville: Westminster/John Knox, 1994), 107.

[5]Frederick J. Murphy, *The Religious World of Jesus: An Introduction to Second Temple Palestinian Judaism* (Nashville: Abingdon, 1991), 334.

[6]W. D. Davies, *The Setting of the Sermon on the Mount* (Cambridge, UK: University of Cambridge Press, 1964; reprint, Atlanta, Ga: Scholars Press, 1989), 102. Margaret Davies, *Matthew* (Sheffield, UK: JSOT Press/Sheffield Academic Press, 1993), 52, also argues that these are not strictly antitheses: In reaction to the command not to commit adultery, Jesus does not endorse adultery; in reaction to the command to take oaths, Jesus does not endorse repudiating oaths, etc. Of course this line of reasoning assumes that the antithesis is with the *letter* of the Torah; if Jesus is targeting the *interpretation* of the Torah, then to speak of antitheses would certainly be expected.

[7]Pinchas Lapide, *The Sermon on the Mount: Utopia or Program for Action?,* trans. Arlene Swidler (Maryknoll, N.Y.: Orbis, 1986), 46. Among others who take this approach of interpreting Torah rather than rejecting it are: Stephen C. Barton, *The Spirituality of the Gospels* (London: SPCK, 1992), 24; Blaine Charette, *The Theme of Recompense in Matthew's Gospel* (Sheffield, UK: JSOT Press, 1992), 83–84; Wayne A. Meeks, "Breaking Away: Three New Testament Pictures of

Christianity's Separation from the Jewish Communities," in *Essential Papers on Judaism and Christianity in Conflict: From Late Antiquity to the Reformation,* ed. Jeremy Cohen (New York: New York University Press, 1991), 104; Jack T. Sanders, *Schismatics, Sectarians, Dissidents, Deviants: The First One Hundred Years of Jewish-Christian Relations* (Valley Forge, Pa: Trinity Press International, 1993), 24; Alan F. Segal, "Matthew's Jewish Voice," in *Social History of the Matthean Community: Cross-Disciplinary Approaches,* ed. David L. Balch (Minneapolis: Fortress, 1991), 21–22.

[8]Robert Mackintosh, in his *Christ and the Jewish Law* (London: Hodder and Stoughton, 1886) wrote to prove this point but conspicuously fails to discuss the Sermon on the Mount as an example of that reliance. Walter Alford's *The Old and New Testament Dispensations Compared* (London: Thomas Hatchard, 1858) only introduces one antithesis, that of the demand that one love rather than hate one's enemies.

[9]Fari Syreeni, *The Making of the Sermon on the Mount: A Procedural Analysis of Matthew's Redactoral Activity. Part I: Methodology & Compositional Analysis* (Helsinki: Suomalainen Tiedeakatemia, 1987), 62.

[10]Robert Obach and Albert Kirk, *A Commentary on the Gospel of Matthew* (New York: Paulist, 1978), 65.

[11]Ibid., 66–67.

[12]John P. Meier, *The Vision of Matthew: Christ, Church and Morality in the First Gospel* (New York: Paulist, 1979), 64. Cf. his earlier assertion of this in his *Law and History in Matthew's Gospel* (Rome: Biblical Institute Press, 1976), 149. He studies the alleged contradictions in detail in *Law and History,* 140–61.

[13]John P. Meier, *Matthew,* The New Testament Message Commentary Series, Vol. 3. (Collegeville, Minn.: Liturgical Press, 1990), 65.

[14]Eduard Schweitzer, *Jesus,* trans. David E. Green (Richmond, Va.: John Knox, 1971), 32.

[15]Francis J. Moloney, *The Living Voice of the Gospel: The Gospels Today* (New York: Paulist, 1986), 135.

[16]R. T. France, *Matthew: Evangelist and Teacher* (Grand Rapids: Zondervan, 1989), 192–93.

[17]The following quoted individuals are a representative sample. There are other ways to verbalize the same basic approach. For example, David L. Balch does not use the term *contradict*, but speaks, rather, of a "change" of an undefined number of the practices Jesus discusses ("The Greek Political Topos…and Matthew 5:17, 19, and 16:19," in *Social History of the Matthean Community: Cross-Disciplinary Approaches,* ed. David L. Balch (Minneapolis: Fortress, 1991), 76.

[18]Lapide, *Sermon on the Mount,* 85.

[19]William Barclay, *The Gospel of Matthew,* Daily Study Bible Series, Vol. 1, Rev. ed. (Philadelphia: Westminster, 1975), 134.

[20]Ibid., 134–135.

[21]C. Milo Connick, *Jesus: The Man, the Mission, and the Message,* 2nd ed. (Englewood Cliffs, N.J.: Prentice Hall, 1972), 247–248.

[22]Herschel H. Hobbs, *An Exposition of the Gospel of Matthew* (Grand Rapids: Baker, 1965), 65.

[23]Jerry F. Basset, *Rethinking Marriage, Divorce & Remarriage* (Eugene, Ore.: Western Printers, 1991), 21–34.

Section One

JESUS ON THE ABIDING AUTHORITY OF THE TORAH

3

Matthew 5:17-20: Interpreting the Antitheses in Context

Our thesis is that Jesus was well aware that much of what he was going to say would be in fundamental contradiction to what the masses had been taught. He recognized that there would be a chasm, an incompatibility, between the prevailing orthodoxy (either popular, clerical, or both) that they had been raised in and that which he was advocating (Mt. 9:16, for example). Hence it was vital for him to impress upon his listeners that no matter how much what he said departed from what they had been taught, it in no way departed from what the Mosaic Law itself demanded. In doing this, he was defying the religious traditions that had evolved, but he was opposing nothing that came from God (Mt. 15:1–9).

At the beginning of the Antitheses, Jesus does this in three ways: (1) by asserting the ongoing permanency of the Mosaic Law (v. 17–18); (2) by asserting the spiritual consequences of releasing others from any provision of that Law (v. 19); (3) by pointing out who his real targets

were: nothing in the Law itself, but the scribes and
Pharisees who were, in reality, departing from the Law
(v. 20). Each of these themes deserves careful attention
in its own right.

1. The ongoing permanence but ultimate removal of the Mosaic Law (verses 17–18)

Do not think that I came to destroy the Law or the
Prophets. I did not come to destroy but to fulfill. For
assuredly I say to you, till heaven and earth pass away,
one jot or one tittle will by no means pass from the law
till all is fulfilled. (Mt. 5:17–18)

[Do not think that I have come to abolish the law or the
prophets; I have come not to abolish but to fulfill. For
truly I tell you, until heaven and earth pass away, not
one letter, not one stroke of a letter, will pass from the
law until all is accomplished. (NRSV)]

Regardless of the point at which "all" is, in fact, "fulfilled," at that chronological point in time, Jesus sees the
need for the existing Mosaic Law to vanish. In short, his
is a *positive* mission—to "fulfill" rather than "destroy."
The latter term would suggest animosity and antagonism, whereas the former presents his work as part of a
process begun (but not completed) by the existing Law.
The end result would be essentially the same (the
removal of the Torah as religious authority), but the purpose and motive would be diametrically opposite.

Laying aside the question of when that completion
point would be reached, the comprehensiveness of the
authority of the Law would remain in effect until that
time. Neither "jot" nor "tittle" would cease to be authoritative until that point. "Jot" is *iota,* the nearest Greek

equivalent to the Hebrew word *yod,* which is "the smallest Hebrew letter."[1] *Iota* and *yod* are "the smallest letters in the Greek and Hebrew alphabets respectively."[2] "Tittle" is keraia and refers to "a little horn…the point or extremity which distinguishes certain Hebrew letters from others."[3] "Grammarians used the word to denote the accents in Greek words."[4]

Hence God demands (as viewed from the human perspective) that even the smallest point of his law must be observed. It cannot be safely set aside; it is just as much deserving of obedience as one that would count as the largest or most significant. Nor is this the only place that Jesus makes this point. Time and again during his ministry, he assails his foes for setting apart, ignoring, and even—in effect—canceling the laws God has ordained.

True, he was especially offended when their callousness and special pleading resulted in injustice to others and in ignoring the fundamental ethical demands of the Law. Their well-intentioned but ultimately Law-undermining interpretive glosses he was quite willing to set aside, but the minutest part of the Law itself and its true intent—never. This is pointed out emphatically in Matthew 23:23, a passage that, oddly enough, is often cited to prove that Jesus was utterly unconcerned with the "secondary" things of Moses' Law: "Woe to you, scribes and Pharisees, hypocrites! For you pay tithe of mint and anise and cummin, and have neglected the weightier matters of the law: justice and mercy and faith."

Mentally, and sometimes literally, the vital closing words are often omitted when this verse is cited: "These you ought to have done, *without leaving the others undone."* This fits in perfectly with the "jot" and "tittle" in Matthew 5:18. Matthew 23 stresses that one could not safely ignore such "technicalities" in God's law, while

Matthew 5 emphasizes that the Mosaic "technicalities" would remain in effect until the prophetic purposes were completely and totally accomplished.

This essentially traditional reading of "jot" and "tittle" has been challenged at least in regard to the latter. Alan Hugh McNeile objects that "to erase one of these may cause an enormous difference in the sense, not a small one as the words [of Jesus] imply."[5] Actually this fits quite well, because it stresses the fact that what seems quite trivial may actually be quite important. When one decides to dispense with some part of divine law because of its seeming insignificance, one may be totally misjudging it in that it carries a bundle of implications that one has been unable to grasp.

Jesus' teaching on the authority of the Mosaic Law implies that what he is teaching is in full agreement with the Torah. On the other hand, if Jesus' intent was to eventually institute dramatic departures from the Mosaic Law along the lines of those implemented by the apostles, then there must have been some time limitation on how long the Torah would remain binding. Hence it is not surprising to find just such a time limitation expressed in our text: "For assuredly I say to you, till heaven and earth pass away, one jot or one tittle will by no means pass from the law *till all is fulfilled*" (v. 18).

Some have argued that the verse must represent an addition by Matthew to create the impression of complete Torah-obedience. This is inherently impossible: If Jesus truly thought along such lines, he could not have added commands that were different from those of the Torah.[6] This line of reasoning falters because it overlooks the fact that the second *till* in the verse implies a termination date for Torah authority. Furthermore, the invention theory assumes that Jesus' demands were radically and irreconcilably different from those imposed by the Old Testament. It is our argument from the many passages that we will examine that this fundamentally mistakes the relationship of the "new" teaching with the "old." The "new" walks distinctly in the path of the "old" and represents a reaffirmation of that centuries-old doctrine of the Torah and the Prophets. Hence one can not fairly dismiss Matthew 5:18 as from "Matthew or the tradition of the primitive church" rather than from the Lord himself.[7]

Having established that a terminal date is clearly in Jesus' mind, the question remains: What is that termination date? Expositors have suggested three approaches.

A. The Law would never, in any part or element, be removed from authority.

Matthew 5:17 has two *till(s):* "till heaven and earth pass away" *and* "till all is fulfilled." By dwelling on the first one, it is easy to come to the conclusion that "Jesus held [the Old Testament] as unchangeable forever and as long as the world exists..."[8]

This approach can take either an "absolutist" (the earth will abide forever) or a "conditional" approach (until earth is destroyed and replaced by the heavenly cosmos). In behalf of the first approach, we read of the permanence of the earth in such texts as Ecclesiasties 1:4: "One generation passes away, and another generation comes; but the earth abides forever." Since the earth abides "forever" and since the Law will not pass away "till all is fulfilled"—and that won't *ever happen*—Jesus is asserting not only the eternal existence of the Torah but also its eternal authority.

Of course the comparison in Ecclesiasties is of an individual generation with the earth. In comparison with any individual generation, the earth does abide forever. It is around long generations after we have perished and are forgotten. But that in no way answers the question of whether there ultimately will be a time when the cycle is broken and this time-cosmos is removed.

The author of Second Peter ardently assures his readers that "the heavens will pass away with a great noise" when the Lord returns and that "the elements will melt with fervent heat; both the earth and the works that are in it will be burned up" (3:10). Even "the elements will melt with fervent heat" (v. 12). Having asserted that such will occur, he refers to the new cosmos that will take its place, the "new heavens and a new earth in which righteousness dwells" (v. 13). Even if one assumes (I believe incorrectly) that he has in mind a rejuvenated current earth purged of its evil decay—rather than the afterworld itself—this "new earth" is still pictured as purged of the iniquity that besieges our world. One wonders how the laws of ceremonial purity would then apply in such a place? Indeed, in the new world to come gender as we know it is abolished, along with sexual reproduction (Mt. 22:29–30). How then would there be any room for the sexual and marital laws of the old covenant? Hence there is immense difficulty in applying the two-testament concept of an abiding earth as evidence that the Torah was designed to be equally long-lived as religious authority.

B. The Law would remain in effect until this physical universe is brought to an end at the return of the Lord.

This certainly solves some of the problems posed by the previous approach, but it leaves inexplicable the clear and dramatic New Testament departures from the practices of the Old. For example, how does one explain the fundamental substitution of Sunday worship for Saturday worship? Christians joined together in their worship on the first day of the week (Acts 20:7; 1 Cor. 16:1–4) whereas under the Law, the seventh day of the week was observed. Some speak of the "Christian Sabbath," but this term is not only alien to the New Testament, but it flies in the face of the careful distinction made between the Sabbath and the first day of the week: "Now *after* the Sabbath, as the *first day* of the week began to dawn, Mary Magdalene and the other Mary came to see the tomb" (Mt. 28:1 [our emphasis]; the distinction is also clear in Mk. 16:1–2 and Lk. 23:56–24:1). Need we speak of a free-will offering (1 Cor. 16:1–4) taking the place of the tithe or of circumcision being classified as nonessential?

In light of such clear differences, it is hardly surprising that a central theme of Hebrews is the replacement of the Mosaic Law by the gospel system. A key argument of that book is that the Old Testament itself predicted that such would occur (Heb. 8:8–13, quoting Jer. 31:31–34). Furthermore, under the Mosaic system, Jesus could not perform the priestly role he is pictured as doing in the gospel age (Heb. 7:11–14). Under the Torah a conditional forgiveness of sin was received, but thanks to the death of Christ, what we might call the promissory note promising forgiveness is stamped paid. Under the Old Testament itself, such final forgiveness was impossible (Heb. 9:15).

Hence large hunks of Old Testament teaching were laid aside in the first century itself. Unless we are to say that the apostles were guilty of excess enthusiasm and conjured up a new religious system in defiance of the actual intent of the Lord himself, we are forced to conclude that they initiated these changes with his full endorsement and approval. Yet if Jesus had such changes in mind, would we not expect some hints or premonitions in his earthly teaching?

This is exactly what we do find in Matthew 5:18: Jesus satisfies the dual purpose of avowing full loyalty to the Law while indicating that a day was coming when his "blank check" endorsement of the Torah would no longer be valid. He has no need to stress the latter because what he teaches in the Sermon are attitudes and moral principles that would remain true in the gospel dispensation. Yet without the passing chronological termination reference, he would have foreclosed his apostles from the dramatic alterations in religion that would enable Christianity to become the universal religion it is.

Both the-earth-abides-forever scenario and the-law-abides-until-the-return-of-Jesus scenario overlook the importance of the second *till* in the verse, and any interpretation of the text hinges on recognizing the existence of both: Jesus teaches that the authority of the Law is unending even to the end of the world but *only* if all has not been fulfilled prior to that point.

There is a way that this difficulty could be overcome, but we end up at the same concept of a termination of Torah authority. We could take both *tills* as providing definite chronological points that must be reached in order for the Law to be removed as authority. At the point that all was "fulfilled," the stage was indeed set for the replacement of one testament by another, the legal prerequisites had been satisfied. But this would not necessarily do away with the actual practice of the existing system. Since most were not convinced by the claims of Christianity, these could only occur through the intervention of an external event, an ending of the world, so to speak. One could argue with considerable justice that though the physical world did not perish, the socio-religious-political world (at least) was indeed done away with in the fall of Jerusalem. The destruction of Jerusalem meant that the Judaism that now existed would be inescapably different in central matters of conduct and behavior from the Judaism that had been. This would provide one terminal date (A.D. 70) for the ending of the authority of the Law; that is, *one* of the *tills* was satisfied. Yet the termination point of the Law could be made even more specific in the second till and its allusion to the death of Jesus on the cross. Hence the first *till* would refer to the *practical* abolishment of the Mosaic religious system, and the second to the earlier, *legal,* abolishment of it through the death of the Messiah.[9]

Although this represents an intriguing way to link together the two *tills* in the verse, it seems far more likely that what Matthew 5:18 has in mind is our third interpretive option. It makes the first *till* represent the generalization and the second *till* a reigning in of the generalization he had just made. Not only does it allow us to explain the presence of both *tills,* but it also has considerable appeal in that the biblical concepts of "prophecy" and "fulfillment" (of prophecy) are natural, interlocking concepts to the student of scripture.

C. The Law would only remain in effect until its prophecies concerning Jesus were fulfilled.

This is the only one of the three traditional approaches that really puts sufficient emphasis on the time limitations provided by Jesus himself, "till all is fulfilled." The other two are, at heart, efforts to make permanent what Jesus indicates is only semi-permanent. Assuming that Jesus was indeed the authority behind the apostolic message of freedom from the Jewish law, the presence of this time limitation explains how he could both bind the Jewish law and have his apostles (not all that many years later) free humanity from the obligation of obeying it. As of then, the "till" reference-point *had* been reached—the prophecies had been fulfilled; hence, the Law could then be safely laid aside. The ceremonial aspects could be ignored because the new system only continued the moral aspects of the old system. The moral teachings were preserved because they represented the abiding ethical principles required for ethical conduct in all ages. It wasn't a matter of picking part of the old covenant and rejecting the rest; it was a matter of having a new system that would henceforth possess all the authority in itself that the preceding one had possessed.

Jesus is presented as having in mind a conscious fulfillment of those prophecies he regarded as messianic. He applied to his listeners the text from Isaiah 6 condemning the lack of spiritual perception in them (Mt. 13:13–17). He also rebuked those who would stop his arrest by pointing out that "the Scriptures of the prophets [must] be fulfilled" (26:56). A theme of Matthew himself, both before (1:22–24; 2:14–15; 2:16–18; 2:23) and after this chapter (8:16–17; 12:16–21; 13:34–35; 21:1–5; 27:3–10; 27:35) is the tying together of Old Testament texts with their fulfillment in the life of Jesus. At least some of these Matthean references come very close to claiming an explicit *intent* of Jesus to be acting as "fulfiller" rather than merely being Matthew's description and interpretation of the events. Hence this usage of "fulfilled" in connection with the carrying out of texts regarded as messianic is rooted both in the author of the gospel of Matthew and in the picture of Jesus himself that is painted by that author.

Similar tie-ins are found in the other three gospel

accounts, sometimes of the same events discussed in Matthew. Of special relevance is Luke 24:44 where Luke quotes Jesus as presenting that which needed to be fulfilled as having been fulfilled by the time of his death and resurrection: "These are the words which I spoke to you while I was still with you, that all things must be fulfilled which were written in the Law of Moses and the Prophets and the Psalms concerning Me." Hence interpreting Matthew 5:18's reference to events that needed to be fulfilled fits in well with both the gospel authors and the Jesus they portray.

It has been objected that if verse 18 "refers to Jesus' death and resurrection, then all of Matthew 5:17–19 would be only of historical interest for early Christians."[10] The same reasoning would dismiss as irrelevant the Old Testament prophecies since they commonly describe events that occurred long before the New Testament was composed. Furthermore, this approach would dismiss as irrelevant the historical narratives of the Old Testament. They are complete, old, firmly in the past. Of what possible value are they? Paul answered the question of the relevance of events in the past by appealing to believers to examine them for lessons that illustrate the teaching they knew was binding in their own day and age (1 Cor. 10:6–14). Old does not necessarily mean outdated or useless, especially in those first few decades when Christians of Jewish ethnic background exercised their personal religious liberty to conform to many of the customs in which they had been raised.

Daniel Patte roots his opposition to our suggested approach by asserting that "[t]here is absolutely nothing in the text up to this point that would suggest an interpretation of this verse in terms of Jesus' death and resurrection. It is only through a retrospective reading of the

Gospel from the perspective of the resurrection" that the view can be maintained. He argues that 5:1-12 concerns rewards that are in the "eschatological future," and therefore verse 18 should be interpreted in a similar manner.[11]

However *none* of the blessings in the first twelve verses are stated in the time-conditional terms of Matthew 5:18; none are presented as true "till" a certain event. Even *implicitly* many of these cannot be interpreted in such terms; humility, meekness, hungering for righteousness, mercifulness, and such like are surely intended to be characteristics of those in the heavenly kingdom as well as a living style for the current earth. In contrast, the authority of the Law is indicated as being "till" a certain point is reached—and no further. The very fact that the early evangelists and apostles taught such dramatically different religious practice from Judaism argues that they interpreted the "till" point as being fulfilled already, in their age. Unless it was grounded in the time-limited wording of Matthew 5, where did they consider that the authority came from to justify their changes?

Nor can one escape by asserting (as is common) that such elements of Jesus' foreshadowing later beliefs were inventions of the later church to justify their changes in practice. The early church clearly believed that miraculous divine revelation was present; hence, there was no need to backdate into Jesus' ministry either ideas or practices to justify what was currently being done. This belief is especially pronounced in First Corinthians in its regulations about the use of tongues-speaking and prophecy (1 Cor. 12:27–31; 14:1–40).

The case becomes even stronger when we turn to the apostles. The very concept of apostolic power to bind and loose (Mt. 16:19; 18:18), a natural outgrowth of belief in apostolic inspiration, certainly carried with it a right to authoritatively initiate even actions that might be perceived as dramatic changes. For example, when Paul discusses the divorce of believer and unbeliever, he makes no pretense that Jesus had dealt with the situation. Instead he contrasts the two-believer marriage that Jesus had dealt with (1 Cor. 7:10–11) with the believer-pagan relationship that Paul needed to discuss (v. 12–16).

2. The spiritual consequences of releasing others from any provision of the Law (verse 19)

> Whoever therefore breaks one of the least of these commandments, and teaches men so, he will be called least in the kingdom of heaven; but whoever does and teaches them, will be called great in the kingdom of heaven. (Mt. 5:19)

> [Therefore, whoever breaks one of the least of these commandments, and teaches others to do the same, will be called least in the kingdom of heaven; but whoever does them and teaches them will be called great in the kingdom of heaven. (NRSV)]

A. The "least" and "greatest" commandments.

Some have thought in terms of the reference being to long versus short commandments. This seems inherently unlikely; when individuals reject a religious teaching, it is its contents, rather than its length, that forms the basis of the rejection.

Others would see here a distinction between the "moral law" and the "ceremonial law" with the latter representing the "least" commandments. Yet the term *least* would seem inappropriate for ceremonial regulations when (in length at least) they often require far more space and detail than the moral ones. Indeed, the two are sometimes so closely intertwined that a valid distinction seems virtually impossible. For example, how does one distinguish between the command to keep the Sabbath holy and the various requirements to enforce that law? In terms of the present question, perhaps the greatest problem lies in the fact that it would lump all the ceremonial laws together as if they were all on the same level of significance and importance. Furthermore, within that alleged body of ceremonial teaching there would still be the temptation to categorize the contents into "lesser" and "greater." Likewise within the body of moral law in the Old Testament. In light of this human desire to categorize, it seems most improbable that Jesus has any specific laws in mind. For his purpose it does not matter what law one counts as "least"—the sin remains the same.

For better or for worse, all ages categorize sins as to relative importance. Sometimes the categorization grows out of the simple fact that the *consequences are greater.* It is bad to slander someone, but much worse to murder them; for the latter destroys both the person's life and any opportunity to attempt to undo the lies. In other cases the categorization is a means of *removing or minimizing guilt:* What I've done "is not as bad as" some other transgression, preferably one you've committed. On a more abstract level, some divine laws *demand more from an individual*—more effort, more time, more commitment, more patience—than others.

Doubtlessly such mental processes were at work in the first century as well. Jesus does not deny that categorization will be an inevitable temptation. What Jesus is teaching is that it is unacceptable, that one cannot rightly play semantic games with the various provisions of God's law. All of it is to be taken seriously and treated with respect. To do otherwise is to endanger one's acceptability to God, to make one "least in the kingdom of heaven."

B. Sharing the whitewashing of sin: "...and teaches men so."

Especially among the religious leadership, it was expected that one would share one's convictions with others. It was part of the job. Yet anyone and everyone who takes their religion seriously does so as well. It may not be in a formal teaching format, it may be the result of questions or casual conversation, but what we believe we share. It's natural and inevitable. And if what we believe is wrong in itself, we are encouraging others to imitate our error. The New Testament warns against putting a stumbling block in the way of others (Rom. 14:13); and when we act this way, we are unintentionally doing just that. John A. Broadus correctly observes that "[i]t is bad to do wrong, but worse if in addition we teach others to do wrong."[12]

C. The consequence of minimalization of sin: such "shall be called least in the kingdom of heaven."

Rudolf Stier notes that this verges on saying that they will "not enter the kingdom at all," though it stops just short of going that far.[13] If a person did such things to the Law—if one looked upon it as proper to divide the revelation into that which had to be obeyed and that which could safely be dispensed with—would not that skepticism encourage an individual to treat Jesus' teaching in a similar manner, of obligatory and non-obligatory? The mentality could also provide a convenient excuse to reject the teaching of such a doctrinal nonconformist as Jesus. Was not his doctrine so different that it could be safely ignored? After all, Jesus was but one individual. Would someone from despised Nazareth, of all places (Jn. 1:46), have a teaching so valuable to be worth the risks that came with discipleship? Surely many would think not.

True as this is, it is not on this ground that Jesus assails the practice. He takes for granted that in spite of this obligatory/optional approach to religion, they will, indeed, become his disciples. And it is to this group that he addresses his warning that their approach to religion will cripple their discipleship. The same mentality that allowed them to set aside part of the Torah as dispensable would permit them to set aside part of Jesus' own teaching as nonessential. They had acted cavaliarly with the Torah; the same mind-set would permit them to act in a similar manner with Jesus' doctrine. They might well be in his kingdom, but their attitude would hobble any aspirations to spiritual greatness. It would not be because he forbade them to become great, but because their own root religious assumptions undid the potential that was within them.

D. This teaching on obeying both the "least" and the "great" commandments was binding on Jesus himself.

The key word is found at the beginning of verse 19, "*Whoever* therefore breaks one of the least of these commandments and teaches men so...." The acceptance of full and faithful adherence to *all* of the Torah grew out of the *authority* of the Torah that he had discussed in verses 17 and 18 (note the "therefore" in verse 19 and how Jesus ties in the necessity of observing all of the Torah with the fact of the *authority* of the Torah). Hence Jesus recognized the need for *himself* to conform to the teaching of the Law and the prophets.

As important in determining Jesus' attitude as his explicit teaching are those references to his personal Torah observance that are introduced as the backdrop for the events of his ministry. Geza Vermes describes a selection of these when he writes,

> As a law-abiding person, Jesus may be presumed to have behaved in respect of these general rules and common customs like everyone else in Galilee. Embracing the accepted way of everyday life, He will have conformed spontaneously to a number of Biblical precepts. The gospels show Him also complying with the laws regulating religious activities proper, participating in synagogue worship on the Sabbath (Mark 1:21; 6:2; Luke 4:16, etc.), visiting the Temple of Jerusalem as a pilgrim (Mark 11:15 and parallels).[14]

Furthermore, in Jesus' teaching to others, we find him enjoining obedience to the demands of the Torah even when it might seem unneeded or when local opinion might be annoyed by it: "After curing several lepers, he orders them to report to the priests and to perform the ceremony prescribed by Moses (Mark 1:44 and parallels; Luke 17:14; cf. Leviticus 14:1–32). He approves of sending gifts to the Temple (Matthew 5:33) and of the tithing laws, which will of course have been far from popular among the Galilean rural communities (Matthew 23:23; Luke 11:42)."[15]

Jesus was at pains to root his teaching in Old Testament precedent *even when what He was doing or saying flew diametrically in the face of the accepted understanding of the Mosaic Law.* A German commentator of the nineteenth century concisely presents several telling examples of Jesus' rooting his teaching in the ancient Law:

> He vindicates the right of the heathen to God's messengers by the examples of Elijah and Elisha, Luke 4:25–26; the incomparably superior importance of the fulfillment of the moral law than the ritual observances, is shown by

quotation from Hosea, Matthew 9:13, 12:7; the right
even to break the Sabbath, when its claims come into col-
lision with moral self-love of our neighbor, is proved from
the example of David and the priests, Matthew 12:3–4;
the summing-up of all the commandments of the moral
law in love to God and thy neighbor, Matthew 22:40; a
future life for the departed patriarchs is demonstrated
from the words of Moses himself, Matthew 23:32.[16]

This is not to deny that he was also willing to cast the
issue in terms of his inherent, divinely-given power. In
the Matthew 12 case of his disciples eating of the grain
in the field in spite of the fact that it was the Sabbath, he
claimed to be "greater than the temple" (v. 6) and "Lord
even of the Sabbath" (v. 8). The Lord (ruler/rule-maker)
surely has the inherent right to determine where and
when to set it aside or otherwise make exceptions to it.
Not only is this an assertion of the personal right to set
aside the provisions of the Mosaic Law, but it is also an
implicit assertion of his own deity, for the only "Lord"
with the legitimate power to set aside divine law would
be God himself.

Even with such explicit assertions of personal power,
Jesus also carefully cited Old Testament precedent both
in the cases of David eating the shewbread on the Sabbath (v. 3–5) and also the fundamental Old Testament
moral principle that God "desire[s] mercy and not sacrifice" (v. 7) if a situation requires that a choice be made
between the two. So we have here the tremendous para-
dox of Jesus' *claiming supreme authority over* the Mosaic
Law while simultaneously *working within* its demands.
Only by carefully doing the latter could he be the faithful
expositor of the true meaning of the Torah rather than
its reckless expunger.

In retrospect, of course, Jesus' inherent authority verifies that he had the right to have his apostles establish the distinct faith of Christianity, a religion that would be dramatically different from existing Judaism. If he had posed his teaching only in terms of the Mosaic Law, his apostles would have had no right to modify one single thing in it after his death and resurrection. On the other hand, if he had not based his personal teaching during his early ministry solely on the Law of Moses, he would have been a transparent hypocrite in calling the people to a faithful obedience to it as in Matthew 5:17–18. Jesus' ministry was two pronged: immediate and long-term. In recognition of these dual purposes lies the reason for these two distinct and different strands of teaching.

3. Jesus' real targets were the scribes and Pharisees rather than the Law itself (verse 20).

> For I say to you, that unless your righteousness exceeds the righteousness of the scribes and Pharisees, you will by no means enter the kingdom of heaven. (Mt. 5:20)

> [For I tell you, unless your righteousness exceeds that of the scribes and Pharisees, you will never enter the kingdom of heaven. (NRSV)]

Jesus would probably have had no problem in insisting that a higher standard of character was necessary than for *some* Pharisees; he might not even have been thought on shaky ground in demanding character superior to *most* Pharisees. Jesus goes far beyond such potential in-house criticism when he speaks in blanket terms of the inferiority of Pharisee morality in Matthew 23, for example. Those who did not fall into the obvious trap of open hypocrisy were extremely vulnerable to less obvious dangers.

For one thing, they were sticklers for the letter of the law even if the *content* and *purpose* were gutted in the process. They were the kind of individuals who gave "proof-texting" a bad name; they always got the doctrine and morality they wanted—they just had to work at it a while and ignore the more obvious meaning. With sufficient "massaging" of the texts, they always obtained the "right" (desired) interpretation.

As if this were not bad enough, the *grounds* for their spiritual pride was open to the gravest question: faithful obedience to the Law—*as interpreted, enhanced, expanded (and even restricted) by their traditions.* In Matthew 15:1–9 Jesus provides a particularly reprehensible example of how they had permitted their traditions to prevent young adults from assisting their parents who were in need even though such "honoring" had been demanded by the Ten Commandments. Jesus demanded superior righteousness to the scribes and Pharisees because any righteousness based strictly on God's law had to be, inherently, a superior righteousness to that produced by human glosses on the divine law.

Closely related to this was the *externalizing* of their religion. Proof of external right conduct tended to be substituted for the rightness of heart that should have been interlocked with it.[17] The heart of Jesus' moral teaching is that outward and inward character are to be but twin reflections of the same faithfulness to the Lord.

Jesus does not deny that the scribes and Pharisees were usually righteous, but he presents it as an inadequate morality. Whatever they knew, they too often found ways to bend, distort, or outright ignore in practice (cf. the scathing rebuke in Mt. 23). This inconsistency was certainly known to the rabbis, and the Talmud comments on it. As a later writer sums up the Talmudic remarks:

There are seven classes of Pharisees:

1. The shoulder Pharisee (who carries his good deeds on his shoulder ostentatiously or, according to another interpretation, tries to rid himself of the commandments).
2. The wait-a-while Pharisee (who says "Wait till I have done this good deed").
3. The bruised Pharisee (who breaks his head against the wall to avoid looking at a woman).
4. The pestle Pharisee (whose head is bent in mock humility, like a pestle in a mortar).
5. The bookkeeping Pharisee (who calculates virtue against vice, or who sins deliberately and then attempts to compensate for his sins by some good deed).
6. The God-fearing Pharisee, who is like Job.
7. The God-loving Pharisee, who is like Abraham. Talmud only regards the seventh class of the Pharisees as acceptable to God.[18]

Hence later rabbis—however much they rejected Jesus—accepted the basic validity of his judgment against the Pharisees: They were generally prone to excesses for which they could rightly be mocked and rebuked. When only one type of the seven possible types of Pharisees was considered acceptable, Jesus could hardly be looked upon as being excessive in his generalizations criticizing the group when he spoke in such terms. If Jesus was breaking new ground on this point at all, it was new ground that many who never left Judaism felt free to walk within.

*   *   *

Before passing into the main body of our discussion, it would be appropriate to analyze three key phrases that Jesus uses throughout the Antitheses: (a) "You have heard;" (b) "to those of old;" and (c) "But I say to you." Each deserves a few passing comments before we get into the body of our discussion.

"You have heard"

Alan Hugh McNeile sees in this phrase an indication that "[t]he mass of the people in Galilee could not read; they learnt the Scriptures by hearing them read and explained in the synagogues."[19] In a similar vein, C. Milo Connick asserts that "the common people were generally illiterate."[20] The assumption of widespread illiteracy is certainly open to vigorous challenge. Henri Daniel-Rops comes to the opposite conclusion: "Generally speaking one has the impression that the majority of the Jews knew how to read and write."[21] He properly introduces the repeated, casual New Testament references to literacy as evidence:

> We find many allusions to this ability, even looking no farther than the Gospels: in the parable of the dishonest steward, the cunning fellow says to a debtor, "'Sit down and write it as fifty." There is Zacharias, who being unable to speak writes the name of his son John, the future Baptist. Christ Himself speaks of the *Jod,* the smallest letter of the alphabet; and when the woman was taken in adultery, He is shown "writing on the ground with His finger," writing no doubt, His answer to the accusers, "Whichever of you is free from sin shall cast the first stone at her."[22]

Ernest DeWitt Burton and Shailer Matthews omit the challengable reference to the degree of illiteracy and are content to state that the natural force of the wording is:

> ...that He is speaking of the teaching to which His hearers have been accustomed to listen [in the synagogue], not to what they have read, [which] shows that Jesus is contrasting His teaching not with that of the Old Testament, but with that of the synagogue teachers—the scribes of the Pharisees. The people of his day sat at the feet of these scribes, and knew even Moses only as the scribes interpreted him.[23]

Although the last sentence may refer to an assumed general illiteracy, it seems more likely to mean that the scribes and Pharisees enjoyed an effective religious monopoly on the religious education of the day. One was either educated by them in the synagogue—or by nobody. That the bulk of their instruction should come orally should not be all that surprising. Even today in the United States—where the vast bulk of the population is literate—most people still learn most or all of what they know of biblical interpretation from what they hear advocated and explained at their place of worship.

It is easy to restrict "you have heard" to strictly Pharisaic/scribal interpretations,[24] but we would be putting too restrictive an interpretation on the words. Today some misinterpretations are propagated by the ministers of a religion; yet others are what might be called "lay heresies." Why should we assume things were any different in those days? Jesus does not waste time arguing over who is to blame for the misuse of the Old Testament; he simply wants his listeners to grasp that these are distortions of the true meaning of the

Torah *regardless* of who originated them and perpetuated them.

"To those of old"

Jesus conspicuously does not assert "Scripture says," "Moses says," or any synonymous term. He simply asserts "it was said to those of old" (Mt. 5:21, 27, 33).

It has been argued that if these expressions are synonyms for the Mosaic covenant and the Prophets, they represent a drastic departure from Jesus' normal terminology. The Dutch scholar H. N. Ridderbos argues that

> When Jesus quotes from the Old Testament, He always uses the words "it is written" (e.g., 4:4, 7, 10; 11:10; Mark 11:17; Luke 7:27; 18:31). Here, however, He says "It was said." His words there obviously do not refer to God's written revelation of the Old Testament but to the oral traditions of the later teachers of the law. The same is indicated by the use of these words in Jewish literature; "it was said" could actually be translated "it was taught."[25]

One could quibble a little with this; there are additional cases where Jesus refers to what a specific Old Testament figure (Moses, David, Isaiah) said, and he even cites statements from "scripture." Yet when he speaks of the body of Scripture without using the term itself, Jesus does indeed speak in the terms Ridderbos stresses. John R. W. Stott reinforces this approach by a linguistic argument: "When [Jesus] introduced a Biblical quotation, both verb and tense were different, namely gegraptai (perfect, 'it stands written'), not errethe (aorist, 'it was said')."[26]

Serious difficulties, exist, however, that require a considerable modification of the argument before it can be accepted. Pinchas Lapide contends that "it was said" is found among the descriptions of scripture used by later rabbis.[27] Even if this were not the case, the nature of the quotations made by Jesus indicates that scripture—at least the interpretation of scripture—is under consideration. When Jesus says "you have heard" and then quotes the injunctions against murder (Mt. 5:21) and adultery (Mt. 5:27), he is directly appealing to the text of the Ten Commandments. Likewise when he introduces the subject of divorce (Mt. 5:31) and punishment (Mt. 5:38), he directly appeals to the text of Deuteronomy (24:1) and Leviticus (24:20) respectively. How then can one introduce "it has been said" as convincing evidence that Jesus is *not* appealing to scripture?

Hence we must seek elsewhere an explanation for the unexpected terminology that Jesus uses. If he had used his usual expressions, then it would have been easy for his listeners to dismiss his words as criticism that was aimed at scripture. By using the vaguer terminology, he is free to quote scripture while simultaneously critiquing the exegetical abuse of the texts. In this light "it was said" could have either of two ideas:

(1) *An affirmation of the antiquity and authority of the Torah.* In rebuking the misuses of it, he is doing nothing less than upholding that which countless generations of Jews had recognized as authoritative. He is not so much introducing a teaching that is new as recovering the implications and requirements of teachings that those "of old" either knew or should have known.

(2) *An affirmation of the antiquity and authority of the interpretative "twists" that he is about to criticize.* Taken this way, the terminology only shows that it was long established teaching, dating back to an unknown (or at least unstated) period of time. Hence it

carried with it all the authority that long-standing acceptance could bestow upon it. In turn, this automatically bestowed on it a kind of semisacredness, just as creedal statements are similarly treated today when centuries have passed since their adoption.

This does not necessarily mean that *all* the rebukes are aimed at "historic" misconstructions of scripture. In two cases the Lord simply stated "it was said" (5:38, 42) and in a single case "it has been said" (5:31). These conceivably could indicate newer interpretations than the others, ones that had not yet gained the antiquity status of the other examples. On the other hand, it is possible that the wording is changed simply to provide verbal variety in the way the teaching is presented. Either way, Jesus rejects the teaching—regardless of the relative newness or ancientness of the error.

Of the two basic approaches, it seems sounder to say that Jesus is impressing upon his audience the antiquity of the Torah and using that to reinforce his critiques of how the texts were being used. He is not out to deliver a "new" teaching so much as to reaffirm that which those "of old" would have recognized—or, at least, should have. The "new" of his teaching is but an expression of the genuine "old," and the two link up to expel the contemporary interpretations that undermined the proper interpretation of Torah.

"But I say to you"

This verbal formula was unprecedented in Jewish usage. If one rejects Jesus' authority to speak, it represents nothing short of arrogance and an excuse to reject his teachings. The Roman Catholic scholar John P. Meier suggests that this willingness to speak on his own authority rather than as a prophet (the word of the Lord

said) or as a rabbi (rabbi Z said such and such) represented an "unheard-of-claim to authority over the Mosaic
Law and over people's lives." It may well have struck to
the heart of sensibilities of "pious Jews and the Jewish
authorities."[28] Certainly this has been the case among
modern Jews who have rejected the credentials of Jesus
of Nazareth. The Orthodox Jew Ahad ha'Am has argued,
"Israel cannot accept with religious enthusiasm, as the
Word of God, the utterances of a man who speaks in his
own name—not 'thus said the Lord,' but 'I say unto you.'
This 'I' is itself sufficient to drive Judaism away from the
Gentiles forever."[29]

In a narrower sense, this can be rebutted by noting
that Jesus seems to have seldom used the contrastive
"but I say to you" since it is only found in the Sermon on
the Mount. Although the phrase is not used in these
other contexts, there is still a clear authoritativeness
implied throughout his teaching, one that was recognized by observers *no matter what verbal wording was
used to express the claim.* We read of the reaction of the
people to one of his parables: "And so it was, when Jesus
had ended these sayings, that the people were astonished at His teaching, for He taught them as one having
authority, and not as the scribes" (Mt. 7:28–29). On
another occasion, we read of the Sabbath day reaction to
his preaching in the synagogue in Capernaum, "And
they were astonished at His teaching, for His word was
with authority" (Lk. 4:32).

If Jesus was more than a mere itinerant rabbi, would
one expect him to teach with different verbal formulas
than they? The use of traditional terminology would
seem to have conceded that he was merely on a par with
them, when in reality—as the Messiah—he was actually
their superior. For that matter, if he was truly the Mes-

siah, should one expect him to speak in terms of "the word of the Lord came to me"? Would that not lower him to that of a mere prophet when he deserved much higher honor?

Hence Jesus' distinctive claim to authority is a natural outgrowth of his messiahship. A unique role (Messiah) quite naturally carried with it the propriety of a unique way of speaking. Grant that he *was* that and none could criticize either the content or mode of his teaching; *deny* it and one would be doubly offended both by his terminology and by his insistence on being the uniquely accurate and authoritative spokesman of God on all things spiritual. It all comes down to whether he was or was not what he claimed to be.

NOTES

[1]"Jot," *Expository Dictionary of New Testament Words,* ed. W.E. Vine. (London: Oliphants, 1953; U.S. reprint), 2:277.

[2]Hobbs, 65.

[3] "Jot," *Expository Dictionary,* 2:277.

[4]"Tittle," *Expository Dictionary,* 4:140.

[5]Alan Hugh McNeile, *The Gospel According to St. Matthew* (London: Macmillan, 1915; 1952 reprint), 59.

[6]Gustaf Aulen, *Jesus in Contemporary Research,* trans. Ingalill H. Hjelm (Philadelphia: Fortress, 1976), 137.

[7]Ibid.

[8]Hermann Samuel Reimarus. *The Goal of Jesus and His Disciples,* trans. George W. Buchanan (Leiden: E. J. Brill, 1970), 60.

[9]Based on the precedent of the Old Testament application of apocalyptic rhetoric to dramatic and nation-changing events, the use of world-ending terminology would certainly be appropriate in describing the fall of Jerusalem. The religious world, the socio-religious-political universe that then existed, *was*

destroyed and had passed away. Or, as the writer of Hebrews argues, the old covenant "is becoming obsolete and growing old [and] is ready to vanish away" (8:13). Even in regard to the *legal* abolishment by being nailed to the cross (Col. 2:13–14), apocalyptic, world-shattering type rhetoric is used (v. 15).

[10]Daniel J. Harrington, *The Gospel of Matthew* (Collegeville, Minn.: Liturgical Press, 1991), 81.

[11]Daniel Patte, *The Gospel According to Matthew: A Structural Commentary on Matthew's Faith* (Philadelphia: Fortress, 1987), 106.

[12]John A. Broadus, *Commentary on the Gospel of Matthew* (Philadelphia: American Baptist Publication Society, 1886), 101.

[13]Rudolf Stier, *The Words of the Lord Jesus,* 4th ed., trans. William B. Pope, and rev. James Strong and Henry B. Smith (New York: N. Tibbals & Son, 1864), 1:53.

[14]Geza Vermes, *Jesus and the World of Judaism* (Philadelphia: Fortress, 1983), 47.

[15]Ibid.

[16]D. Tholuck, *Commentary on the Sermon on the Mount,* 4th ed., trans. R. Lundin Brown (Philadelphia: Smith, English, and Co., 1860), 128.

[17]Cf. this as a warning to Christians in John R. W. Stott, *Christian Counter-Culture: The Message of the Sermon on the Mount* (Downers Grove, Ill.: InterVarsity Press, 1978), 75.

[18]H. Loewe, *Rabbinic Anthology,* 485, as quoted by Jakob Jonsson, *Humour and Irony in the New Testament* (Leiden: E.J. Brill, 1985), 97–98.

[19]McNeile, 60.

[20]Connick, 244.

[21]Henri Daniel-Rops, *Daily Life in the Time of Jesus,* trans. Patrick O'Brian (New York: Hawthorn Books, 1962; paperback edition: New York: New American Library, 1964), 270.

[22]Ibid.

[23]Ernest DeWitt Burton and Shailer Matthews, *The Life of Christ,* 5th ed. (Chicago: University of Chicago Press, 1904), 102.

[24]Horace Marriott (*The Sermon on the Mount* [London: Society for Promoting Christian Knowledge, 1925], 31) stresses the rabbis as the villains in Jesus' rebuke.

[25]H. N. Ridderbos, *Matthew* (in the *Bible Student's Commentary* series, trans. Ran Togtman (Grand Rapids: Zondervan, 1987), 103.

[26]Stott, 77.

[27]Lapide, 85.

[28]John P. Meier, "Reflections on Jesus-of-History Research Today," in *Jesus' Jewishness: Exploring the Place of Jesus within Early Judaism,* ed. James H. Charlesworth (New York: American Interfaith Institute/Crossroad Publishing Company, 1991), 95.

[29]As quoted by Donald A. Hagner, *The Jewish Reclamation of Jesus* (Grand Rapids: Academie Books/Zondervan Publishing House, 1984), 102–3.

4

Examples of Jesus Allegedly Rejecting the Authority of the Torah

In light of Jesus' teaching in Matthew 5:17–20, we would expect to find him faithfully following all the provisions of the Mosaic Law—both its moral provisions and its ceremonial elements—and encouraging others to do so as well. We find this to be the case. Jesus takes for granted that gifts would be presented at the altar of the temple in Jerusalem (Mt. 5:23), that alms would and should be given (Mt. 6:2), and that fasting would be practiced (Mt. 6:16).

Indeed, the fact that his adversaries could not find any genuinely serious accusations to lodge against him with the Roman governor indicates that, overall, they found nothing that could credibly be interpreted as a major moral blot to either the Gentile or to Jews not already committed to the anti-Jesus clique. The fact that nothing of real substance could be dragged up even at the "Jewish trial" bears silent witness that no clear-cut

infractions of the Jewish law—moral or ceremonial—
could clearly and convincingly be laid at his door.

Some of Jesus' conduct and doctrine lies on the bor-
derline between these two divisions of the Jewish law
(using them for convenience rather than for strict accuracy, the relationship of moral and ceremonial being far
more intertwined than any simplistic analysis would
indicate). For example, when Jesus cleared the
Jerusalem temple (the only authorized center for the
sacrificial ceremonies required by the Law), he did so
both because of the unethical practices of traders ("you
have made it a den of thieves") and because they had
subverted the central purpose of the temple ("My house
shall be a house of prayer," quoting the Old Testament;
see Mt. 21:13).[1]

A commitment to obey even the clearly ceremonial elements in the Mosaic system is also clear in Jesus' ministry. When he cleansed the lepers, he promptly sent
them where they were supposed to go when leprosy disappeared—to the priests: "See that you tell no one; but
go your way, show yourself to the priest, and offer the
gift that Moses commanded, as a testimony to them"
(Mt. 8:4). Although he had touched the leper (v. 3) and
thereby technically violated the Law, he touched him to
heal him. Even the priests would have to do this in
examining him to be sure that he was, indeed, freed
from that terrible health scourge. Both Jesus and the
priests would technically violate the Law so that its
greater purpose of healing and restoration to full Jewish
citizenship might be fulfilled.

Such conformity to Jewish precedent is not explicitly
asserted in all situations, and one could conceivably
argue that the silence indicates a lapse on Jesus' part in
some or all such nonexplicit cases. It is far sounder to

argue from the *known* cases and conclude that this was at least his normal course of action and probably his uniform course as well. Certainly any established pattern of defiance or dissent would have brought censure in the most explicit terms, for it would have offered an inescapably attractive tool to use against him. The very fact of its absence reinforces the reasonableness of our deduction that Jesus was a faithful practitioner of the Jewish law, under any and all circumstances.

Throughout his teaching in the Sermon on the Mount (and throughout his ministry) Jesus labored to make his listeners recognize that obedience to the *letter* of the Law was never to be substituted for doing what the Law *intended.* For example, the Law taught the need to pray, but Jesus had nothing but censure for those who would "for a pretense make long prayers" (Mt. 23:14).

Closely related to this was his insistence that the letter of the Law not be used to escape what was taught by other parts of the Torah. It wasn't a matter of either/or but of either/and. In the narrative of the forty days of temptation in the wilderness, the Devil quoted scripture correctly, but Jesus rebutted with other scripture to show that an interpretation was being put on the texts that would result in the transgression of the other passages. Jesus vigorously rebuked the Pharisees for playing the either/or game with biblical injunctions: "Woe to you, scribes and Pharisees, hypocrites! For you pay tithe of mint and anise and cummin, and have neglected the weightier matters of the law: justice and mercy and faith. *These you ought to have done, without leaving the others undone"* (Mt. 23:23 our emphasis).

Jesus' argument makes plain that one did not have to choose between obeying the "minor" points of the law and obeying the "major" commands: one both could—

and should—observe both. And one could not properly use the obedience to one set of commandments as justification for ignoring the other set of commands. In light of this attitude, it is clear that Jesus could not imagine any *real* contradiction between obeying the various points of God's law.

But what if one came across a situation where it appeared that one had to choose? In Matthew 9:13 Jesus deals with this when he says, "But go and learn what this means: 'I desire mercy and not sacrifice.'" Even here Jesus roots his teaching in the old covenant by citing Hosea 6:6. Hence he is not an innovator—however much he might seem such to his foes—but is moving clearly within the orbit of prophetic teaching. In Matthew 9 he is dealing with opposition between what tradition asserted was essential (abstaining from social dealings with "tax collectors and sinners," v. 10) and what true faithfulness to God required, rather than with allegedly contradictory instructions from different commandments of God.

Likewise when Jesus again quotes the admonition from Hosea in Matthew 12:7, it is to justify his defiance of the rabbinical *interpretation* that working on the Sabbath forbade such a trivial act as "plucking heads of grain...to eat" (v. 1). Pushed to its logical extreme, such a view would even forbid the breaking of bread into pieces since that would also be "work." Again Jesus raises "mercy" to the level of vetoing any non-Torah tradition or custom.

Indeed, it is hard to believe that as strong an advocate of the divine origin of scripture as Jesus (see John 10:35, for example) could really imagine even the possibility of irreconcilable demands flowing from the Torah and the Prophets. When he advocates in Matthew 5:18 the comprehensive authority of the

Mosaic regulations, he implicitly accepts that the individual parts are fully compatible (rather than contradictory) with each other. In light of Matthew 9, however, if he actually encountered a contradictory situation—or one that people *thought* was such—he would certainly have favored the path of greater mercy—not as a substitute for obedience to the other command, but as a matter of temporary delay so that both could ultimately be carried out.

One could contend that the contrast of mercy and sacrifice represents just such a choosing, since both are presented in the Pentateuch as commanded by God. Mercy, though, was to take precedence only to whatever limited degree that one could not simultaneously carry out both commandments. Indeed, virtually any sacrifice demanded by the Law was postponable; the *sacrifice* was commanded rather than the exact timing of the sacrifice. Whether it was in the morning or the evening or even the next day was an irrelevancy. In contrast, a situation demanding mercy was one that demanded *immediate* mercy; it was something that was not postponable. It was not a matter of contradictory demands but of which needed to be carried out first so that it all would be done.

We can also look at this from a slightly different angle. When we examine the context of Hosea's admonition (6:6), we find that in its original historical setting it was a case of mercy being ignored while the people felt confident that they were safe because they were offering the required sacrifices (cf. v. 7–11). The actual situation was choosing between *meaningless ritual* (sacrifices) that exhibited no commitment beyond the superficial and the *mercy* that does exhibit a real-life commitment to carrying out God's law in daily life. What is not contrasted by Hosea are *meaningful* sacrifices with mercy;

it is meaning*less* sacrifices that are contrasted with mercy. Meaningless sacrifices had never been commanded by God, and when one had to choose between such sacrificies and mercy, mercy naturally enjoyed a higher priority.

Yet there are five lines of evidence that can be introduced to undermine our conclusion. Each of them represents a type of conduct that has been viewed by a varying number of writers, commentators, and other scholars as evidence that Jesus, in some very fundamental ways, rejected the implementation of the Jewish law. Yet if they turn out to be true, that in no way alters the evidence we have already examined or will examine in future chapters. We would have to seek some other means to reconcile the conflicting data rather than simply rule out one stream of documentation.

Jesus was walking an intellectual and spiritual tightrope. Because the Mosaic Law was still in effect, he was morally obligated to uphold it in his life and teaching; yet because he was also the Messiah, the promised prophet/lawgiver like Moses (Dt. 18:18–19), he was to prepare the people for a new religious system (Jer. 31:31–34). Hence he needed to be faithful to the old, while consistent with the new. This goes far to explain why so much that is useful to later non-Jewish audiences was included in the four Gospels: Jesus' ministry centered on what would be of *continuing* value. The approach that argues that Jesus clearly, vigorously, and even vehemently contradicted the clear instructions of the Torah carries with it the implicit claim that Jesus "fell off" of his intellectual tightrope. Again, this would require a dramatic revision of our evaluation of the success of his ministry and his intentions.

1. Healing on the Sabbath

The Pharisees collided with Jesus more than once about the requirements of true Sabbath observance. Jesus in no shape or form felt obligated to follow these well-intended but misguided human accretions to the divine law. "As many others have done," Burton and Matthews observe, "they identified their interpretation of the Scripture with the Scripture and Divine law itself, and because He opposed the interpretation they charged Him with hostility to the Scriptures."[2]

The Sabbath controversies arose over two topics: healing on the Sabbath and eating on the Sabbath. Both revolved around the accusation that Jesus had violated the Mosaic prohibition against "working" on that day of the week.

The healing came in two varieties. The first concerned cases where Jesus did not touch the individual. In Mark 3:1–5 we read of a man with a withered hand.[3] The crowd was upset at the Lord's insistence on healing him even though it was the Sabbath: "And when He had looked around at them with anger, being grieved by the hardness of their hearts, He said to the man, 'Stretch out your hand.' And he stretched it out, and his hand was restored as whole as the other" (v. 5). Since Jesus had not *touched* him, even the most nit-picking critic would have found it impossible to brand him a violator of their traditional glosses on the meaning of Sabbath "work."[4] Of course one could conceivably have argued that he *spoke* words to heal, but since his critics also spoke words on the Sabbath, any such accusation would have been transparently hypocritical. Jesus had to physically "do" something to give them a leg to stand on, and he conspicuously did not.[5] Perhaps this "mousetrap" element of Jesus' conduct—

placing them in a position where they couldn't criticize him without looking foolish—partly explains their immediate extreme reaction of seeking to destroy him (v. 6).

In other cases, the critics had more to work from, for Jesus *did* touch the person who was healed. He had performed "work" of some sort. For example, in Luke 13:10–17 we read of a physically bent woman who had been suffering from her affliction for eighteen years (v. 11). "And He laid His hands on her, and immediately she was made straight, and glorified God" (v. 13).

The alert leader of the synagogue promptly proceeded to label this inadmissible Sabbath-day "work": "There are six days on which men ought to work; therefore come and be healed on them, and not on the Sabbath" (v. 14). Note that the criticism is not explicitly targeted at Jesus; it is aimed at those who would come to be healed by him. Inconsistently enough, the synagogue leader saw no violation of the Sabbath in coming to the synagogue that day for worship, but it was wrong to come that same distance and to that same place in the hope of being healed!

Jesus recognizes that the *implicit* target of the rebuke was himself for carrying out the healing. He critiques the leader's insensitivity to the needs of his fellow humans by pointing out that he would tolerate kindness towards an animal on the Sabbath (pulling it out of a ditch, v. 15) but was forbidding mercy to a hurting human. On a positive note, he stresses the inherent and constructive good of his act; a woman in pain so long deserved to be healed, Sabbath or not (v. 16). The hardheartedness of his critics was so blatant that they "were put to shame" (v. 17). Their "logic" might have been compelling in a meeting of rigid-minded interpreters who considered the human impact of interpretation as an irrelevancy, but it sounded foolish when vocalized in public before a commonsense-minded audience.

It should be noted that there *was* a strain of thought among "liberal" rabbinical interpreters (some of which probably goes back deep into the first century), that would have found no trouble with Jesus' conduct. (If there had been no sympathy for his attitude and conduct, would he have found even the modest degree of support among the clerics that was provided him?)

Some based health-preserving "violations" of the Sabbath on the grounds that such observance was a generalization that permitted exceptions. It was an ongoing demand; hence God understood that it might not be possible to observe *every* Sabbath, though one did observe the Sabbath normally and regularly.

The more generous approach was buttressed by appeal to Scripture. Some noted the declaration in Leviticus 18:5 that the divine laws were to be followed and that an individual was to "live by them." Hence *life preservation* was the central thrust of those laws, including the Sabbath ordinance. Others read the Sabbath text in Exodus 31:14 and stressed that the Sabbath was to be "holy *to you*," that is, the Sabbath was to be human centered; *human needs came first.* That attitude (if not that particular text) can be found in Jesus' advocacy that "the Sabbath was made for man and not man for the Sabbath" (Mk. 2:27). One judgment in the Mishnah goes so far as to state, "If a man has a pain in his throat, they may drop medicine into his mouth on the Sabbath, since there is doubt whether life is in danger, and whenever there is doubt whether life is in danger this overrides the Sabbath."[6]

Even if Jesus was willing to go further in putting healing first, the fact remains that he was walking within a line of precedent that many rabbis would have acknowledged and perhaps even accepted. In one sense, how much they agreed with him or not matters little. The real question is: Was Jesus right in his interpretation of what was permitted on the Sabbath? That is what determines whether Jesus was living by or contradicting the Mosaic system. *If Jesus was "correct" in his analysis, he was truly faithful to the Law of Moses even if every single rabbinical interpreter had disagreed with him!* (And, as we have seen, there is a good deal of evidence that many would not have been.)

2. Plucking of Grain on the Sabbath

In Matthew 12:1–7 (and its parallels in Mark 2:23–29 and Luke 6:1–5), we find Jesus and his disciples passing through the fields of grain. "And His disciples were hungry and began to pluck heads of grain and to eat" (Mt. 12:1). "And His disciples plucked the heads of grain and ate them, rubbing them in their hands" (Lk. 6:1).

There may or may not be significance in the fact that Jesus is neither pictured as personally doing this nor accused of such: "Look, Your disciples are doing what is not lawful to do on the Sabbath" (Mt. 12:2). In Mark 2:23–24 he is challenged about what "they" are doing. The original challenge was to the disciples: "Why are you doing what is not lawful on the Sabbath" (Lk. 6:1–2) and Jesus answered in their defense beginning in verse 3.

The Jewish scholar David Flusser believes that this was "the one and only act of transgression of the Law recorded in the synoptic tradition."[7] (W. D. Davies notes that "most Christian scholars" have interpreted the account to be a "rejection of the Law itself.").[8] Flusser concedes that the Jews of the era considered it proper to both pick up fallen grains and to rub them together and eat them. The transgression would have been considered the actual *plucking* of them.[9] Of course why rubbing the grains was not working and yet the plucking was represents a distinction that would seem virtually impossible to justify. On any other day of the week, the conduct of the disciples would have been regarded as beyond challenge.[10] By falling on the Sabbath, however, the hostile critic could look upon it as "technically, 'reaping' and forbidden" on that weekly day of rest and religious worship.[11]

Furthermore, note that this type of objection to Jesus only reveals—at the most—that his conduct would have been in defiance of *traditional interpretation*. Once again, the real question must be whether this was "work" in genuine defiance (and defilement) of the Sabbath. Was breaking a loaf work? Why then would be the casual picking of some grains? If it had been *harvesting* that would have been a thoroughly different story. But it wasn't that at all.

Jesus did not respond with legalistic nit-picking (and his action was certainly justifiable on that score, as noted above), but instead he cast the question in terms of a broader principle. David was a man after God's own heart, but when moved by hunger, he felt it legitimate to eat the shewbread which was supposed to be just for the priests (Mt. 12:3–4). He didn't do it daily or regularly—or probably even once again in his entire life—any more than the disciples made a *custom* out of plucking the grain and eating it. Sabbath law was important, but hunger was even more so. There would be many a Sabbath left to "keep holy" in the future—but only if human life were preserved from the hunger that could destroy it.

As to "working" on the Sabbath, the priests did that each and every Sabbath in their ministering in the temple.

Yet this was a work that was clearly "blameless" (v. 5). Implied here is that the motive and intent behind the work is the standard for praise or condemnation.

Jesus briefly alludes to his own status as authority figure ("in this place there is One greater than the temple," v. 6). The Old Testament prophet Hosea taught that humanitarian consideration was of greater importance than sacrifice (v. 7). And who can more rightly interpret what is prophetically endorsed mercy than the one who is himself "Lord even of the Sabbath" (v. 8)? Jesus aligns his teaching (v. 8) with that of the prophets (v. 7). So far as he was concerned, it was a matter of carrying out the *principles* and *intents* of the Old Testament. His critics might deny that his interpretation was correct, but one could hardly read verses 3-7 without recognizing that it was his intent to advocate a doctrine totally consistent with the true meaning of the old covenant.

3. The Woman Taken in Adultery

The case of the woman taken in adultery (Jn. 8:1–11) may seem a clear-cut example of Jesus' refusal to carry out the demand of the Torah when (a) the demand of the Law was quite clear and (b) the guilt of the accused was equally certain. Yet Jesus refused to countenance her proposed execution:

> But Jesus went out to the Mount of Olives. And early in the morning He came again into the temple, and all the people came to Him; and He sat down and taught them. Then the scribes and Pharisees brought to Him a woman caught in adultery. And when they had set her in the midst, they said to Him, "Teacher, this woman was caught in adultery, in the very act. Now Moses, in the

law, commanded us that such should be stoned. But what do You say?"

This they said, testing Him, that they might have something of which to accuse Him. But Jesus stooped down and wrote on the ground with His finger, as though He did not hear. So when they continued asking Him, He raised Himself up and said to them, "He who is without sin among you, let him throw a stone at her first."

And again He stooped down and wrote on the ground. And those who heard it, being convicted by their conscience, went out one by one, beginning with the oldest even to the last. And Jesus was left alone, and the woman standing in the midst. When Jesus had raised Himself up and saw no one but the woman, He said to her, "Woman, where are those accusers of yours? Has no one condemned you?" She said, "No one, Lord." And Jesus said to her, "Neither do I condemn you; go and sin no more." (Jn.8:1–11).

[...while Jesus went to the Mount of Olives. Early in the morning he came again to the temple. All the people came to him and he sat down and began to teach them. The scribes and the Pharisees brought a woman who had been caught in adultery; and making her stand before all of them, they said to him, "Teacher, this woman was caught in the very act of committing adultery. Now in the law Moses commanded us to stone such women. Now what do you say?"

They said this to test him, so that they might have some charge to bring against him. Jesus bent down and wrote with his finger on the ground. When they kept on questioning him, he straightened up and said to them, "Let anyone among you who is without sin be the first to throw a stone at her."

And once again he bent down and wrote on the ground. When they heard it, they went away, one by one, beginning with the elders; and Jesus was left alone with the woman standing before him. Jesus straightened up and said to her, "Woman, where are they? Has no one condemned you?" She said, "No one, sir." And Jesus said, "Neither do I condemn you. Go your way, and from now on do not sin again." (NRSV)]

Laying aside the question of the degree to which the death penalty could be carried out without Roman approval, a careful consideration of the text raises several questions that point to Jesus being merciful not in spite of the demands of the Torah, but because the demands of the Torah had not been satisfied.

Note carefully that the scribes and Pharisees prove the woman's guilt by stressing that "this woman was caught in adultery, *in the very act*" (v. 3). They correctly noted that in such cases "Moses, in the law, commanded us that such should be stoned" (v. 4). Then, apparently in hope of getting him to endorse a procedure in contradiction to the Law of Moses, they queried, "But what do *You* say?" (v. 5) (By the way, if Jesus had a reputation of normally acting in defiance of the Old Testament, there would have been no need for such entrapment. The fact that it was required strongly implies that Jesus was very well known for his steadfast adherence to the Torah.)

Although the Law provided for the death penalty, it demanded quite a bit more than what her prosecutors were asserting: "If a man is found lying with a woman married to a husband, then *both of them shall die*—the man that lay with the woman, and the woman; so you shall put away the evil from Israel" (Dt. 22:22, our emphasis).

The critics of Jesus were indicted by their own words as demanding one-sided pseudojustice rather than the strict equity that the Torah demanded. For Jesus to have acceded to their insistence would have been to permit only part of the Law to be observed while allowing an equally guilty individual to escape unharmed. Such was in direct defiance of Deuteronomy 22:22.

Yes, Jesus showed mercy, but it was mercy fully grounded on the insistence of the Torah that the same crime be punished in the same way when two people shared equal guilt. (The fact that the man was to be punished by death should also lay to rest the odd claim that under the Mosaic system only a married woman and not a married man could be guilty of adultery. The Law provided for the death of the man involved, whether married or not.)

Then there is the matter of one of the most misused verses in the entire Bible, Jesus' rebuke in verse 11: "He who is without sin among you, let him throw a stone at her first." *Something* in these words clearly embarrassed them: "Then those who heard it, being convicted by their conscience, went out one by one, beginning with the oldest even to the last" (v. 9). Standing by itself, the words are an obvious truism, blatantly unable to provoke such an extreme reaction. Who is not a sinner? If we were to avoid punishing someone because in some way we too are sinners, no one would ever be punished for any evil no matter how base or depraved.

So there must be more going on here than is recognized when we misuse the passage into a convenient text to urge tolerance and understanding for others. There must be something *in the immediate circumstances* that made them feel an overpowering guilt. One obvious possibility would have been that they were sufficient students of the Torah to recognize that only one of the two guilty parties had been brought for punishment. But does even that go far enough to incite the kind of overwhelming guilt implied by our text? Does not the intensity of their reaction require that they too had been engaged in similar sin? Perhaps even with this very woman? Or perhaps it was even one of their own number who had been caught in this particular illicit mating.

J. Duncan M. Derrett suggests two possible sources of guilt that would be slightly less soul-indicting, though ominous in their own right. He suggests the possibility that they had received a bribe to avoid hauling along the guilty male to the bar of justice.[12] Furthermore, since at least two witnesses were required, the "discovery" seemingly had to have represented a trap, set up with the purpose of bringing accusations against the woman. This would be unsavory in itself, but since they had sprung the trap while she was engaged in actual intercourse, *it had been within their power to stop it from happening.* As Derrett comments, "The whole affair reeks of [causes for judicial] doubt, but the witnesses' sin in not attempting to prevent what might easily have been prevented admits of little doubt."[13]

In our judgment, the fact that the entire crowd started to drift away—not just her direct accusers— implies an even more serious ethical breach, such as we suggested earlier. Whatever we trace their guilt to, it must have some kind of direct bearing on the sin they were accusing the woman of. Even if we limit this to being a "put-up case" where they raided the house of a known prostitute for the purpose of bringing the accusation (a far less reasonable supposition), a guilty root was still present. For their rage was aimed not so much at the adultery, but far more at the Jesus whom they desired to entrap.

While we are on the subject, we should perhaps draw attention to another ill-used text found in the same passage, "But Jesus stooped down and wrote on the ground with His finger, as though He did not hear....And again He stooped down and wrote on the ground" (v. 6, 8). How many expositors have spoken of Jesus being embarrassed by the accusation, as if he were some kind of urban Victorian who liked to pretend that human sexuality did not exist. As most people of his day, Jesus probably knew more of the "facts of life" at an extremely early age (what else when teenage marriage was customary?) than many raised in the first half of our own century.

There is no way of proving what he wrote,[14] but I have often wondered whether it wasn't something directly relevant and humiliating to the woman's accusers—like the names of prominent individuals she was known to keep company with, or perhaps even the names of certain members of the present company who had been her bed mates in the past. Now wouldn't that be a powerful reinforcer of the Lord's rebuke, "He who is without sin among you, let him throw a stone at her first"!

There is one last aspect to consider: It seems to be generally conceded that by the time of Christ the death penalty for adultery was no longer being enforced. If that is so, the hypocrisy of Jesus' critics stands out in even harsher light. They are demanding that he enforce a law that they themselves were no longer willing to carry out. The confrontation, then, becomes even more an attempt to find something—anything—to criticize Jesus about. The proper punishment was not really an issue to them, nor was the correct interpretation and usage of Moses' law. What *was* of overwhelming concern was uncovering some accusation that could be used against Jesus to make him appear to contradict the scriptures of old. The punishment, or lack of punishment, of the woman was an irrelevancy; the ability to use her sin to undermine the credibility of Jesus was all that mattered.

4. Clean Versus Unclean Food

In Matthew 15:1–20 and its parallel account in Mark 7:1–23, Jesus gives instruction that can easily be taken as a denial of the Mosaic prohibition of eating certain foods. For example, R. T. France argues that "this was not just an attack on scribal *halakah,* but on a principle of the Mosaic law (even though Jesus has just accused the scribes of undermining the authority of that same law by their traditions!)"[15] (his emphasis). (But does not that *un*-innovative avowed intention of Jesus itself constitute a mighty argument against the interpretation?)

But let us look more closely at the text. Jesus is quoted as telling his listeners, "Not what goes into the mouth defiles a man; but what comes out of the mouth, this defiles a man" (Mt. 15:11; cf. Mk. 7:15). Hence, in context the issue is not over the eating or not eating of specific meats, but over whether one had to ceremonially wash hands before eating.

The challenge was hurled at him, "Why do Your disciples transgress the tradition of the elders? For they do not wash their hands when they eat bread" (Mt. 15:2). Once again we see that the controversy was not over whether Moses' law about what foods could be consumed was valid, but over why Jesus' disciples so stubbornly departed from the authoritative tradition that accompanied the eating of permitted foods. This *tradition* was not only an established endorsed custom, but it was the dominant practice in all parts of society: "For the Pharisees and all the Jews do not eat unless they wash their hands in a special way, holding the tradition of the elders" (Mk. 7:3).

Such customs were not wrong in themselves, but they neither morally improved nor morally lowered the food that was consumed. Only that which came voluntarily from within the power of the individual to control could inflict moral defilement: "Are you thus without understanding also? Do you not perceive that whatever enters a man from outside cannot defile him, because it does not enter his heart but his stomach, and is eliminated, thereby purifying all foods?" (Mk. 7:18–19). Does this mean that Jesus was abolishing the difference between clean and unclean foods decreed by Moses in the Law? For that matter, is this the remark of Jesus or the interpretation put on it by Mark in retrospect?

The red print found in many Bible editions represents the editor's best judgment, but there is nothing in the manuscripts to show where Jesus' words begin or end. Usually it is not a difficult question, but reconciling these words with Jesus' upholding of the Mosaic Law makes one wonder whether a mistake might not have been made in this particular case. In defense of the possibility that they are Jesus' words is the fact that the words are addressed to the disciples, in private and not in public (Mk. 7:17). Hence one could argue that Jesus was preparing them for the future change. Yet two considerations argue that at this point in the text we go from the actual words of Jesus to a Markan interpretation:

(1) Jesus' disciples might be quite willing to defy a rabbinically established custom since they were not tied in with the religious power structure of the day. To ask them to accept the abolishment of kosher/unclean distinctions would surely have sparked a further discussion that would have required some type of additional textual reference. Indeed, even among these, his friends, this would have seemingly undermined Jesus' public

stance of being a dedicated upholder of Mosaic Law. More would have been required to justify this divergence from his public position.

(2) Furthermore, *the apostles did not interpret Jesus' words in this way until substantially after his resurrection.*[16] As late as his vision in Acts 10, Peter was still convinced that it was wrong to eat those foods forbidden by the Old Testament (10:11–16 and 11:5–10, where Peter himself summarized the incident). If Jesus had personally and explicitly dealt with the matter, would Peter have felt so strongly against partaking of the "unclean" food? Or been so defensive when the Jewish believers in Jerusalem challenged him on going to the Gentiles?

Hence we conclude that we are dealing with Markan interpretation rather than with the personal words of the Lord. This is certainly *early* interpretation, assuming that the general consensus that Mark was the first written gospel account is correct. On the other hand, it comes from a date *after* the vision Peter had in Acts, since a stern vigor against departing from food distinctions still existed at that date. It seems safest to conclude that as a result of this vision, the Jewish Christians (or at least the ones under the influence of the apostles) came to accept that all foods were now on a moral par regardless of whether they personally exercised the liberty that fact gave them.

Reading Christ's rebuke of the scribes and Pharisees, it would have been easy to see in retrospect—just as we do today—that the *principle* Jesus gave could apply not just to the eating of foods with unwashed hands, but to the very distinction of foods into clean and unclean categories. But that is far different from saying that his immediate listeners understood it that way or that he *intended* his immediate listeners to so understand.[17] So far as immediate practice was concerned, Jesus asserted nothing in any way different than what the Mosaic Law demanded; his eventual intentions for his disciples after his resurrection and the removal of the Mosaic system represents a different topic altogether.

We have assumed a Markan authorship; but if one insists that the words came from Jesus, they still do not require the repudiation of clean/unclean distinctions. This is not the same thing as saying that Jesus did not intend his later listeners/readers to deduce from the text that conclusion, just that he himself could not use the arguments (which so effectively argue that case as well) while the Mosaic Law itself remained authoritative. One can read and re-read the text a hundred times and still one is faced with the fact that only one topic is under immediate discussion: whether an individual could eat food without ceremonially washing his hands. The question of the clean/unclean food distinction was in no way under consideration.

Yes, "He purif[ied] all foods" (Mk. 7:19) *so far as eating them with unwashed hands.* Again, only in retrospect and after Peter's vision was it natural to grasp that the arguments Jesus used had a far wider scope. With humanity freed from Moses' Law, Jesus' arguments then cried out for the repudiation of the kosher/unclean food distinction. But this was true only at that point in history and not during the earthly ministry of the Lord himself.

5. Let the Dead Bury the Dead

In Matthew 8:18–21 and Luke 9:57–62, we read of an individual apparently wishing to follow Jesus in his travels (cf. Mt. 8:16). He already was a follower, for he is

called "another of His disciples" (Mt. 8:21). This man
Jesus urged to "follow Me" (Lk. 9:59). It was the *immedi-
acy* of this demand that the disciple wished to postpone:
"Lord, let me first go and bury my father" (Lk. 9:59; cf.
Mt. 8:21). Many a sermon has been preached from these
texts about "putting Jesus first" even above one's close
family. Jesus rebuked the divided heart of this disciple
by telling him, "let the [spiritual] dead bury their own
[physical] dead" (Lk. 9:60; cf. Mt. 8:22).

Such sermonic elaboration certainly represents "fair
use" of the passage, but what is nearly always understated is just how drastic a demand Jesus gave. To us it
is startling, but to the Jew far, far more so. As E. P.
Sanders has written, "What is important here is to see
the force of the negative thrust: Jesus *consciously*
requires disobedience of a commandment understood by
all Jews to have been given by God"(his emphasis)[18] "At
least [this] once Jesus was willing to say that following
Him superseded the requirements of piety and the
Torah."[19] After examining other cases of Jesus' allegedly
defying the Law, Sanders concludes that this is the only
clear-cut case of Jesus doing so.[20]

Jewish exegesis traditionally interpreted the fifth
commandment to require the offspring to bury their parents.[21] Later rabbis even went so far as to demand that
the Nazarite and high priest ignore the rigid laws
against ceremonial uncleanness attached to their positions in order to prepare their loved ones for burial.[22] In
the book of Tobit (6:15), a marriage proposal is rejected
lest the groom be struck dead and his parents be left
without any child to bury them.

Now let us look at the other side of the coin. All would
agree that the Torah demanded obedience to God above
any other loyalty, even to kinsmen. Would not Jesus'

demand—assuming he truly was who he claimed to be—
be an exercise of such divine prerogatives? Of putting
God first and even kinspeople second?

Laying aside that reasonable assertion, there is something distinctly odd in the incident itself: *What was the
man doing with Jesus in the first place on that day of
family tragedy?* According to Daniel-Rops, in Jewish
communities of that day and age "[t]he burial usually followed eight hours after the death: in a hot climate it cannot be delayed."[23] Even if we stretch this a bit, it is
inconceivable of much more than a day passing prior to
burial. The two cases of burial in the four Gospels were
clearly done promptly and quickly. Jesus was buried
within hours of his death. Lazarus was also buried the
day of his death. He had been "dead four days" by the
time the Lord arrived at his burial site (Jn. 11:39), yet we
read that "he had already been in the tomb four days" (v.
17). In other words, he was buried the day he died.

In light of the tradition of same-day internment, what
in the world was he doing there listening to Jesus, especially if we have read the implication correctly that he
was seeking to travel with Jesus in his ministry? Where
was the time found in the matter of hours between death
and burial? How? In light of this incongruity, the suggestion may not be unsound that his father was not dead at
all, that what he was really asking was permission to
join Jesus when his father eventually died. This would
explain both his ability to be present to pose the request
and the unexpected intensity of Jesus' demand.

Another factor to be considered is this: Did Jesus *expect*
the man to accompany him? The dialogue has certainly
been interpreted that way, and it is a reasonable construction. After all, Jesus does say, "Follow me." He certainly
demands more of the man than passive listening, but is it

a call as well to join Jesus in his travels? When we hear preachers of today speak of our "following Jesus" does that mean we are being urged to become itinerants?

It could mean that in the present text. Yet note the wording in Luke 9:60: "Let the dead bury their own dead, but you go and preach the kingdom of God." Not "come with me and preach the kingdom" but "you go and preach the kingdom." The implication here is, seemingly, that he would be teaching *elsewhere than as part of Jesus' traveling company.* Hence Jesus' admonition would be perfectly consistent with the individual remaining until the burial was over with. What Jesus is doing, in this reconstruction, is urging him to rearrange his priorities: "Let the spiritually dead take care of and worry about the burial, but you must center your mind on something far, far different—not death, but the message of God's kingdom." This becomes a particularly attractive scenario if we believe that the father was still alive; then he could both go immediately and be available for that sad day when his father eventually perished. But in neither case would he be traveling with Jesus. He would be working in his own area and be available both for both teaching and for more immediate family obligations.

NOTES

[1]The Talmud indicates that in the days of Caiaphas, the high priest under whom Jesus died, "there was considerable controversy over the siting of cultically related commercial activity" (Chilton, *A Galilean Rabbi,* 18). Jesus' action was his acted-out interpretation of what was right and wrong on the subject and bears witness to his stern determination to avoid all the supposedly incidental commercial uses of the site in order to fully implement the spiritual purposes of the temple.

[2]Burton and Matthews, 101.

[3]Chad Myers argues that Jesus' prior public healings are conspicuously set as occurring when the Sabbath was over (1:21, 1:32) and suggests that the emphasis is to alert the reader that when he decides to heal on the Sabbath itself, the decision is going to be a controversial one (*Binding the Strong Man: A Political Reading of Mark's Story of Jesus* [Maryknoll, NY: Orbis Books, 1988], 140).

[4]Hagner, 111; Irving M. Zeitlin, *Jesus and the Judaism of His Time* (Cambridge, UK: Polity Press/New York: Basil Blackwell, 1988), 73.

[5]Cf. on this theme Morna D. Hooker, *The Gospel According to St. Mark* (London: A & C Black, 1991), 108; and Howard F. Vos, *Mark: A Study Guide Commentary* (Grand Rapids: Zondervan, 1978), 31.

[6]Yoma 3:6, quoted by Zeitlin, 75–76. For a discussion of the various "liberal" rabbinic views, see Zeitlin, 74–76. On the same theme see also I. Abrahams, *Studies in Pharisaism and the Gospels,* First Series (Cambridge, UK: Cambridge University Press, 1917; reprint edition: New York: KTAV, 1967), 129–35.

[7]Quoted by Hagner, 110.

[8]Davies, *Setting of the Sermon,* 103.

[9]Cited by Hagner, 110. Hagner notes that Flusser believes that because of the unacceptability of the plucking aspect of the text, that this was an element added by a writer unacquainted with local customs on the subject.

[10]John Hargreaves, *Guide to St. Mark's Gospel,* Rev. Ed. (London: S.P.C.K., 1995), 53, citing Deuteronomy 23:25 as support.

[11]An interpretation that Wilfrid Harrington concedes is valid in her *Mark* (Wilmington, Del.: Michael Glazier, 1979), 35.

[12]J. Duncan M. Derrett, *Law in the New Testament* (London: Darton, Longman & Todd, 1970), 163–164.

[13]Ibid., 164.

[14]For a concise survey of various opinions on the subject see

Raymond E. Brown, *John,* in the Anchor Bible series (Garden City, NY: Doubleday, 1966), 333–34.

[15]R. T. France, *Divine Government: God's Kingship in the Gospel of Mark* (London: S.P.C.K., 1990), 59.

[16]On this theme see John J. Kilgallen, *A Brief Commentary on the Gospel of Mark* (New York: Paulist, 1989), 134–135.

[17]Stephen Westerholm (*Jesus and Scribal Authority* [Coniectanea Biblica: New Testament Series Number 10. Doctoral Thesis at Lund University. GWK Gleerup, 1978], 82) comes to a somewhat similar conclusion when he writes, "What we have here is a general statement, the *implications* of which seem clear to us, as indeed, they did for Mark (7:19c) and Paul (Romans 4:14), but in the absence of any specific applications to the laws of Leviticus 11, may not have been immediately so clear for the entire church." We may add that an *explicit* reference to the dietary laws themselves was precluded by his intention to live in full conformity with the existing Mosaic system. The most he could do was to give teaching that would be compatible with both the existing system *and* the one he intended to have his apostles proclaim.

[18]E. P. Sanders, *Jesus and Judaism* (Philadelphia: Fortress, 1985), 255.

[19]Ibid.

[20]Ibid., 267.

[21]Ibid., 253. Luke T. Johnson, concurs in this as a valid deduction from the commandment to honor one's parents, in his *The Gospel of Luke* (Collegeville, Minn.: Liturgical Press, 1991), 163.

[22]Sanders, 253.

[23]Henri Daniel-Rops, *Daily Life in the Time of Jesus,* trans. Patrick O'Brian (New York: Hawthorn Books, 1962; paperback edition: New York: New American Library, 1964), 322.

Section Two

RELATIVELY OBVIOUS
OLD TESTAMENT PARALLELS

5

Adultery and Lust (Matthew 5:27-30)

"It isn't wrong so long as you don't actually go out and do it. It only becomes sin if you actually sleep with the other person." That attitude is the bedrock on which rests the acceptance of extreme sexual explicitness in literature and photography and in its toleration in its less restrained younger brother, outright pornography. It is easy to consider such attitudes as uniquely the product of the modern world, perhaps even of our own lifetime. But anyone who has either seen or heard of the wall frescoes found in the ruins of Roman Pompeii has to doubt whether such an attitude is either peculiarly modern or the result of the particular culture we live in. In the case of Pompeii, many of the possessors of such pornography probably made no distinction between thought and act and considered it one unbroken continuum: what one *wants* quite naturally leads to what one *does*—provided the right opportunity and playmate/victim is available. Less callous souls need a way of reconciling the immoral they *want* to do with what they feel it proper to do. Hence the attractiveness of separating fantasy life from actual conduct. Jesus apparently had such individuals at least partly in mind in the second half of the second of his antitheses:

> You have heard that it was said to those of old, "You shall not commit adultery." But I say to you that whoever looks at a woman to lust for her has already committed adultery with her in his heart.[1] (Mt. 5:27–28)

> [You have heard that it was said, "You shall not commit adultery." But I say to you that everyone who looks at a woman with lust has already committed adultery with her in his heart. (NRSV)]

The Meaning of Jesus' Assertion

Note the stress on *intent* in Christ's teaching: "whoever looks at a woman to lust after her," i.e., with that intent and purpose. The idea is not that of desire that spontaneously wells up without warning—though Christ's teaching would be an implicit warning to suppress such when it occurs—but at the individual who is setting out to look at women with such a purpose.

Horace Marriott suggests that the immediately preceding rejection of unjustified anger is an absolute prohibition, whereas this one is conditional or limited. "There our Lord began with 'whoever is angry with his brother' simply, here He does not condemn the feeling of lust *apart from* some yielding to it."[2] Connick has a similar idea when he writes, "What is the lustful look? It is persistent purposing. It is not the consummation (adultery) or the consideration (glance, thought, desire) but the commitment (conscious choice, will)."[3]

Sexual desire is an inherent part of our nature; therefore, it cannot be wrong in itself, but it must be regulated to keep it within proper boundaries. Desire, however limited, may spring almost instinctively when faced with an attractive person. What Jesus condemns is looking in order to lust. According to Frederick D. Brunner,

> The differene may seem subtle. But something important is protected by the difference: to see a person *with* desire is the result of a God-given drive (Genesis 1:27–28; 2:18–24), to be enjoyed in the marriage relation; to stare at another person in order to desire that person is proscribed, for it uses another person, and it takes what God has given in creation—the created desire for the opposite sex—and uses it outside God's plan of marriage. The lustful stare goes beyond the desiring look like hate goes beyond prophetic anger or like theft goes beyond admiration.[4]

In light of the emphasis on *sustained* looking, Brunner suggests that the Greek verb found here might well be rendered "staring."[5] He suggests that a great deal about interpersonal attitudes is implied here. "The other person is no longer really a unique human being; she or he is now simply kindling, tinder, a thing, a way for one to enjoy oneself, to express oneself, to feel one's powers."[6] By rejecting such a self-centered ethic, Jesus is enjoining "an ethic of other-honoring and of other-protection."[7]

Nothing is said here indicating any fault on the woman's part. Jesus is targeting his teaching specifically at those who are determined to mentally exploit a woman *regardless.* In light of Proverbs' very explicit warning of how certain types of women could lead one astray, Jesus was surely aware of the possibility of mutual culpability. Jesus, however, puts it in the simplest and bluntest form so that the male will understand his responsibility *regardless* of how the desire arises.

Although the verb for lust that Jesus uses in Matthew 5:28 is not found elsewhere in the New Testament in any explicitly visual context (however, see on Romans 7:7 below), the noun form *(epithumia)* is so found. In 1 John 2:16 we read of the three-fold stumbling blocks of "the lust of the flesh, the lust of the eyes, and the pride of life." The first two, combined together, can certainly produce the kind of mental imaginings that Jesus condemned. For that matter, does not the "pride of life" also enter in? To seek to be the object of such desires caters to our pride and to seek to have at least in our fantasy one whose physical allure would increase our worldly status, isn't that a form of pride-seeking as well?

The noun form is also found in the rogue's gallery of mainly sexually related sins found in Colossians 3:5: "Therefore put to death your members which are on the earth: fornication, uncleanness, passion, evil desire *[epithumia],* and covetousness, which is idolatry."

All Women or Just Married Women?

The word for woman in Matthew 5:28 can mean either unmarried or married. Two things argue for the latter. First, Jesus is reacting to the commandment against extramarital sex (adultery). Second, since he labels the sin of sexual fantasizing as "adultery" (rather than "fornication"), the most natural understanding is that the woman is *married.*[8] This line of reasoning would seemingly have to be carried a step further: because the term *adultery* is used, would this not also require that only the married *male* is under consideration?

On the other hand, both betrothal (a firm, binding

commitment to marriage) and marriage itself were undertaken at a much younger age in that day than in modern industrial nations. Any woman who was old enough to incite such desire was almost inevitably in one of these two interlocked categories. Even if the marriage had not yet taken place, she could be anticipated to be *betrothed* in marriage, which would cause the transgression to bear a similar moral taint. Hence, even if we give the text the "narrower" reading, the practical implications governed all adult male-female relationships.

Old Testament Precedents and Similarities

Many have used this text to prove that, at least on this point, both the Old Testament in general and the Ten Commandments in particular permitted something that Jesus explicitly prohibited. The founder of the modern social gospel movement in American Protestantism, Walter Rauschenbusch, worded it this way: "The old law forbade adultery, the infringement of family life, and stopped there. Jesus goes back of the act to the lustful imaginations and the wandering eye..."[9] I, myself, had repeatedly insisted through decades that "What mattered under the Old Testament was your outward conduct, not what was in your heart. The Old Testament targeted the external act; the gospel of Christ the state of your heart. Here we have a direct quotation from the Ten Commandments and we find Christ rejecting it as inadequate, saying that, good as the instruction was, the gospel demands far more."

In part this is true: comparatively, the Old Testament *did* stress the external more than the internal. Yet the demand that the inner person be put right was not missing either, and this antithesis of Jesus is an example of the application of that principle. In quoting the seventh commandment, Christ is not denying that the Old Testament prohibited unrestrained, unlimited, uncontrolled lust; he is only saying that this particular commandment specifically singles out one type of sexual sin (adultery) and does not contain all of the divine will on human sexuality.

Indeed, the tenth commandment quite specifically orders, "You shall not covet your neighbor's house; you shall not covet your neighbor's wife, nor his male servant, nor his female servant, nor his ox, nor his donkey, nor anything that is your neighbor's" (Ex. 20:17). What does it mean to "covet"? To want to have for yourself, to possess as your own, sometimes to the point of obsession. And what can it mean to "covet your neighbor's wife" than to either desire her as your wife and to have the ongoing sexual relationship that comes with marriage or to have that relationship with her even while she remains married to someone else? Either way it comes down to sexually desiring a relationship that the Torah prohibits.

F. F. Bruce is not pleased with such an exegesis. He contends that the prohibition is mentioned in the context of "items of...property" and must be interpreted strictly in such a relationship. "In a property context one might 'covet' someone else's wife not by way of a sexual urge but because of the social or financial advantages of being linked with her family."[10] In our own day and age, individuals sometimes engage in hunting down someone else's spouse as a means of upgrading their own financial status or public image. So the suggestion is not completely unfounded. On the other hand, when it comes to intergender relationships, and when the gender relationship of "wife" is under specific consideration, it is hard to see how it can avoid including the desire for an unlawful sexual relationship. Even when other factors are also present, it is hard to see how anyone of normal sexuality could avoid seeking that person, at least partly, through sexual self-interest as well.

Paul quotes the tenth commandment as "You shall not covet" in Romans 7:7 and uses the same verb *(epithumeo)* that Jesus uses in Matthew 5:28 and that is rendered "lust." It is a word that refers to any strong, powerful, potentially overwhelming desire. Since Paul had just been speaking of adultery (v. 3) and since he uses terminology most commonly (though not exclusively) pertaining to sexuality ("passions," v. 5; "desire," v. 8), it is quite possible that Paul is reading the tenth commandment as meaning sexual coveting or at least applying it primarily to sexual coveting. If this be the case, our reading of the tenth commandment as prohibiting lusting would be confirmed.

Be this as it may, other passages also deal with the matter and also censure, condemn, or outright prohibit the same conduct that Jesus did in his antithesis. In Proverbs we find quite explicit admonition on the subject. In chapter 6 we find the young man being warned to avoid the prostitutes of his day: "Do not lust after her beauty in your heart, nor let her allure you with her eyelids" (v. 25). Here is specifically condemned sexual lust aimed at someone you are not married to. It even combines that idea with the desire being in the "heart"—the very two ideas Christ joins together in his antithesis. One text effectively functions as a commentary on the other.

Job made the conscious decision not to follow a lifestyle in which he would fantasize the pleasures of a relationship with other women: "I have made a covenant with my eyes; why then should I look upon a young woman?" (Job 31:1). For the word *look,* the marginal reading suggests as alternatives, "look intently or gaze." Moffatt's modern speech translation sums up the thought rather well, "I laid an interdict upon my eyes, never to look with longing on a maiden." Is not this the idea of "lusting after" that Jesus condemned?

Verse 9 finds Job wishing calamity upon his own house if he had given in to this way of thinking: "If my heart has been enticed by a woman, or if I have lurked at my neighbor's door." Just as Jesus noted the heart as a potential breeding ground for lust, Job referred to how the heart could be "enticed" by the sexual appeal of the other gender.

In Ezekiel 6:9 the Lord rebuked the people "because I was crushed by their adulterous heart which had departed from Me, and by their eyes which play the harlot after their idols." In this case, lusting after false gods led to spiritual idolatry; but is not the obvious, earthly basis the fact that looking with lusting eyes after a woman leads to carnal adultery?

A major practical objection to unrestrained sexual fantasizing is that it breaks down the barriers to *doing* what one is dreaming about doing. Genesis 34:2 seems to imply such a sequence. Shechem the Hivite, a nobleman among the Hivites, "saw" Dinah and then raped her. He desired her so much that he allowed desire to be translated into assault. David "saw" the naked Bathsheba, and she "was very beautiful to behold." The text draws a straight line between this and David's adultery (2 Sm. 11:2–4) and all the tragedy that it ultimately produced. Again, desire was allowed to go unrestrained, and it was transformed into transgression.

Jeremiah 5:8 has such an idea in mind: "They were like well-fed lusty stallions; every one neighed after his neighbor's wife." They were "hot" after others; they were aroused and sought out the opportunity to translate desire into action. Hence they chased their neighbor's wife (v. 8) and frequented the prostitute (v. 7)—all of which they would ultimately be punished for (v. 9). First came a desire they refused to curb—then came translating fantasy into reality.

In Ezekiel 23:16–17 a similar imagery is used in regard to Israel entering into unlawful foreign alliances that betrayed a lack of trust in Jehovah: "As soon as her eyes saw them, she lusted for them and sent messengers to them in Chaldea. Then the Babylonians came to her, into the bed of love, and they defiled her with their immorality." Based on the psychology all can recognize, the picture is that of being sexually "turned on" and then "consummating" that desire. Desire and act, stimulation and fulfillment, are linked together just as they are in real life. It is of some interest, though, that the rebuke here pictures *feminine* lust while most other texts speak in terms of *masculine* desire. The Bible mainly targets the male on such matters, but it is well aware of the danger of uncontrolled desire from either gender.

Another practical objection to such daydreaming is that, like any other weakness, it can become an unyielding slavemaster. Rather than being a pleasant departure from the norm, it can become an all-consuming, overwhelming compulsion that cannot be controlled. Second Peter makes this connection when that author rebukes those who "hav[e] eyes full of adultery and that cannot cease from sin" (2 Pt. 2:14). They had given up their freedom of choice and now were enslaved to those unrestrained desires that they had once cultivated. Implicit in some of the Old Testament condemnations seems to be a similar thought: once we *surrender* our control of our desires, we become the slaves of those desires.

Interestingly, Jesus does not rebuke sexual lusting

because of its fruit, but on its own, by itself. Could it be that—unlike a normal sexual relationship between two people, which always has at least the *potential* for love—sexual fantasizing sees the person in a one-dimensional role, simply as someone to be used? Worse than that, as a "something" to be used and discarded? In short, it appeals to the worst instincts of self-centeredness and selfishness.

The Need for Self-Control Because of the Consequences of Its Loss

Having presented his antithesis, Jesus elaborates on the need to conform to it even though it may be extraordinarily difficult for some individuals:

> And if your right eye causes you to sin, pluck it out and cast it from you; for it is more profitable for you that one of your members perish, than for your whole body to be cast into hell.
> And if your right hand causes you to sin, cut it off and cast it from you; for it is more profitable for you that one of your members perish, than for your whole body to be cast into hell (5:29–20).

> [If your right eye causes you to sin, tear it out and throw it away; it is better for you to lose one of your members than for your whole body to be thrown into hell.
> And if your right hand causes you to sin, cut it off and throw it away; it is better for you to lose one of your members than for your whole body to go into hell. (NRSV)]

Note that Jesus did not deny that such a way of thinking might be difficult to control—just like any other debilitating habit. But he argued that so important is such control that (figuratively speaking) it would be better to lose an eye or a hand than to allow uncontrolled sexual desire to warp us and cause us to lose favor with God (v. 29–30). The significance of this injunction may easily be overlooked. It comes immediately after the prohibition of unrestricted sexual desire (v. 27–28); hence, in context, it must have sexuality especially in mind.

One might even find a reference to this need for self-control (or, at least, an application of the same principle) in Matthew 19:12, where Jesus refers to those who figuratively become "eunuchs for the kingdom of heaven's sake." As least so far as the mind is concerned, such figurative "enuchanizing" is necessary if the alternative is unrestricted fantasizing. One must guard against literalizing when the text did not intend it. Literal self-castration would remove only the physical ability to carry out the sexual act, but it would not tame the uncontrolled mind that helped originate those desires.

Some find a semantic equivalent between the enuchanizing in Matthew 19 and the reference to the "hand" in the current text. J. Enoch Powell contends that this is a euphemism for the male sexual organ, since it is used in this way "in several Semitic languages."[11] If a euphemism is involved at all, the connection between the "eye" of the previous verse and the "hand" in the present verse would seem more likely to be the sexual fantasizing involved in masturbation. Margaret Davies suggests a more conventional approach and at least as credible. It is with the eye that one visually "catches" the woman to lust after her, and it is with the hand that one "catches" her to carry out the fantasy.[12]

The hyberbolic use of such terminology in Aramaic continued long afterward. George M. Lamsa observes that even into the twentieth century the Aramaic adage

about "cut[ting] off your hand" was never taken literally
but as a demand that one stop one's offensive conduct.
For example, one would demand that you "cut off your
hand from my vineyard," and that meant "do not gather
grapes from my vineyard." Stay out of it. Stay away
from it.[13]

Consistency with Rabbinical Thought

Many rabbis would have found nothing to censure in
Jesus' antithesis aimed at uncontrolled inward desire, at
least based on the rabbinical records that have survived
from different periods. For example, a rabbinic interpretation of Genesis 6:5 fits in well with Jesus' assertion:
"Sinful imagination leads to desire; desire to intent;
intent to pursuit; pursuit to deed. This is to have you
know how difficult it is for a person to turn back from
one to the other."[14]

Another rabbi went so far as to assert that,
"[u]nchaste imagination is *more* injurious than the sin
itself."[15] Likewise the *Pesiqta Rabbati* quotes Rabbi
Simeon ben Lakish as saying, "You are not to say that
only he is called adulterer who uses his body in the act.
We find scripture saying that even he who visualizes
himself in the act of adultery is called an adulterer. And
the proof? The verse, 'The eyes of the adulterer wait for
the twilight' (Job 24:15)."[16]

The tractate Kallah (which is post-Talmudic) comes
the closest to what Jesus says when it argues, "Whoever
looks lustfully at a woman is like one who has had
unlawful intercourse with her."[17]

Nonrabbinic sources concurred in such attitudes. The
Dead Sea Scrolls repeatedly stress how a combination of
inward desire and desiring eyes can lead to various

types of sin.[18] Likewise, the historian Flavius Josephus spoke of the interlocking of desire and action: "To us...the only wisdom, the very virtue consists in refraining from every action, from every thought, that is contrary to the laws originally laid down."[19]

In light of such remarks, one wonders how much Jesus' rebuke was aimed at a male popular gloss on the text rather than at specific Pharisaic or rabbinic teaching. On the other hand, every age has found that the "sins of the pew" are soon "whitewashed by the pulpit." Hence a certain degree of toleration or tacit approval seems inevitable by a greater or lesser number of rabbis. Official condemnation but unofficial toleration is a well-known phenomenon, and there is no reason to expect it did not exist in that day and age. Even assuming a reasonably consistent united front on the matter among the Pharisees, other sectarians may have been more broad minded. The Sadducees, in their denial of existence beyond death, certainly espoused a creed that could be used to destroy the inhibitions imposed by the Law on both mental and literal philandering.

Regardless of what these various individuals and groups taught, the most important thing here is that *Jesus' teaching was identical with that of the Torah and the Prophets.* This is extremely important. When Christ says, "But I say to you," (in regard to lusting), he is not substituting his own tighter, more restrictive law. He could not be doing this, because the old covenant had *already* enjoined such behavior. Hence Jesus' antithesis is aimed at bringing the individual's doctrine and conduct in line with existing Torah, not in replacing it with something different. And in light of Christ's solemn declaration that not "one jot or one tittle" would pass away until all was fulfilled (Mt. 5:18) and that one would demean one's status in the kingdom by teaching any doctrine different from the Law (v. 19), this is what we would expect to find.

NOTES

[1]Zimmermann notes that in Aramaic there would be a wordplay between "lust" and "committed adultery" (77).

[2]Marriott, 187.

[3]Connick, 245.

[4]Frederick D. Brunner, *The Christbook: A Historical/Theological Commentary, Matthew 1–12* (Waco, Tex.: Word, 1987), 183–84.

[5]Ibid., 183.

[6]Ibid.

[7]Ibid.

[8]Hans D. Betz, *The Sermon on the Mount* (Minneapolis: Fortress, 1995) notes that "[a]ccording to the consensus of scholarship, this term [woman] refers to the married woman" (232), a view with which he concurs. Additional advocates of this view include Robert H. Gundry, *Matthew: A Commentary on His Handbook for a Mixed Church under Persecution,* 2nd ed. (Grand Rapids: Eerdmans, 1994), 88; and Ulrich Luz, *Matthew 1–7: A Commentary,* trans. Wilhelm C. Linss (Minneapolis: Augsburg, 1989), 294.

[9]Walter Rauschenbusch, *The Social Principles of Jesus* (New York: Association Press, 1911; 1919 printing), 85. Others imply, rather than directly affirm, a contradiction between Jesus and the Old Testament on this theme. For example, Joseph A. Fitzmyer refers to Matthew 5:27 as an example of how Jesus "differ[ed] with the legal attitudes of old and some widespread beliefs and customs rooted in the Old Testament..." The next sentence notes that this grew out of his attitude toward Moses, the scriptures, and God himself. (*A Christological Catechism: New Testament Answers,* rev. ed. [New York: Paulist, 1991], 47.

[10]F. F. Bruce, *The Hard Sayings of Jesus* (Downers Grove, Ill.: InterVarsity Press, 1983), 53.

[11]J. Enoch Powell, *The Evolution of the Gospel: A New Translation of the First Gospel with Commentary and Introductory Essay* (New Haven: Yale University Press, 1994), 82.

[12]Margaret Davies, *Matthew* (Sheffield, UK: JSOT Press/Sheffield Academic Press, 1993), 53.

[13]George M. Lamsa, *Gospel Light: Comments on the Teachings of Jesus from Aramaic and Unchanged Eastern Customs* (Philadelphia: A. J. Holman Company, 1939), 36.

[14]Kalla Rabbati II, 6, as quoted by Lapide, 47.

[15]Quoted by Samuel T. Lachs, *A Rabbinic Commentary on the New Testament: The Gospels of Matthew, Mark, and Luke* (Hoboken, N.J: KTAV Publishing House/New York: Anti-Defamation League of B'nai Brith, 1987), 96–97.

[16]24:2, as quoted by Geza Vermes, *The Religion of Jesus the Jew* (Minneapolis: Fortress, 1993), 164. Joseph Klausner renders this (or a different preservation of the rabbis' thought): "For thou mayest not say that everyone that committeth adultery with his body is called an adulterer; he that committeth adultery with his eyes is also to be called an adulterer" (*Jesus of Nazareth: His Life, Times, and Teaching,* trans. Herbert Danby [New York: Macmillan, 1925; 1945 reprint], 385). Klausner provides other antilust rabbinical quotations as well.

[17]Quoted by Vermes, 17.

[18]For citations see Vermes, 32.

[19]*Contra Apionem* ii. 183, as quoted by Vermes, *Jesus the Jew,* 32.

6

Love and Hate
(Matthew 5:43-48)

In the sixth and final "but I say," we read of the war between love and hate that can wage in the human soul:

You have heard that it was said, "You shall love your neighbor and hate your enemy."
But I say to you, love your enemies, bless those who curse you, do good to those who hate you, and pray for those who spitefully use you, and persecute you. (Mt. 5:43–44)

[You have heard that it was said, "You shall love your neighbor and hate your enemy."
But I say to you, Love your enemies and pray for those who persecute you…. (NRSV)]

It has been noted that the word *hate* can be used in the less passionate sense of "loving less" or "regarding of little or no importance in *comparison with* someone else."[1] We find Jesus speaking of the need to hate parents and relatives and even one's own life in order to become his disciple (Lk. 14:26). This kind of hate for one's own life "in this world" will result in "keep[ing] it for eternal life" (Jn. 12:25). The Old Testament speaks of how, comparatively, "Jacob I have loved, but Esau I have hated" (Mal. 1:2–3), a passage that Paul quotes in Romans 9:13. In Deuteronomy 21:15 we read of a polyg-amist who "has two wives, one loved and the other unloved," or, in other translations, "hated."

Since Jesus *enjoins* hatred in the broader sense of "lesslove," it is hardly likely that hatred in that limited sense is under consideration. In the Antitheses the hatred is of such a nature that it must be *rejected* rather than embraced. Hence hatred in the pure sense of "vehement animosity and rejection" makes the best textual sense.[2]

Although one might feel pressed to prove that the old covenant *explicitly* demanded that one should "love one's enemy," there certainly was never any command or ordi-nance that the opposite course was to be followed, that one should "hate your enemy." From this factor alone, one would suspect that in this case Jesus was once again rebuking a tradition—a traditional gloss on the mean-ing of the sacred text. He was pointing out that not only did the Mosaic system not *require* hatred, but that such a frame of mind was an outright violation of the com-mand to love.

That the contrastive element "but I say to you" does not always carry the idea of presenting a new, previously unrevealed command is well illustrated in the present case. In the parallel account of this teaching found in Luke 6:27–28, Jesus uses "but I say to you" in regard to the very statement that he himself had just given in verses 24–26. He certainly was not rejecting the instruc-tion he himself had just given, nor is there any need to take Matthew 5:43 as meaning that Jesus was rejecting any doctrine of the Old Testament. Indeed, by stressing the need to love those one would prefer not to love (v. 44), he was rejecting the gloss that permitted hate while reaffirming the very command for love that was presented by the Torah itself.

Since the demand for love is found in both testaments, we see the uniformity we expect after reading that nothing was to pass from the Law until all was fulfilled. Yet there is a tendency among students of the sacred text to assert that Jesus has gone far beyond the Torah and universalized love.[3] Presumably with such a thought in mind, A. E. Breen writes that "Christ is here not correcting the falsity of Pharisaic teaching, but perfecting the weakness of the Law itself."[4] M. D. Goulder gives this as an example of one of the antitheses that "overturn provisions of scripture...."[5] But is this exegesis correct? To answer the question, we begin with the issue of the identity of the "enemy" under consideration within the text.

Hatred as Targeted at Romans?

Some have interpreted the "enemy" in the passage in a *political* sense, as an allusion to the Roman occupiers of the land.[6] Perhaps Marcus J. Borg presents the case best when he contends that "in the late twenties of the first century" the "political implication" of the teaching would be inescapable.[7] Although the Romans were certainly perceived as the foe, this represents a depersonalizing of the text that safely removes most of its daily application. In real life—then and now—one's enemies are more likely to be, if not kith and kin, certainly one's fellow co-religionists (at church or synagogue), colaborers (in the businessplace), and competitors.[8]

Some appeal to the fact that Jesus referred to impressment (Mt. 5:41) as evidence that the Romans are under consideration.[9] However, this was in the previous antithesis rather than the current one, and even there purely private actions were also considered (v. 42). Indeed, barring cases of major military movement, impressment was as often as not likely an action of an individual soldier or official. Hence the antagonism would be far more at the power-user as an individual than as a representative of the occupying nation. Jesus had the whole person in mind, not just one's political relationships. Hence the principle applies to the Romans but also to all such adversarial relationships that occur in life.

Hatred as Targeting the Gentiles in General?

A variant of this approach, which enjoys the advantage of depoliticizing the question, makes the contrast between loving *Jews* and hating *Gentiles*. There is an immediate problem in attempting to propound this approach; especially in the days the Torah was written (and again in the days of Jesus), there is every indication that Jews were the overwhelming ethnic group in the land. Hence one's enemy was nearly always one's fellow Jew!

Many of the same difficulties that weighed against the Roman/political approach caution against this one as well. Once again, consider the experience of those we know today. Who is an individual's most likely *real* enemy? Some foreigner or one's conational whom one happens to live next to or work with?

Hence Jesus is talking about hatred toward the same ethnic group the Torah has primarily in mind, one's fellow Jew. Again, Jesus reaffirms the same doctrine as the Torah. They were seeking a scriptural justification for hatred of those they rubbed shoulders with every day.

Since the Torah only commanded love of neighbor, but said nothing specifically of enemies, the quibbler could make the deduction that this was a case where the love imperative did not apply. This was a reasonable deduction[10] but an unnecessary one, because it effectively tore the guts out of the command to love one's neighbor since most (all, probably) of one's enemies were in that category. Jesus refused to accept such a twist of scriptural teaching and pointed his listeners back to the true meaning of the text: love is required toward all.

Hence the question of love toward Gentiles does not arise in this context. Monteflore says it well:

> Jesus in this section is not definitely thinking of the public enemy and of non-Jews. He is not thinking of non-Jews one way or the other. I do not mean that he is consciously and deliberately excluding them. I only mean that He is not consciously and deliberately including them.[11]

This is not to deny that there is implicit evidence in other verses that Jesus considers neighbor obligations to extend to the Gentiles. But as we will soon see, the old covenant made a similar extension of the demand to love. Continuity, not rupture, is what we confront.

The Torah Demanded Broader Love than Just of Friendly Neighbors— Whether Jews or Gentiles

The text Jesus cites only has God's then-covenant people specifically in mind, "*You* shall not take vengeance, nor bear any grudge against the children of *your* people, but you shall [*not* should] love your neighbor yourself: I am the Lord" (Lv. 19:18). In all the talk about how desirable "universal" love would be, an important fact can easily get lost: Considering the hostile relationships that exist in many communities, would not even this level of love represent a considerable improvement and be a vast promoter of civic peace? Indeed, how could a "universal" love ever occur unless one loves those one has an immediate relationship with? (Cf. the challenge found in 1 John 4:20b.)

In that day and age, one's neighbor would most commonly be one's fellow Jew. This deduction is reinforced by the specific reference that "the children of your people" is under discussion. Yet one must tread cautiously indeed in any effort to limit the teaching to this narrowest possible category: If this teaching is limited to one's fellow Jew, why not other "neighbor" teachings as well? As Stier points out, "Where is the expositor who would venture to say that it was lawful for Israelites dwelling in heathen lands to bear false witness against the heathen man outside the land of Israel, or to covet his wife or his house?"[12] In the few occasions when there was a specific difference in how fellow Jews and Gentiles were to be treated (for example, in cases of usury) the text is quite clear in asserting the difference. The very lack of such language in regard to love creates the natural assumption that this and other ethical demands were to be practiced toward one and all.

Furthermore, the same Old Testament chapter gave quite explicit teaching to regulate one's attitude toward the non-Jew: "The stranger who dwells among you shall be to you as one born among you, and you shall love him as yourself; for you were strangers in the land of Egypt: I am the Lord your God" (Lv. 19:34). The degree of love toward this non-Jew could hardly be greater: "you shall love him as yourself." Your frame of mind is to be the same toward him as yourself. You love yourself, so you love him. You don't curse yourself but say good things about yourself; you should do likewise of the other person. You pray for your own well-being; likewise you should pray for his. The implications interlock the text perfectly with Matthew 5:43-44. Coming in the same chapter as the command to love one's neighbor, how could one avoid the conclusion that the Gentile neighbor was to be loved as well?

In a similar vein, in Deuteronomy 10 we read that God "shows no partiality" (v. 17) and "loves the stranger" (v. 18). "Therefore *love* the stranger, for you were strangers in the land of Egypt" (v. 19). Since the "stranger" was *any* non-Jew (or, in later age, even a Jew born in Diaspora), God wanted them to have the same attitude toward any of mankind that crossed their paths.

Jesus agreed with his contemporaries that one had to live by the Leviticus 19:18 demand that one was to "love your neighbor as yourself" (Lk. 10:27–28). Jesus was asked to interpret the scope covered by the expression "neighbor" in Leviticus 19:18, and he responded with the parable of the Good Samaritan (Luke 10:30-37). In these verses, Jesus interpreted "neighbor" to include *anyone an individual comes in contact with regardless of ethnic background.* This was not a "but I say to you" teaching, but a direct interpretation of the correct meaning of Leviticus 19:18. How could Jesus' "but I say" be a rejection of some hypothetical narrowness of Leviticus 19:18 when in Luke he specifically embraces that Law's doctrine of who a neighbor is?

Furthermore, Jesus' teaching was in conformity with the intent of Leviticus 19, for just a few verses later (v. 34). Leviticus embraced a love of the alien as thoroughgoing as one feels toward oneself. No doubt there were hate-loving individuals who ignored the Gentile-love of Leviticus 19:34, but Jesus refused to tolerate any such doctrine. He refused to exclude from neighborly love anyone who was included by the Torah.

At this point a person could object that the text only demands love for the *resident* alien and not the alien living somewhere else. One wonders whether this is a very realistic objection when considered from the standpoint of human psychology. Certainly one can hate the "foreigner" regardless of where he lives, but it would seem very difficult to positively love the alien who lives next door while hating his physical brother who lives across the national boundary.

Even if one disagrees with this judgment, one fact should not be overlooked: Neither Leviticus 19 nor Jesus is discussing international attitudes. Both are talking about one's neighbor, *the individual one comes in contact with*. The question Jesus dealt with in Matthew 5 was that of trying to exclude one's enemies from the definition of the neighbor one was supposed to love. The answer would apply to Gentiles only if they might be the neighbor one is outraged with.

Jesus is not giving a lesson in international peace attitudes. He is giving down-to-earth admonitions on not excluding our troublesome and annoying "enemy" from the rank of "neighbor" toward whom we are obligated to cultivate positive attitudes and positive conduct even though he or she is trying our patience to the limit. They remain our enemies,[13] but they are to be given more consideration than we are receiving from them.

Both the Torah and the Prophets As Well As the New Testament Demand Loving "Conduct" Rather Than "Feeling Good" Sentimentality

One reason that we have difficulty in accepting the need to love our enemies who are our neighbors is because of our modern Western tendency to define love in terms of gushy sentimentality. Although love can and does involve an emotional element, the heart of love lies in conduct rather than the emotions. In 1 Corinthians 13 Paul very effectively shows that true love is *manifested* love, love *in action,* love being of benefit to others.

We may or may not like the other person, and we may or may not be affectionate toward the other individual, but we have love toward them because we are exhibiting toward them the kind of positive and beneficial conduct that we would show to those we emotionally think well of. *The Old Testament demanded exactly this kind of this-world, concrete, acted-out love.* It is almost impossible to be affectionate toward a devout enemy, but one can act justly toward them even when under provocation. And the Old Testament hits hard on demanding exactly this kind of love.

For example, one is to do what one can to protect the enemy's possessions from coming to harm. In Exodus 23:4 the Jew was instructed: "If you meet your enemy's ox or his donkey going astray, you shall surely bring it back to him again." The following verse provides a different illustration but with the same point, "If you see the donkey of one who hates you lying under its burden, and you would refrain from helping it, you shall surely help him with it." The words "you would refrain from helping" are intriguing. In other words, you don't really want to assist. And then God implores, in effect, "Help him anyway!" God recognizes that *emotionally* we have resentments about our treatment and that if we did what we preferred, we would let our foe suffer the loss. And quite a foe this individual is! He is described not only as an "enemy," but as "one who hates you." Yet even under that kind of provocation one is to remember to put practical helpfulness above natural animosity.

Basic humanitarianism is to conquer one's hostility. When an enemy is hungry, one is to protect him from starvation: "If your enemy is hungry, give him bread to eat; and if he is thirsty, give him water to drink" (Prv. 25:21). When one is hurting, it seems only natural to seek revenge. And the Proverbist immediately interprets this helpfulness as a form of revenge—*constructive* revenge: "For so you will heap coals of fire on his head and the Lord will reward you" (v. 22). The idea of the first words is probably that having the need to accept help from you—of all people!—will burn at him like hot coals from the fire. He can't avoid accepting because he desperately needs assistance, but lo, how he wishes he could!

Then the Proverbist points out the personal advantage: "The Lord will reward you." One may never receive a kind word from the person who has been assisted—though who knows? It might just be the first step in healing the breach. The writer does not want to raise false hopes; he doesn't even suggest the possibility of reconciliation as a motive. Rather, he stresses that it is the type of conduct that pleases God and that he will reward. The Old Testament provides an example of such conduct in regard to the treatment of enemy prisoners (2 Kgs. 6:17–23).

Such conduct is hard enough to practice, but the Old Testament went beyond the outward and demanded that attention also be given to one's *inner* attitudes toward personal enemies. In Proverbs 24:17-18 we read the admonition, "Do not rejoice when your enemy falls, and do not let your heart be glad when he stumbles; lest the Lord see it and it displeases Him, and He turn away His wrath from him." The point is to leave wrath to God rather than gloating over it when it happens—but, oh, how hard a virtue to practice!

Although the word *enemy* is not in Proverbs 17:5, the frame of mind is certainly found there: "[H]e who is glad at calamity will not go unpunished." Here the thought is that if we are so thrilled by the idea of punishment, perhaps we would like some of it as well. Edom was denounced for having "rejoiced over the children of Judah on the day of their destruction" (Ob. 12).

Job lived by the standard demanded in such texts: "If I have rejoiced at the destruction of him who hated me, or lifted myself up when evil found him (indeed I have not allowed my mouth to sin by asking for a curse on his soul)" (Job 31:29–30). Job neither gloated in the hour of his enemy's anguish nor wished a disaster ("curse") on him. It is hard for us to avoid making the mental leap of more than a millennium to the later words of Paul, "Bless those who persecute you; bless and do not curse" (Rom. 12:14).

Samuel T. Lachs insists, "Nowhere in Biblical or rabbinical Judaism is one called upon to transcend human nature and to love one's enemies."[14] Yet he promptly goes on to assert that "[t]his does not, however, preclude positive moral actions toward those who are your enemies."[15] This seems to be another way of asserting that though the *emotion* of love is psychologically impossible, *acts* of constructive love are within our capacity. Yet there is nothing in Jesus' antithesis demanding emotional love; all he is demanding is love of the same kind and same quality as that demanded by the Torah and the Prophets. And since that love was to include substantial restraints on *attitudes* as well as *behavior,* the Old Testament demanded considerably more than Lachs seems to recognize, and the New Testament teaching of Jesus considerably less. It is this tendency to exaggerate the meaning of love in the New Testament and minimize it in the Old that has led to the accusation of a grave contradiction between the Lord and the Torah on love of one's fellow human beings.

Just as the old covenant demanded loving conduct and a loving mind—positive good will and helpfulness in mind and action, if you will—so does the New Testament. Peter joins together an admonition that the Christian exhibit both types of conduct toward one's brethren who have become alienated: "not returning evil for evil or reviling for reviling" (i.e., in neither action nor word is one to treat them the way they themselves have acted). "But on the contrary, blessing, knowing that you were called to this, that you may inherit a blessing" (1 Pt. 3:8–9). Likewise, Paul urged the Thessalonians to control their temptation to strike back: "See that no one renders evil for evil to anyone, but always pursue what is good both for yourselves and for all" (1 Thes. 5:15).

When Paul, in Romans 12:18–21, wished to impress upon his readers the need to avoid retaliating for past injustices, he appealed to both the triumphant potential of good (v. 21) and also to two Old Testament principles: that God will punish the unjust (v. 19, quoting Dt. 32:35) and the need to extend positive good to our enemies (v. 20, quoting our already examined text of Prv. 25:21–22). Note that Paul did not treat this doctrine of love as something new introduced by Jesus, but as already directly demanded by the old covenant itself.

Punitive Language in the Old Testament

The Old Testament does contain considerable punitive language, such as threats against the native (and corrupt) possessors of the promised land and prayers that the wicked be smashed not merely in the next world but also in the present life. When introduced by themselves and used in contrast with Matthew 5:43–44, one can erect a very impressive but quite misleading "proof" that the Old Testament taught hate, whereas Jesus, in marked contrast, taught love.

This artificial construction overlooks two very important facts. First, the Old Testament itself required loving conduct and a loving attitude in such passages as those we have already examined. Second, the New Testament also teaches the propriety of crying out for divine vengeance upon the wicked in this life. The New Testament emphatically does not see divine punishment as having to wait for eternity to begin. We read of such prayers in Revelation 6:10, and we find Jesus himself endorsing the propriety of them in Luke 18:7. Likewise considerable vehement language is used in regard to punishment in the next life. The idea of hell being a burning fire where punishment lasts forever surely threatens a degree and intensity of retribution that is rarely, if ever, explicitly found in the Old Testament! Jesus is even pictured as the Final Judge who pronounces the sentence that sends the convicted there (Mt. 25:41).[16]

So the problem is not in reconciling a punitive Old Testament with a loving New Testament, but in reconciling the punitive and loving strains found in *both* testaments. *However one explains the coexistence of these two patterns of thought in the New Testament, one simultaneously provides an explanation for their presence in the old covenant as well.* Providing such an explanation is beyond the scope of this work, but one point surely deserves at least passing consideration. There is a vast difference between just retribution and unjust vindictiveness, between an individual receiving the due fruits of his evil and his being punished simply because we are on the outs with him or his family. In one case his evil behavior is reaping proper justice; in the other, our *own* excessive frustration may itself be inflicting an injustice upon someone else. The great danger in the retaliation we initiate ourselves is that it will be far too much vengeance and far too little justice.

Clerical or Popular Doctrine?

Of the known teaching of the various Jewish sects, only among the Essenes do we find anything approaching the teaching Jesus rebukes.[17] One of the Dead Sea Scrolls explicitly enjoins hatred of the reprobate:

> All those who devote themselves to do the ordinances of God, shall be brought into the covenant of mercy for the community, into the council of God. He shall walk perfectly before Him according to all the things which have been revealed at the times fixed for their revelations. He shall love each one of the sons of light according to his lot in the council of God, and hate each one of the sons of darkness according to his guilt at the time of God's vengeance.[18]

Although hatred is enjoined, it seems to be proportional in intensity "according to his guilt" (i.e., the greater hostility is due to the one whose misconduct has most earned it). The reference to "the time of God's vengeance" could place this hatred as one to be felt only at that time. It is also open to the interpretation that the current hate is to be proportional to the apparently obvious guilt they will face at "the time of God's vengeance." The latter is almost certainly intended since it is known that formal curses were issued against the followers of "Belial" by those who entered the Qumran community.[19] However theoretically full of "hate" toward the Gentile, the Essenes were not permitted personal acts of retribution against others simply because they were Gentiles.[20]

Although the Dead Sea Sect is of special interest because so much is known of them, any major impact on the populace at large is purely conjectural. Hence there is far too little evidence to assert that Jesus is specially targeting the doctrinal peculiarities of that movement, although his criticism obviously includes their beliefs.

This indicates the high probability that Jesus is targeting not some priestly or scribal[21] distortion of the Jewish law (nor that of the ascetic Qumran group), but one that had taken root among the masses. The blunt truth is that "hatred of enemies seemed natural"[22]—both then and today. Hence it did not require clerical encouragement; it was the natural human reaction to injustice. It represented popular attitudes even if not explicitly verbalized teachings.[23]

As in the case of lust, Jesus is taking on not *official* opinion but *mass* opinion. And in doing so, he is squarely aligning himself with the Torah. Rather than radically rejecting its demands, he is embracing it and demanding that the people strip away from their doctrine of neighborliness the claim that annoying and obnoxious neighbors did not come under its provisions. Hatred might please the heart, but it represented a frame of mind and action that Torah firmly prohibited and that Jesus is firmly prohibiting as well.

Prayer for Enemies, Doing Good to Them, and the Search for Moral Perfection

Although we have been stressing the central controversy surrounding this antithesis (love versus hatred), the remainder of Jesus' admonition deserves attention both for the argument it presents and for its Old Testament precedent. To take up the text at the beginning of Jesus' antithesis,

> But I say to you, love your enemies, bless those who curse you, do good to those who hate you, and pray for those who spitefully use you and persecute you, that you may be sons of your Father in heaven; for He makes His sun rise on the evil and on the good, and sends rain on the just and on the unjust.
>
> For if you love those who love you, what reward have you? Do not even the tax collectors do the same?
>
> And if you greet your brethren only, what do you do more than others? Do not even the tax collectors do the same?
>
> Therefore you shall be perfect, just as your Father in heaven is perfect. (Mt. 5:44–48)
>
> [But I say to you, Love your enemies and pray for those who persecute you, so that you may be children of your Father in heaven; for he makes his sun rise on the evil and on the good, and sends rain on the righteous and on the unrighteous. For if you love those who love you, what reward do you have? Do not even the tax collectors do the same? And if you greet only your brothers and sisters, what more are you doing than others? Do not even the Gentiles do the same? Be perfect, therefore, as your heavenly Father is perfect. (NRSV)]

We have stressed the Torah roots of love; it is also germane to note that several other concepts mentioned in these verses also have strong Torah and prophetic roots.

Old Testament Precedents for Praying for Enemies

A number of Old Testament examples exhibit the frame of mind that prays for one's enemies, the attitude Jesus enjoins. Pinchas Lapide points out that even though the

Egyptians had "brutally subjugated the people of Israel and intended eventually to exterminate them," Moses prayed for the Pharaoh, no less than *five times* even though Pharaoh kept wavering between a cooperative policy and vehement opposition (Ex. 8:24–27, for example). Lapide notes that Job prayed for his enemies (Job 42:9) and that David is well known for his prayers for Saul, who so unjustly sought his life. Indeed, Saul's life was in David's hands—and he let him live (1 Sm. 24:12). (Might we not introduce this as an example of turning the other cheek—not as literal ritual, but as shaping actual conduct in everyday life? At a minimum, of love of enemies.) Likewise in the subjugation and exile imposed by Nebuchadnezzar, the people had every earthly reason to hate the Babylonians. Instead, Jeremiah urged the people to pray to God for them (Jer. 29:7).[24]

God as Bestower of Good on Those Who Hate Him

Recognizing that the mere quoting of scripture rarely settles a matter for one who wants to do the opposite (after all, the Torah had made the blanket statement to love one's neighbors and that had not been sufficient to keep people from finding a way around its injunction), Jesus appeals to the commonsense judgment of his listeners. He does this by appealing to the nature of the heavenly Father who gives blessings to both the good and the bad (v. 45), by pointing out that their level of morality in their two-level method of treating people is no better than those they despise (v. 47), and by concluding that they should imitate the moral perfection of their Father in heaven (v. 48).

A repeated theme of the Old Testament is the abiding willingness of God to love those who had rejected him—often his own people! Not only did God preserve a remnant, but he kept the door open wide for one and all to return if they but would. It was because "I do not change" that they escaped from destruction. Such long-suffering was imperative, for "from the days of your fathers you have gone away from My ordinances and have not kept them. Return to Me, and I will return to you" (Mal. 3:6–8; cf. Is. 65:2–3 and 2 Chr. 6:36–39). Love under provocation–repeated provocation. The door for a return to favor was always left open. Like-wise Jesus urges his disciples, by positive and con-structive conduct, to always leave the door open for reconciliation to their earthly enemies.

Nor is the Old Testament without precedent on the *human* level for such conduct. Perhaps the best example of this is David's sparing Saul's life even though Saul was in hot pursuit. David did sneak into where Saul was sleeping and, rather than strike him dead, merely cut off a piece of his garment (cf. 1 Sm. 24 above).

The Search for "Perfection"

This last admonition—to seek to be "perfect"—can be taken in either (or both) of two ways. Since no one can ever attain true perfection it always remains *a goal to be sought.* Not reached, but sought. The very act of rec-ognizing our falling short of it makes us conscious of our imperfections and keeps us from being puffed up with unholy zeal that castigizes all others as beyond the pale of potential redemption. We can make a valid judgment that their present conduct falls short of divine accept-ability, but because we are all too painfully aware of our own failures, we happily leave the eternal ramifications to the judgment of a righteous and fair God. We can give *our* judgment of their destiny, but God will one day give his final judgment, which may be in complete conformity with our understanding—or totally different.

The Old Testament puts front and center human sinfulness and the need to come to terms with it. Not only is the species pictured as deeply mired within sin's grasp, but even the most righteous of the patriarchs and kings are candidly pictured with their blemishes and imperfections. The prototype ideal king, David, is rebuked for his affair with Bathsheba. And the Psalter pictures him pouring out his sense of guilt before the God who will forgive.

It is perhaps more common to look upon the perfection enjoined as more reachable than this—that is, *as the perfection of maturity rather than the perfection of reaching sinlessness.* R. Gregor Smith presents this approach when he writes,

> In the LXX the word [teleios] is frequent, usually as a translation of *tamim.* Three typical usages are Deut. 18:13, 1 Kings 8:61 and 11:4. In these passages *tamim* is used as an expression of the cult, and means whole, or sound, or unblemished, like the sacrificial offering. To be perfect means, therefore, to be whole or sound or true; and to be perfect as the heavenly Father is perfect (Matthew 5:48, the main NT reference) means to be wholly turned, with the whole will and being, to God as He is turned to us.[25]

To be "perfect" in such a sense does not indicate that sin has been left behind but that one has reached the level of being what one can and should be—on the moral and spiritual levels. Our behavior is not erratic and irregular, but constant and resolute. How we believe and act is no longer merely a reflection of what we were *taught;* it has become so fully assimilated it is now what we are. To use a Pauline analogy, one is no longer a child—one has grown up (1 Cor. 13:11).

This fits in well with the Aramaic usage of the equivalent word. A native-born speaker of that tongue wrote,

> The Aramaic word *gmera* means perfect, comprehensive, complete, thorough and finished. In this verse it does not mean perfect in character as God is perfect but perfect or complete in understanding. Jesus knew that no one could be perfect like God. A learned man is called *gmera biolpana,* which means that he is acquainted with every branch of learning. *Gmera bnamosa* means one who is well versed in the law. Also, when a young man reaches the age of maturity he is known as *gmera* which means that he has become a man of understanding.[26]

The Old Testament certainly held a similar view, that maturation in spiritual matters is to be sought and ultimately obtained. For example, the whole concept of religiously and morally educating a child in the way he should go (Dt. 6:6–9; 31:12–23; Ps. 34:11; Prv. 22:6) carries with it the idea that the end result is an individual able to grasp right and wrong and live by it. The book of Proverbs, in particular, aims at training the youth into a mature adult (Prv. 3:1–4, 4:1–4, 5:1–2, 8:32–33, etc). Hence the concept of full moral and spiritual maturity as a desirable and attainable goal goes back to firm roots in the pentateuchal and prophetic works. And Jesus walks within that tradition.

NOTES

[1]The following illustrations come from Lapide, 86.
[2]Cf. the remarks in Lapide, 86.

[3]The scholar of rabbinic thought, C. G. Montefiore (*Rabbinic Literature and Gospel Teachings* [London: Macmillan, 1930], 59) suggests, "About no section [of the Sermon on the Mount] are Christian commentators and theologians more sensitive. In none are they more anxious to prove and maintain *the absolute originality* of Jesus" (our emphasis). Hence the generalization that Jesus is preaching in conformity with the Torah yields to the apologetic purpose of proving the uniqueness of his teaching. One cannot consistently ride both horses at one time.

Stier (76) implies that the Jew-only application of the Old Testament love commandment was dominant in his own age, though he personally rejects it. Among those who accept the validity of such a severe limitation of that covenant's teaching are McNeille (71) and Archibald M. Hunter, *A Pattern for Life: An Exposition of the Sermon on the Mount,* rev. ed. (Philadelphia: Westminster, 1965), 61.

[4]A. E. Breen, *A Harmonized Exposition of the Four Gospels,* Vol. 2, rev. ed. (Rochester, N. Y.: John P. Smith Printing Company, 1908), 185.

[5]M. D. Goulder, *Midrash and Lection in Matthew* (London: S.P.C.K, 1974), 20. Others who see an anti-Torah stance in this teaching of Jesus include Sister Audrey, *Jesus Christ in the Synoptic Gospels* (London: SCM Press Ltd., 1972), 119.

[6]Helmut Merkel, "The Opposition Between Jesus and Judaism," in *Jesus and the Politics of His Day,* ed. Ernst Bammel and C. F. D. Moule (Cambridge: Cambridge University Press, 1984), 140; and David Winter, *The Search for the Real Jesus* (Wilton, Conn.: Morehouse-Barlow, 1982), 62.

[7]Marcus J. Borg, *Conflict, Holiness & Politics in the Teaching of Jesus* (New York: Edwin Mellen, 1984), 130; cf. 234.

[8]On the need not to lose sight of the intended personal and immediate relevance of Jesus' teaching on the matter, see Donald Senior, *Jesus: A Gospel Portrait,* rev. ed. (New York: Paulist, 1992), 90–91.

[9]William J. Lunny, *The Jesus Option* (New York: Paulist, 1994), 162.

[10]Patte (though not with the current text in mind) contends that "Scripture would allow you to hate your enemies" (82). He seems to imply that all of these antitheses are between the Old Testament and the teaching of Jesus. He clearly argues that the old interpretations *were* valid but that Jesus has changed the correct understanding of Scripture (83). If Scripture were *this* flexible—so that we can have two equally true but contradictory interpretations—aren't we edging into the idea that Scripture can mean anything we please to make it mean: i.e., *we read into* it the truths we wish to find rather than *interpret out of it* the truths that are actually there?

[11]Montefiore, 61.

[12]Stier, 76.

[13]A point often overlooked but which John R. Meier brings to our attention (*Matthew,* 54).

[14]Lachs, 108.

[15]Ibid.

[16]We are using the argument to show that Jesus' teaching is far more complex than the simplifier acknowledges. The way Jesus' love doctrine is so broadened by some, there would be no room left for such passages to exist at all. An *antagonistic* over-simplifier also finds no room for a "loving" Jesus to function as judge. Hagner, *The Jewish Reclamation of Jesus,* 149–50, discusses how Jesus' role as judge and his scathing indictment of the Pharisees in Matthew 23 is considered by such individuals as a clear-cut contradiction of Jesus' instruction demanding love. Such critics are also guilty of the same fundamental error: they insist on an either/or reading of the Lord's doctrine when it actually demands an either/and approach. It is not a matter of Jesus contradicting himself, but of his doctrine having a greater depth and fullness that refuses to fit inside the boundaries of a narrow over-simplification by either his friends or foes.

[17]Hagner, 147; Thaddee Matura, *Gospel Radicalism: The Hard Sayings of Jesus,* trans. Maggi Despot and Paul Lachance (Maryknoll, N. Y.: Orbis Books, 1984), 113; Georg

Strecker, *The Sermon on the Mount: An Exegetical Commentary,* trans. by O. C. Dean, Jr. (Nashville: Abingdon, 1988), 87.

[18]Quoted by W. D. Davies, 245–46. Cf. the quote in Lachs, 106.

[19]For citations, see W. D. Davies, 246.

[20]Hagner, 147.

[21]Michael Green suggests that the hatred represented a scribal gloss on the Old Testament text and was carried out as an effort to become less "unrealistic" and to come to terms with "human fraility" (*Matthew for Today: Expository Study of Matthew* [Dallas: Word Publishing, 1988], 78).

[22]Margaret Davies, 55.

[23]Barclay W. Newman and Philip C. Stine, *A Handbook on the Gospel of Matthew* (New York: United Bible Societies, 1992), 152.

[24]These scriptures are cited, along with 1 Kings 20:30–34 in Lapide, 89–90.

[25]R. Gregor Smith, "Perfect," in *A Theological Word Book of the Bible,* ed. Alan Richardson (New York: Macmillan, 1950; 1964 printing), 167. For a book length discussion, see the South African scholar Paul Johannes Du Plessis, *Teleios: The Idea of Perfection in the New Testament* (South Africa: Uitgave J. H. Kok N. V. Kampen, 1979). To Du Plessis, the essence of the meaning in Matthew 5:48 is to be "whole," to be perfectly consistent in the application of one's moral attitudes to all, whether friend or foe (170–71).

[26]Lamsa, *Gospel Light,* 43.

7

Murder and Anger
(Matthew 5:21-26)

In the first of Jesus' antitheses, he struck out at the
attitude that merely avoiding the *act* of murder was adequate to make one morally acceptable in God's sight. To
enjoy *that* status, one must go further and avoid the very
anger that can erupt in the destruction of another's life:

> You have heard that it was said to those of old, "You
> shall not murder, and whoever murders will be in danger
> of the judgment." But I say to you that whoever is angry
> with his brother without a cause shall be in danger of the
> judgment. And whoever says to his brother, "Raca!" shall
> be in danger of the council. But whoever says, "You fool!"
> shall be in danger of hell fire. (Mt. 5:21–22)

> [You have heard that it was said to those of ancient
> times, "You shall not murder"; and "whoever murders
> shall be liable to judgment."
>
> But I say to you that if you are angry with a brother
> or sister (note: other ancient authorities add, without
> cause), you will be liable to judgment; and if you insult a
> brother or sister, you will be liable to the council; and if

you say, "You fool," you will be liable to the hell of fire. (NRSV)]

Before analyzing how the two Testaments interlock in the matter Jesus discusses, several other interpretive questions first deserve our consideration.

"Without a Cause"

Although the phrase "without a cause" is found in a number of important manuscripts and is quoted by various of the ancient church writers, it is missing in a sufficient number that its presence in the biblical text has been challenged[1] as well as its origin in the actual personal teaching of Jesus.[2]

It is true that the phrase is lacking in certain ancient manuscripts where one would normally anticipate finding it. If it is an interpretive addition, it probably arises from the fact that anger *in itself* need not be wrong and that even Jesus himself was known to get angry (explicitly stated in Mark 3:5, and implied in the accounts of the chasing of the money-changers out of the temple). Hence it would seem unlikely that Jesus would condemn all anger when his own life occasionally exhibited it and since there are blatant circumstances that clearly call for it. Even if we prefer to substitute a milder term, such as "righteous indignation," this would still remain anger though under a different name.

Yet the omission of the phrase would hardly turn Jesus into a violator of his own teaching, for nowhere in the verse does he actually call anger an inherent sin. What he does assert is that anger is always *dangerous.* He does not say that one will be the subject of "judgment," "the council," or "hell fire" for anger *alone,* but that one would be "in *danger of.*" Even when one is right-eously angry, there still remains a potential risk, and Jesus was too worldly-wise to deny it. Hence, he sets out to demand the control of anger rather than the *elimina-tion* of it. For if one does not control the emotion, the day will inevitably come when an individual is going to want to reach out in uncontrolled temper to do bodily damage to others. To avoid that potential, anger must be repressed and kept on a tight leash or it will become the excuse for the very murder that the Law prohibited.

Another approach can be taken as well: Carl G. Vaught observes that *"origzo* is the word for 'anger' in this case, and it means not those momentary fits of anger that come upon us unexpectedly, but the smoldering, festering cauldron within from which violent action springs." In short, Jesus targets not anger per se, but "the kind of anger that smolders until it sometimes explodes: for even if the explosion never occurs, we will be guilty before the court because of the anger itself. And this is so, first because the seething anger *will* overflow, if not in mur-der, in other ways; and in the second place, because anger of this kind will destroy the soul in which the anger itself occurs."[3] If anger is taken in this sense, then the argument that "without a cause" is a later textual addition is enhanced; it seems inconceivable that *this* kind of "anger" could ever be anything but morally crip-pling. If, however, this reads too much into the expres-sion, and anger in the broader and more traditional sense is under consideration, then some type of limita-tion would be expected in light of Jesus' own conduct.

Let's examine the verse from yet a different perspec-tive. Assuming the traditional text in verse 21 is valid, we have two different kinds of anger under discussion. The first is the type that is "without a cause"—the irrational, unthinking, punitive anger that is perhaps the most dangerous of all. Since there is no real reason behind it, there is nothing even the most temperate and peace-seeking can do to calm the complainer or eliminate the grievance. In verse 22 Jesus passes on to a second kind of anger: the insult throwing type, with "Raca" and "you fool" being the then-contemporary epithets the Lord singles out. Jesus censures both and thereby shows that they can ultimately be brought under self-control. That does not mean it can be done without effort, pain, or (perhaps) even professional counseling.

Degrees of Insult? "Raca" and "Fool"

Various commentators have suggested varied rough English equivalents for *Raca*. "Empty-headed" is the most common one.[4] Close variants of this are "empty head,"[5] and "hollow head."[6] Carrying on similar imagery, others opt for "bonehead"[7]or "blockhead."[8] Yet others prefer "numskull,"[9] "nitwit"[10] and "stupid."[11] *Raca* is an Aramaic loan-word transliterated into Greek letters.[12] In its literal Aramaic meaning, some make it refer to "the sound a person makes as he clears his throat before he spits in someone's face."[13] Others make it an Aramaic idiom that refers to the actual *act* of spitting.[14] Hence it would carry the connotation of a verbal equivalent to spitting in someone's face, a grievous slur and insult demeaning to the other's dignity and self-respect.

One would therefore expect the terminology to carry deeper connotations than any literal meaning attributed to the word. Several scholars have attempted to ponder what those might be. The German scholar Georg Strecker argues that "'Raca' declares one incapable of interpersonal relations, while 'fool' means that a person is incapable of relating to God, that is, disobedient, god-less."[15] T. W. Manson theorizes that "*Raca* suggests a defect of intelligence" while fool "makes the much more serious charge of moral defect."[16] To Frederick D. Brunner, *raca* questions "the mental competence of the other person" while the other term "pierces still deeper and questions the competence of the other."[17]

Thus we may see an escalating severity in the insults: first *raca,* and then an even worse censure, *fool.* On linguistic grounds—the meaning of the terms themselves—others have challenged the claim of any significant difference in the *degree* of insult between the two terms.[18] However equivalently insulting the two terms may appear, societies often consider one insult more grievous than another even when there is no objective criteria in the literal meaning and significance. That such would be the case in first century society would be hardly surprising. Hence the intensification argument cannot be quite so easily ruled out of court.

On the other hand, possible confirmatory evidence of *non*-intensification comes from a consideration of whether Jesus intended the term *fool* to imply as negative a portrayal as those who stress a distinction between the two terms suggest. We could easily understand the use of *fool* as equivalent to "unfaithful" when it is used by Jesus of the Pharisees (Mt. 23:17). Yet he also uses the same word (rendered as "foolish") in Luke 24:25 to apply to his own disciples. *They* certainly weren't devoid of loyalty to God as the term has been theorized to mean by some. But they *were* being devoid of perception and insight. And isn't that close to the colloquial translations of *raca* given above?

Perhaps when used together, there is intended an intensification of insult. Then again, perhaps not. For our purposes, both served as severe censure, and that was enough to make his point. Doubtless there were other derogatory terms Jesus could have substituted, if he had preferred. It was not so much the specific words that Jesus was concerned with but the attitude that underlay the expressions, especially when the emotions aroused were so passionate that the use of the insults could egg one on to outright violent conduct as well.

Types and Places of Punishment

We read of threatened "judgment," of the "council," and of "hell fire." These have been placed in three different chronological frameworks by various interpreters.

1. *The first two could refer to potential earthly punishments and the last to divine wrath in eternity.* The idea would then be that it matters little whether it be verbalized or unverbalized anger—both run the danger of severe repercussions. Some will occur in this life and others in the next. Both temporal and eternal punishments represent potential risks for the individual who refuses to control his (or her!) temper.

2. *All three could refer to the consequences of anger in the present life.* Unjustified anger runs the risk of judicial judgment, open insult the danger of condemnation by even higher councils or courts, and the other insults the risk of being figuratively consigned to the city dump where refuse was burned. (*Gehenna,* translatable "hell fire" in contexts speaking of future punishment, originally referred to the site outside Jerusalem where garbage was burned).[19]

Of course one would not literally be thrown on the refuse heap with the other garbage—but many would want to do it just to silence the mouth of the incurable and insufferable troublemaker. This would fit in well with the hyperbole of the earlier part of the verse as well. It would have been extraordinarily difficult in Jesus' day to mount a successful legal prosecution for the use of insulting language such as Jesus cites.[20] Hence Jesus uses *exaggerated consequences* to get over the danger of *exaggerated indignation*.

3. *All three could refer to the future life.* When one accepts the difficulty or impossibility of prosecuting such verbal ridicule, one can understand the appeal of referring all three punishments to the realm of eternity. Gehenna would most naturally belong in such a context, and the Final Judgment would certainly be picturable in terms of either a court or an appeals/supreme court or ultimate Sanhedrin (to use a Jewish term of reference), because it is the court of last resort, so to speak.[21] In such a case, we have three different ways of describing the same ultimate answerability rather than any distinction being made between them.

Even so, two of the three descriptions would most naturally fit the earthly context. Even if a person could not literally prosecute an individual for his or her obnoxious insults, he might still be lying in wait until something was done that *was* legally actionable. Even if the legal action were technically not for the insults, a straight line might still exist between the affront and the ultimate prosecution. (The contemporary equivalent would be the frame of mind, "Don't get angry, get even.") In light of such factors, the original suggestion remains the soundest: Jesus is trying to convey that animosity—expressed or unexpressed—carries the gravest danger of unwanted consequences in both the present and the future life.

Both the Act and the Underlying Anger Are Condemned in Both Testaments

Many are convinced that we find in the current text—the very first of the antitheses—a direct contradiction between Jesus and the teaching of the old covenant. Archibald M. Hunter provides an exegesis of the text of the kind I myself might have given a few years back: "Jesus begins with the sixth commandment, which prohibits murder. Murder, He says, under the Old Order was liable to trial and punishment as prescribed in the Law—in this case death (Exodus 21:12; Leviticus 24:17). In the New Order, he says, not merely the overt act of murder but the inward passion of anger will expose a man to judgment, i.e., by God."[22]

The French Franciscan Thaddee Matura writes, "To the Fifth Commandment forbidding murder, Jesus *opposes* (my emphasis) His own law, which condemns even bad feelings toward others."[23] Georg Strecker, though conceding that there are other views, sums up his own sentiments in one concise sentence, "Jesus pits His authority against that of Moses!" (his emphasis)[24]

On the other hand, a true antithesis with the Law itself would have been an affirmation that homicide was permissible.[25] Jesus is obviously moving profoundly in the *other* direction, reining in excess rather than permitting it. He must, therefore, be rejecting something else—the narrow, legalistic definition that restricted the prohibited conduct to the physical act of murder. The antithesis is between murder *alone* being prohibited and the attitudes and emotions leading to murder being also prohibited.

Linking the breaking of the chains of restraint to an outburst of even worse excess is a form of reasoning the rabbis would have understood. For example, one midrash on Deuteronomy 19:10–11 argues that unless one has love of neighbor to begin with, there is nothing to restrain one from ultimately committing physical violence.[26]

All are agreed that the Old Testament was emphatic that the murderer was to be punished. Indeed, the principle is presented in the Pentateuch as in existence long before Moses was even born: "Whoever sheds man's blood, by man his blood shall be shed; for in the image of God He made man" (Gn. 9:6). Since this was before Abraham and the birth of the Jewish nation, it may well be regarded as intended to represent prototype law designed for the entire human race.

When Israel became a nation, it was warned that to refuse to execute the individual clearly deserving of death was to permit a moral blot to remain upon the land: "So you shall not pollute the land where you are; for blood defiles the land, and no atonement can be made for the land, for the blood that is shed on it, except by the blood of him who shed it" (Nm. 35:33). Witnesses were required to establish that the accused was indeed guilty of a capital crime (Nm. 35:30–31), but once the guilt was established the penalty was mandatory rather than optional. And this was supposed to be the authoritative pattern throughout the history of Israel and not just at that particular time (Nm. 35:29).

One can easily take this and play it off against Jesus' teaching on anger, but to do so is to ignore the clear evidence that the Old Testament itself joined in Jesus' condemnation of uncontrolled anger. How can one with even a modest knowledge of the book of Proverbs make this kind of mistake? (Perhaps because Proverbs is usually discussed in one context and the Sermon on the Mount in an entirely different one?)

Yet Proverbs is quite clear on this matter. For example, it brackets together the two ideas of uncontrolled anger and being a fool: "[w]hat is in the heart of fools is made known" (14:33), implying that only the fool is unaware that there are some things better left unsaid and some emotions better left unexpressed. This is made explicit in 29:11: "A fool vents all his feelings, but a wise man holds them back." The New American Bible renders the text, "A fool always loses his temper, but a wise man holds it back." Furthermore, "A fool's wrath is known at once..." (12:16). Note that the lack of control is so great that not even a temporary ascendancy over temper is permitted; the fool strikes out without thought or restraint. "A stone is heavy and sand is weighty, but a fool's wrath is heavier than both of them" (27:3). It is hurtful without real purpose or goal; the hurting is all that counts—whether it accomplishes anything constructive matters not at all.

Anger is rebuked as being the seedbed of needless strife. "For as the churning of milk produces butter, and as wringing the nose produces blood, so the forcing of wrath produces strife" or, as the NASB has it, "so the churning of anger produces strife" (30:33). Unchecked anger feeds on itself, producing additional sin: "An angry man stirs up strife, and a furious man abounds in transgression" (29:22). So extreme is the anguish and discomfort that such a person can generate, that the proverbist suggests that if one has the misfortune to be married to such a woman it would be better to hide in the wilderness out of her sight (21:19)!

In light of the way anger is portrayed in such passages, what else can we conclude than that the proverbist of old considered anger as carrying the potential for sin—the same doctrine as Jesus in the Antitheses?

We can see a similar frame of mind in other Old Testament books as well. For example, Psalm 37:8 detects so much danger in this temperament that the verse urges listeners to avoid a life characterized by it: "Cease from anger, and forsake wrath; do not fret—it only causes harm." The text does not deny that anger will occur, but making it a lifestyle is something entirely different and receives the rebuke. Perhaps Ephesians 4:26 would be a good commentary, "Be angry and do not sin; do not let the sun go down upon your wrath." Indeed, Paul's idea here is found in the Old Testament as well: "Be angry, and do not sin. Meditate within your heart on your bed, and be still" (Ps. 4:4).

There are other passages along this line that indicate that anger is to be controlled, limited, and regulated rather than abolished. Ecclesiastes 7:9 urges, "Do not hasten in your spirit to be angry, for anger rests in the bosom of fools." Proverbs stresses the need to be "slow to wrath" (14:29) and, repeatedly, "slow to anger" (15:18; 16:32; 19:11).

The anger may take the form of retaliatory conduct or retaliatory words. As to the latter, Jesus warns in Matthew 5:22 that inappropriate and improper language may put one "in danger of hell fire." The Old Testament as well repeatedly warns of the need to control one's tongue. To give only one example, "A soft answer turns away wrath, but a harsh word stirs up anger. The tongue of the wise uses knowledge rightly, but the mouth of fools pours forth foolishness" (Prv. 15:1–2). Excessive and uncontrolled anger provides no guarantee that our supposed foe will retreat; it may only ignite counter anger and an even more explosive conflagration.

Reconciliation Comes Before Religious Worship

Jesus illustrates his plea for abstaining from anger by two examples. The first deals with reconciliation with a brother with whom one has been at odds and—in this context, for there to be a logical relationship with what has just been said—anger must have resulted in things being said and done to have caused or widened the initial rift.

> Therefore, if you bring your gift to the altar, and there remember that your brother has something against you, leave your gift there before the altar, and go your way. First be reconciled to your brother, and then come and offer your gift. (Mt. 5:23–24).

> [So when you are offering your gift at the altar, if you remember that your brother or sister has something against you, leave your gift there before the altar and go; first be reconciled to your brother or sister, and then come and offer your gift. (NRSV)]

We could hardly ask for better evidence than this that Jesus' teaching in this antithesis was aimed at those *living under and practicing the Mosaic Law.* The individual is assumed to have brought some type of sacrifice to the temple in Jerusalem—sacrifices could not properly be offered elsewhere. Hence Jesus was addressing his antithesis to upholding what the Torah required rather than toward initiating new practices and doctrines. He was interpreting *existing* law rather than providing *new and contradictory* ones.

The individual whose anger has *caused* the rupture in friendship is under discussion (note the "therefore" that introduces verse 23). Furthermore, the person seeking the reconciliation is described as one who "your brother has something against." Hence the theoretical "you" under discussion is the guilty individual, and is the same "you" who is to take the initiative in healing the breach. It is very easy both to speak and act unjustly toward others and to be so full of pride (or shame) that one is unwilling to admit the blunder. Jesus is assuming that somehow the problem-causing individual had come to recognize and admit his central responsibility and, hence, the moral responsibility to take the initiative to heal the breach. It is so important to act that even the demands of public worship come second.

This breach-healing principle is found in other New Testament teaching as well. Jesus urged his listeners to "have peace with one another" (Mk. 9:50). So far as we have control over it, we should "live peaceably with all men" (Rom. 12:18). Believers are to "pursue" those attitudes and actions that encourage "peace" with others (Rom. 14:19). Indeed, heavenly wisdom is characterized by being "peaceable" and "willing to yield" (James 3:17; context, verses 16-18), attitudes which make reconciliation possible.

The seriousness—not to mention the embarrassment—of leaving a sacrifice unoffered argues that Jesus is speaking of an extraordinary breach of human relationships rather than the minor upheavals that characterize life. It would be a step that one would not normally even consider doing—like leaving during the observance of communion—but a step that an individual *should* be willing to carry out if and when necessary. It should also be noted that the individual is clearly labeled the transgressor rather than the injured party. The very extraordinariness of the transgressor coming to the admission of his guiltiness would itself justify a departure from the normal completion of the sacrifice.

Would this actually happen in real life? Jackob Jonsson cites the rabbinical parallels and the communion analogy as evidence that the entire discussion is hypothetical and ironical rather than one that could be expected to actually arise.[27] This overlooks the fact that there is a profound difference between what one would normally do and what one *should* do in an extraordinary situation. Bruce Chilton reads the rabbinical evidence in a very different direction, as indicating that delays in the offering of sacrifice *did* periodically occur and that regulations existed to cover it.[28] Again, whether specific precedents existed or not, Jesus is discussing the most appropriate and most proper course of action rather than one that would be expected to routinely occur. Hence there might or might not be specific regulations germane to leaving the sacrifice behind—in any case, reconciliation was so important it was something that must be undertaken immediately.

Furthermore, though there is no explicit recognition of interrupted sacrifice in the Torah, there is the demand that *after* reconciliation, sacrifice is to be offered, implying that the reconciliation and a guilt-free conscience is the moral prerequisite of acceptable sacrifice offering. Hence in Leviticus 6:1–7 we read,

And the LORD spoke to Moses, saying:
"If a person sins and commits a trespass against the Lord by lying to his neighbor about what was delivered to him for safekeeping, or about a pledge, or about a robbery, or if he has extorted from his neighbor, or if he has found what was lost and lies concerning it, and swears falsely—in any one of these things that a man may do in which he sins: then it shall be, because he has sinned and is guilty, that he shall restore what he has stolen, or the thing which he has deceitfully obtained, or what was delivered to him for safekeeping, or the lost thing which he found, or all that about which he has sworn falsely. He shall restore

its full value, add one-fifth more to it, and give it to whomever it belongs, *on the day of his trespass offering.*

And he shall bring his trespass offering to the Lᴏʀᴅ, a ram without blemish from the flock, with your valuation, as a trespass offering to the priest. So the priest shall make atonement for him before the Lᴏʀᴅ, and he shall be forgiven for any one of these things that he may have done in which he trespasses. (our emphasis)

[The Lord spoke to Moses, saying: When any of you sin and commit a trespass against the Lord by deceiving a neighbor in a matter of a deposit or a pledge, or by robbery, or if you have defrauded a neighbor, or have found something lost and lied about it—if you swear falsely regarding any of the various things that one may do and sin thereby—when you have sinned and realize your guilt, and would restore what you took by robbery or by fraud or the deposit that was committed to you, or the lost thing that you found, or anything else about which you have sworn falsely, you shall repay the principal amount and shall add one-fifth to it. You shall pay it to its owner when you realize your guilt. And you shall bring to the priest, as your guilt offering to the Lord, a ram without blemish from the flock, or its equivalent, for a guilt offering. The priest shall make atonement on your behalf before the Lord, and you shall be forgiven for any of the things that one may do and incur guilt thereby. (NRSV)]

In none of the hypothetical cases discussed in Leviticus is there an explicit mention that the lie has been exposed. In none of the hypothetical cases is there direct evidence that the matter has been brought before a court of law and the individual has been exposed as a transgressor. (Indeed, one wonders about the moral validity of a sacrifice in such a case, since it would seem to be a mere obeying of a prescribed ritual rather than out of sincerity of heart.) *So far as what is written,* we seemingly have an individual who has treated his neighbor deceptively and has come to a recognition of his misconduct. He sets out to restore to the victim the lost property or money and then offers a sacrifice to God.

There is but a modest step from this to what Jesus demands: In Jesus the sacrifice is interrupted by the reconciliation and then completed afterwards; in Leviticus the reconciliation occurs and then the sacrifice. What Jesus seems to have in mind is that the very act of religious worship has caused the individual to openly confront his own responsibility. Recognizing the guilt, he moves to heal the breach, and then offers the sacrifice in the spirit God intended. The Torah would have had no problem with this. Neither did Jesus have any trouble with the Torah. Both spoke in terms of reconciliation first, then sacrifice. Indeed, the Leviticus text speaks of the reconciliation occurring "on the [same] day of his trespass offering" being presented (v. 5).

Reconciliation Needed While There Is Still Time

Since the first illustration involves the obligation of the individual in the wrong to put first priority on reconciliation, it is only natural to take the second example as an additional case in which one's foe is in the right. Once again it is imperative that the guilty party seek a healing of the breach. Here the case is even more extreme. It is no longer a more or less private dispute; this time one's anger-produced misconduct has so upset the other individual that he is about to use the judicial process to obtain retribution. In this context the emphasis is not just on reconciliation, but on the need to seek it *while there is still time for it to occur.*

The sad fact is that some disputes are allowed to become so deeply rooted and bitter that the victim is no longer willing to accept the mere correction of the injustice, but feels that nothing less than judicial punishment will be adequate. (Some aren't even happy then.) The same irreparable breach can also occur over issues that are impossible to judicially decide; the issue stumbles on so long, and the heart becomes so hard, that the time for peace has, sadly, long ago faded into the past. Jesus' plea is that pride (or whatever else the stumbling block might be) needs to be overcome before the feud has become so bitter that peace is beyond restoration. And once again the responsibility is placed not on the injured, but on the injuring party:

> Agree with your adversary quickly, while you are on the way with him, lest your adversary deliver you to the judge, the judge hand you over to the officer, and you be thrown into prison.
>
> Assuredly, I say to you, you will by no means get out of there till you have paid the last penny. (Mt. 5:25–26).

> [Come to terms quickly with your accuser while you are on the way to court with him, or your accuser may hand you over to the judge, and the judge to the guard, and you will be thrown into prison.
>
> Truly I tell you, you will never get out until you have paid the last penny. (NRSV)]

The reference to paying "the last penny" suggests that the dispute is over finances of some type. This fits in well with the historical environment in which Jesus lived. The most likely cause for financial conflict with a

neighbor in a rural society—one that would lead to judicial intervention—was debt in one form or another.[29]

Since "you" are the one in the wrong, "you" have
inflicted some kind of real (or, less likely, *apparent*) chicanery that has cost another money. Maybe money has
been borrowed dishonestly or the credit been conned into
some money-making scheme that is shady or outright
dishonest. It doesn't really matter what form the evil
took, the key thing is "you" are in the wrong.

True, "you" might try to beat the rap before the judge.
But Jesus assumes that the case is so clear-cut that your
hide is about to be removed from society. "You" are about
to face the public humiliation of being jailed[30] for what
you are unable to pay. (In those days one wasn't released
until one paid in full, and since the imprisoned person
wasn't able to earn money while in jail, the result was
easily an indeterminate—even permanent—stay in con-
finement.) Yet there are those whose stubbornness
would keep them from seeking reconciliation even at
this last, desperate stage. Jesus tells them, in effect,
don't let pride rule over your best interests: you have
sinned, now go and straighten it out.

The Talmud also urges an individual in danger of losing a legal case to seek out a solution with the adversary
while on the way to court. In the Talmud's case the
agreement is to be secured through verbal intimida-
tion,[31] a methodology conspicuously absent in the case
Jesus presents. Indeed, since the implication is that the
seeker of an agreement is in the wrong, pleas and
beseeching would seem the appropriate course of conduct, not to mention possible concrete actions that would
heal the breach.

That Jesus was not dealing with some kind of
uniquely *new* teaching in this antithesis can be seen in

the fact that the Old Testament enjoined attitudes that, if carried out, required reconciliation: principles such as personal and business honesty, not carrying grudges, love of others, and so forth. When we come specifically to the second example (reconciliation under threat of a court fight), it is interesting that the old covenant *specifically endorsed such an effort:*

> Do not go hastily to court; for what will you do in the end, when your neighbor has put you to shame? Debate your case with your neighbor himself, and do not disclose the secret to another; lest he who hears it expose your shame, and your reputation be ruined. (Prv. 25:8–10).

> [What your eyes have seen do not hastily bring into court; for what will you do in the end, when your neighbor puts you to shame? Argue your case with your neighbor directly, and do not disclose another's secret; or else someone who hears you will bring shame upon you, and your ill repute will have no end. (NRSV)]

What further evidence do we need that Jesus was not giving uniquely *new* teaching, but reaffirming a legacy of moral conduct deeply rooted in the Old Testament itself?

NOTES

[1]For a summary of the textual and citation evidence, pro and con, see Betz, 219, note 156.

[2]John Bligh, *The Sermon on the Mount* (Slough, England: St. Paul Press, 1975), 79, is illustrative of those who consider the phrase a scribal addition.

[3]Carl G. Vaught, *The Sermon on the Mount: A Theological Interpretation* (Albany [New York]: State University of New York Press, 1986), 66.

⁴See Betz, 198, 220; Margaret Davies, 99; Green, 75; Daniel J. Harrington, *Matthew,* 85; Hobbs, 65; Menninger, 117.

⁵Gundry, 84.

⁶Luz, *Matthew 1–7,* 282.

⁷Citations given by Stott, 65.

⁸Citations given by Stott, 65.

⁹Citations given by Stott, 65.

¹⁰Citations given by Stott, 65.

¹¹Hobbs, 65.

¹²Vaught, 66. Cf. Betz, 220.

¹³Vaught, 66–67.

¹⁴George M. Lamsa, *Idioms in the Bible Explained and a Key to the Original Gospels* (San Francisco: Harper & Row, 1931, 1971, 1985), 50, 94. He notes that even into the twentieth century "heated arguments" in the Aramaic-speaking culture of his birth would often degenerate into the exchange of such insults.

¹⁵Strecker, 67.

¹⁶T. W. Manson, "The Sayings of Jesus," in *The Mission and Message of Jesus: An Exposition of the Gospels in the Light of Modern Research,* ed. H. D. A. Major, T. W. Manson, and C. J. Wright (London: Macmillan, 1937; 1940 reprint), 448.

¹⁷Brunner, 175.

¹⁸Riddderbos, 104; A. E. Harvey, *Strenuous Commands: The Ethic of Jesus* (London: SCM, 1970), 80. Betz argues that "fool" is basically just the Greek equivalent of the Aramaic "raca," rather than representing a more intense insult as is usually assumed (*Sermon on the Mount,* 220). Cf. the similar argument of Bligh, 83. Luz suggests that Jesus may have used an Aramaic word that could be rendered as "insane" or "crazy." "There is no significant difference in meaning, let alone an intensification between the two" (*Matthew 1–7,* 282).

¹⁹Brunner, 176–77, argues along this line that the entire reference is to this-earthly repercussions of uncontrolled anger.

²⁰Harvey, 80, argues that there was no grounds at all for such prosecution under the law and tradition as then understood.

W. D. Davies argues that the Sanhedrin of mainstream Judaism would not have touched such a case. In contrast, the Essenes *did* provide for the punishment of their members who used abusive language against each other (237.). Hence Jesus' threat of punishment of language insults would have brought to mind the practice of that contemporary sect. On the other hand, we have no certainty of how familiar outsiders were with that group's internal arrangements.

[21]Harvey, 80, uses such reasoning to date all the prospective punishments as referring to events beyond this earth.

[22]Hunter, 50.

[23]Matura, 109. This is surely a misstatement of Jesus' point: Jesus does not condemn "bad feelings;" rather he condemns unjustified and insulting anger. To feel *disturbed* at perceived injustice is only natural, but to allow it to evolve into anger that strikes out at others (verbally or physically) is something quite a bit different.

[24]Strecker, 65.

[25]Cf. the remarks of Vermes, *Jesus the Jew,* 31.

[26]The Tannaitic midrash Sifre says on this passage:

On this account it has been said: A man who has transgressed a light commandment will finish by transgressing a weighty commandment. If he has transgressed "You shall love your neighbour as yourself" (Leviticus 19:18), he will finish by transgressing "You shall not take vengeance or bear grudge" (Ibid), and "You shall not hate your brother" (Leviticus 19:17), and "That your brother may live beside you" (Leviticus 25:36) until he comes to shedding blood (quoted by Vermes, *Jesus the Jew,* 31).

[27]Jackob Jonsson, *Humour and Irony in the New Testament* (Leiden, E. J. Brill, 1985), 98–99.

[28]For discussion and Tamudic sources (in accompanying footnote) see his "Forgiving at and Swearing by the Temple," in *Judaic Approaches to the Gospels,* ed. Bruce Chilton (Atlanta: Scholars Press, 1994), 114–15.

[29]Eric F. F. Bishop, *Jesus of Palestine: The Local Background to the Gospel Documents* (London: Lutterworth, 1955), 74. The reference to remaining imprisoned till the "last penny," even laying aside the broader historical context, fits in well with the debt hypothesis (Harrington, *Matthew,* 87). Newman and Stine, however, think the expression "more likely…means 'paid off all the money the judge fined you (or, said you must pay)' " (136).

[30]Some find in Christ's warning that one might "be thrown *(ballo)* into prison" (Mt. 5:25), a possible implication of a place of underground imprisonment (Bishop, 74).

[31]b Sanh. 95b, as summarized by Jonsson, 99.

Section Three

OLD TESTAMENT ROOTS OF JESUS' MORE "RADICAL" TEACHING

8

Divorce (Matthew 5:31-32)

The fundamental authorizing passage for divorce in the Pentateuch was Deuteronomy 24:1–4:

> When a man takes a wife and marries her, and it happens that she finds no favor in his eyes *because* he has *found some uncleanness in her,* and he writes her a certificate of divorce, puts it in her hand, and sends her out of his house, when she has departed from his house, and goes and becomes another man's wife, if the latter husband detests her and writes her a certificate of divorce, puts it in her hand, and sends her out of his house, or if the latter husband dies who took her to be his wife, then her former husband who divorced her must not take her back to be his wife after she has been defiled; for that is an abomination before the LORD, and you shall not bring sin on the land which the LORD your God is giving you as an inheritance. (our emphasis)

> [Suppose a man enters into marriage with a woman, but she does not please him because he finds something objectionable about her, and so he writes her a certificate of divorce, puts it in her hand, and sends her out of his house; she then leaves his house and goes off to become

another man's wife. Then suppose the second man dislikes her, writes her a bill of divorce, puts it in her hand, and sends her out of his house (or the second man who married her dies); her first husband, who sent her away, is not permitted to take her again to be his wife after she has been defiled for that would be abhorrent to the Lord, and you shall not bring guilt on the land that the Lord your God is giving you as a possession. (NRSV)]

How did the age of Jesus understand the implementation of the provisions of this law? Robert A. Guelich notes that the procedure for granting a divorce was quite "straightforward." Rabbinic teaching required "the necessity of two witnesses to the writing of the bill, [regulated] the content of the bill, the manner of delivering it, and the possibility of withdrawing it.... [T]he right to divorce belonged exclusively to the husband, although a woman could under certain conditions require her husband to divorce her..."[1] This was done by her convincing a rabbinical tribunal that a divorce was the only proper or just remedy left for her and by the tribunal, in turn, ordering the husband to grant the divorce.[2]

Varying First-Century Interpretations of the Deuteronomy Text

The "conservative" and the "liberal" rabbinical views overlapped on the subject of divorce. On the basis of Deuteronomy 24:1 the school of Shammai restricted divorce to cases of sexual misconduct.[3] The rabbinic schools or movements of both Shammai and Hillel agreed that the text unquestionably applied to such cases. The followers of Hillel went far beyond this and considered virtually *any* professed reason as adequate "scriptural" grounds for the dissolution. Hence, while there was general agreement that the Torah was describing adultery as a proper grounds for divorce, the issue in dispute between the advocates of Shammai and Hillel centered around how many *additional* reasons, if any, represented adequate grounds.

In maximizing the number of justifications for divorce, however, rabbis aligned with the school of Hillel appealed to the very same text. Much of their case was accomplished by shifting from the exception reason provided ("uncleanness") and rooting their claims in the first part of the verse where the reference is to how the relationship has reached the point where the wife "finds no favor" in the eyes of her husband. Isolating this from the "uncleanness" that is mentioned afterwards, a creative mind could authorize virtually any divorce.

Hence it comes as no surprise that the Hillel school could use Deuteronomy 24 to justify divorce on the most tenuous grounds. For example, "even if she spoiled the cooking," the text justified divorce.[4] Rabbi Akiva went so far as to say, "Even if he has found another more beautiful than she is." He explicitly tied this in with the earlier part of Deuteronomy 24 referring to her no longer finding favor in her husband's eyes.[5]

The Shammai form of Judaism (which restricted divorce to sexual misconduct) dominated the religious power structure before A.D. 70. Hillel-style Judaism came into ascendancy only afterward.[6] Because of the dominance of Shammai Judaism, a restrictive divorce doctrine likely dominated in the days of Jesus. On the other hand, the permissive nature of Hillel divorce theory certainly maximized the appeal of that aspect of their doctrine, even among those perhaps not formally aligned with them.

The most famous example of an advocate of divorce for any reason during this period is the historian Josephus (not a rabbi). He interpreted the Torah to his Gentile readers as permitting divorce "for whatever cause" and comments that "with mortals many such may arise."[7] He invoked this right in his own life, divorcing his wife because he was "displeased with her behavior."[8]

Modern commentators and scholars in the past have been prone to discuss the issue in terms of the relative degree of permissiveness among rival factions of first century Judaism. Manuscript discoveries in the mid-twentieth century have made it possible to argue that there was also a far more absolutist, anti-divorce trend among the Jews of Palestine and Syria: one that did not deny that a legal right existed but that was convinced that the right ought not to be exercised.

The Temple Scroll found at Qumran provides an ideal for the king of Israel that explicitly prohibits polygamy and seemingly embraces a no-divorce position as well:[9]

> He shall not take a wife from among all the daughters of the Gentiles, but take for himself a wife from his father's household, from his father's family. He shall have no other wife in addition to her, because she alone shall be with him *all the days of her life.* If she dies he shall take for himself another [wife] from his father's household, from his family. (57:17–18, emphasis mine)

Divorcing her is effectively prohibited. Remarriage is conditional upon death having destroyed the relationship. Since it was common for the ideal of the king to be the ideal for the citizenry as well, this may imply that the Essenes considered unbreakable marriage for life to be the norm for all God's people as well.[10] Caution is appropriate: The Temple Scroll presents the regal *ideal.* It does not discuss whether there are any circumstances when it is proper to violate the ideal. In the lack of an exception-type clause among the Qumran documents, an "absolutist" reading of their divorce convictions is a quite reasonable one. On the other hand, this could be the result of the quirk of which documents have survived and which have been discovered.

The probability of an absolutist view being advocated is enhanced when we consider another related movement in the ancient Jewish community. At Damascus there existed a sectarian group often assumed to be Essenic even if lacking an organizational or formal linkage with the Dead Sea Sect at Qumran. In the *Damascus Document* we read that the supporters of the "Sprouter" of lies "shall be caught in fornication twice by taking a second wife while the first is still alive, whereas the principle of creation is, Male and female he created them."[11]

In light of these facts, whether we conclude that Jesus totally banned divorce or whether we decide that Jesus limited divorce to cases of sexual misconduct, *both positions represent attitudes for which precedent could be found in then contemporary Jewish thought.* The question once again becomes not whether what Jesus taught was consistent with Jewish interpretation, but whether whatever that interpretation *was,* was truly rooted in the Torah. In *either* case, there is no question that Jesus was fundamentally hostile to divorce, even if he permitted it. Hence it is appropriate to examine the anti-divorce strain of thought found in the Old Testament in order to show that this attitude was based on Old Testament precedent as well.

The Old Testament Permitted Divorce Without Being Enthusiastic About the Practice

The central thrust of Jesus' teaching is against divorce, to discourage the practice by limiting it—and this is so regardless of how we read the exception clause found in Matthew 5:32 and 19:9. This was the attitude of the Old Testament as well. The classic evidence of this disgruntlement can be found in Malachi 2:13–16:

> And this is the second thing you do: You cover the altar of the LORD with tears, with weeping and crying; so He does not regard the offering anymore, nor receive it with good will from your hands. Yet you say, "For what reason?" Because the LORD has been witness between you and the wife of your youth, *with whom you have dealt treacherously;* yet she is your companion, and your wife by covenant. But did He not make them one, having a remnant of the Spirit? And why one? He seeks godly offspring. *Therefore take heed to your spirit, and let none deal treacherously with the wife of his youth.* For the LORD God of Israel says, *that He hates divorce,* for it covers one's garments with violence, says the LORD of hosts. "Therefore take heed to your spirit, that you do not deal treacherously." (our emphasis)

> [And this you do as well: You cover the Lord's altar with tears, with weeping and groaning because he no longer regards the offering or accepts it with favor at your hand. You ask, "Why does he not?" Because the Lord was a witness between you and the wife of your youth, to whom you have been faithless, though she is your companion and your wife by covenant. Did not one God make her? Both flesh and spirit are his. And what does the one God desire? Godly offspring. So look to yourselves, and do not let anyone be faithless to the wife of his youth. For I hate divorce, says the Lord, the God of Israel, and covering

one's garments with violence, says the Lord of hosts. So take heed to yourselves and do not be faithless. (NRSV)]

One could hardly ask for better evidence that the Old Testament not only could frown upon divorce but could even be brutally blunt in regard to how individuals could misuse the divorce "right" and thereby abuse their (ex)spouses. Since both Deuteronomy 24 and Malachi 2 are presented as *God himself speaking,* the interlocking of the two texts well demonstrates that God may permit what he does not like and tolerate for human weakness' sake what he would prefer to prohibit. If people treated each other the way they should—rather than treacherously and despicably, as Malachi rebukes them—then precious little divorce would ever occur. Jesus provides an excellent commentary on the Malachi text when he speaks of divorce being permitted "because of the hardness of your hearts" (Mt. 19:8). Here again, he walks in conformity with the old covenant rather than in rebellion against it.

Could Malachi represent some later "evolution" of Old Testament thought, at variance with the provisions of Deuteronomy 24? Marriage preservation texts occur time and again in the Old Testament and make any such theorizing untenable. The ancient patriarchs (for all their faults) are conspicuously pictured as having maintained their marriages over extended periods of time.[12] The theme of marriage preservation is likewise implicitly endorsed in the Wisdom Literature of the Old Testament. Setting one's spouse aside because she is getting older is implicitly rebuked by the admonition to "rejoice with the wife of your youth" (Prv. 5:18). It isn't time to replace her with "a new model," as the jaundiced phrase goes, but to look back on what you've been through together and been able to accomplish as a team. The blessing of "a prudent wife" is praised (Prv. 19:14) and the hard-working and effective spouse praised at length (Prv. 31:10–31). The idea of a spouse as a disposable item finds no countenance or comfort from such texts from the Wisdom Literature; indeed, they are antithetical to such a way of thinking.

When Jesus reins in the popular (and Hillelian) tradition endorsing divorce for any cause, he is walking in the implicit steps of the proverbist and the explicit steps of Malachi. Furthermore, Deuteronomy 24 was not the "blank check" permitting divorce for any and every reason that it was (and still is) commonly presumed to have been. As we will soon see, it was actually a rather restrictive law, and Jesus was attempting to convince his audience to accept the severe restriction of the divorce "right" found in that Torah text. Innovation was not his cause; preservation of original intent was.

The Antithesis and Its Common Interpretation

In the third of his contrastive teachings, Jesus discusses this question of divorce and remarriage:

> Furthermore, it has been said, "Whoever divorces his wife, let him give her a certificate of divorce."
> But I say to you that whoever divorces his wife for any reason except sexual immorality causes her to commit adultery;[13] and whoever marries a woman who is divorced commits adultery (Mt. 5:31–32).

> [It was also said, "Whoever divorces his wife, let him give her a certificate of divorce."
> But I say to you that anyone who divorces his wife except on the ground of unchastity, causes her to commit adultery; and whoever marries a divorced woman commits adultery. (NRSV)]

In Deuteronomy 24:1 a divorce was to be for "uncleanness." In saying "except sexual immorality" is Jesus making the two expressions *equivalent,* or is he contrasting a much broader divorce right with his own extremely narrower formulation of the grounds? We have already indicated that our judgment favors the first approach; however, it should be noted that most commentators opt for the second.

Thaddee Matura argues that the gospel writer included this contrast specifically because "[t]he evangelist thus wanted to demonstrate how Jesus' teaching on the indissolubility of marriage not only transcends but contradicts and abrogates the law authorizing divorce (Deuteronomy 24:14 [sic])."[14]

Ben Witherington III speaks of how "Jesus' divorce ruling…is at odds with Mosaic law…"[15] Stanley B. Marrow speaks of how Jesus "seems to have said something quite different from what the Old Testament allowed."[16] Jesus "abrogates" the Old Testament provision according to Daniel J. Harrington.[17] Jesus is "denying" the Old Testament teaching according to Barclay W. Newman and Philip C. Stine.[18]

These are not uncommon views.[19] Although he is a tad more cautious in his own view, Robert Banks notes that most commentators take Jesus' teaching to be contradictory to the divorce law of Deuteronomy 24 and are convinced that the exception clause cannot be considered a perpetuation of the Old Testament teaching on the matter.[20] W. D. Davies refers to how "many,"[21] indeed "most Christian scholars"[22] have interpreted this as a rejection of the Old Testament regulations on the subject.

Two categories of interpreters constitute this consensus against Jesus being compatible with the teaching of the Torah on divorce. Both groups take for granted that the Old Testament provided a blanket authorization for divorce for any reason imaginable. They are divided, however, over whether Jesus substituted divorce only for sexual misbehavior or whether he substituted a complete prohibition of divorce. In our judgment, both groups are mistaken in their reading of Jesus' intent; they incorrectly read him as a religious revolutionary rather than as a prophet calling the people back to their historic, fundamental Law.

The Case for Interpretation Rather than Substitution

Whether Deuteronomy's "uncleanness" and Matthew's "sexual immorality" are synonyms for the same type of behavior has been vigorously argued both pro and con based on the meaning of these two terms.[23] Laying aside the linguistic argument in its narrowest sense, an examination of the text itself demonstrates that it was Jesus' purpose to be interpreting the intent of the Deuteronomic teaching even if one might quibble as to its strict linguistic equivalence.

For example, one easily overlooked indication that Jesus is not contrasting his "sexual immorality" with the Mosaic "uncleanness" can be seen in the fact that the Deuteronomic description of the woman's sin is *not mentioned at all*. (The same conspicuous omission is also found in the lengthy divorce discussion in Matthew 19:1–9). The contrast is between sexual immorality only and a blanket divorce right, rather than between sexual immorality and uncleanness. How can Jesus be repudiating the Torah's "uncleanness" divorce grounds when it is not even mentioned?

So what Jesus is dealing with is the assertion of a

divorce right *regardless* of whether the Pentateuch's demand for "uncleanness" is present. "Whoever divorces his wife, let him give her a certificate of divorce." *That* is the assertion he is analyzing. The contrast, then, must be between when divorce is accepted as proper for any reason and whether there is a limitation on that supposed "right." His questioners wanted to frame the divorce question in terms of the right to divorce; but the Torah had framed it within the standard of "uncleanness" being present—and Jesus insists on taking the whole Deuteronomic text into consideration by demanding "sexual immorality" as the prerequisite.

This is true no matter how broadly one construed "uncleanness." The husband couldn't just get up one day and order his wife out of the house by giving her a writing of divorcement. Under the terms of Deuteronomy 24, such foul play was prohibited—though doubtlessly the high-handed and well-placed were able to get away with it. To make it acceptable under that text, "uncleanness" had to have been present. This was the *only* time when divorce could properly occur. In light of Jesus likewise specifying only one situation in which a divorce could rightly occur among God's people, does this not indicate that the two expressions were intended as equivalents?

Consider also the fact that in the first two antitheses Jesus had been reaffirming Mosaic Law. In the third has he suddenly decided to reverse his previous approach? It takes what—a minute or so?—to read from Jesus' fervent avowal of the Mosaic Code (v. 17–18) and condemnation of those who taught others to break its teachings (v. 18) to the present discussion of divorce. Would he then dare to so quickly openly repudiate the Torah as so many imagine he was doing? Doesn't it boggle the mind to so interpret Matthew 5:32 in such a way as to require this conclusion?

"But I say" *does* imply a contrast, and that contrast is with the popular understanding of the Mosaic system: an interpretation that permitted one to cite *part* of the text (give her a writing of divorcement) as authority to ignore the *remainder* of the text (that it be for "uncleanness"). Hence the contrast was not with the Deuteronomic provision itself, but with the selective partial citation of scripture that produced a meaning totally at odds with its true intent.

This can also be found in the dialogue in Matthew 19. The question is, once again, What does *Moses'* law demand? (v. 4, 7, 8)—not how Jesus' teaching is new and unique and supposedly replaces that law. In discussing the meaning of the Old Testament divorce law, Jesus' opponents again only cite the divorcing part of the Torah text (v. 7, summing it up rather than quoting it). In the following verse, Jesus refers to Moses authorizing divorce (v. 8). Presenting his own teaching, Jesus words it, "And I say to you" (v. 9); the contrastive "*but* I say to you" is not used. Jesus is not contrasting himself to Moses; with Moses He has no problem. Again, his objection is to the popular editing of the text that allowed virtually any giving of divorce to be regarded as proper.

Jesus again insisted that the *reason* for the divorce be put front and center: "sexual immorality" (v. 9) to use his own words; "uncleanness," to use the words of the Old Testament text being analyzed. In both cases *intent* was central to the moral propriety of a divorce. His foes were determined to ignore this demand of the Law, and Jesus was not going to let them succeed.

Some contend that in rejecting unrestricted divorce, Jesus is replacing it with the original creation pattern of divorce for sexual immorality alone. Of course there is not the slightest textual evidence in Genesis of *any* provision for divorce in that inaugural epoch of the human species. Indeed, as pictured by the Genesis text, with whom was Adam to commit the sin at the time of creation when this pattern was supposedly established? Wouldn't it have been a strange law to have been given at a time when he did not yet even recognize what sin was? (Perhaps one might stretch the argument to include "immediately after the Fall," but even in that context, a divorce right is absent from the list of consequences for man's original transgression.) To the extent that we can safely reach any conclusion about the creation intention at all, it was one man/one woman/for life with no provision for divorce at all. Indeed, Jesus' point in saying concerning divorce that "from the beginning it was not so" (Mt. 15:8) was to stress this very fact. Yes, Jesus cites God's original purpose for marriage (v. 4–6) as evidence—but not evidence for the *grounds* of divorce but evidence that he desired that it be *permanently binding on both individuals*. Divorce was authorized "because of the hardness of your hearts" rather than because of divine happiness with the practice (v. 8).

Furthermore, however one interprets the application of the Genesis precedent for the permanency of marriage, Jesus is *still* speaking in terms of letting the Pentateuch interpret itself rather than replacing it with a contradictory doctrine.[24] In effect, what Jesus is doing is protesting against an empty "proof-texting" approach to the Torah doctrine of divorce. Rather than basing one's conclusions on isolated words alone, one must interpret the Deuteronomy "permissive" text in light of the entire text and not in a way that is contradictory to what the Torah advocated in other passages. Scripture is to interpret scripture and is to limit (or broaden) one's conclusions about a specific passage.

Not only did both Jesus and Deuteronomy both demand the same justification for divorce (sexual misconduct) but in doing so *both* represented departures from the prototype creation pattern. God had not failed, but mankind had failed; the heart had become stubborn and thick-skinned. As a result, under both covenants, God had permitted the divorce he so deplores. In short, God is realistic of (generic) man's failures and makes provision for it. But that does not mean he encourages his creation to exercise that divorce prerogative.

When speaking in blanket opposition to divorce (i.e., when the exception clause is omitted), Jesus was still willing to express himself in terms of *being faithful to the Mosaic Law!* How then could Jesus have believed Deuteronomy permitted divorce for any and all reasons? In this connection we should examine Jesus' teaching in Luke 16:

> And it is easier for heaven and earth to pass away than [for] one tittle of the law to fail.
>
> Whoever divorces his wife and marries another commits adultery; and whoever marries her who is divorced from her husband commits adultery. (Lk. 16:17–18).
>
> [But it is easier for heaven and earth to pass away, than for one stroke of a letter in the law to be dropped
>
> Anyone who divorces his wife and marries another commits adultery, and whoever marries a woman divorced from her husband commits adultery. (NRSV)]

By going immediately and without any interruption from the authority of the Law (v. 17) to his teaching against divorce (v. 18), Jesus leaves the impression that his own teaching matched that of the Deuteronomic code in being (fundamentally) opposed to the disintegration of marriages. How then could Deuteronomy 24 have granted a *general permission* for divorce? Must it not be construed, like Jesus' teaching, as an exception to the *general indissolubility* of marriage? (If we attribute the juxtaposition of the authority of the Law with the prohibition of divorce to the hand of Luke, we do not resolve the difficulty; that merely shows that in the mind of Luke, Jesus saw no irreconcilibility with the Mosaic teaching on divorce.)

Hence, if one may correctly read "except sexual immorality" as an exception to the general banning of divorce among God's people, may not one equally correctly interpret the specifying of the cause of "uncleanness" to be—in a similar fashion—the exception to a general disapproval of the practice? Indeed, if God "hates divorce" (Mal. 2:16) one would most naturally assume that any permission that is granted is just that—an exception to the general disapproval.

Paul also taught against the theory that the old covenant permitted divorce for any and all reasons. In Romans 7:1–4, the apostle presents teaching that has been commonly used to prove that Paul himself (and presumably Jesus himself as well) was opposed to all divorce:[25]

> Or do you not know, brethren (for I speak to those who know *the law*), that *the law* has domain over a man as long as he lives?
>
> For the woman who has a husband is bound *by the law* to her husband as long as he lives. But if the husband dies, she is released from *the law* of her husband.
>
> So then if, while her husband lives, she marries another man, *she will be called an adulteress:* but if her

husband dies, she is free from that law, so that she is no adulteress, though she has married another man.

Therefore, my brethren, you also have become dead to *the law* through the body of Christ, that you may be married to another, even to Him who was raised from the dead, that we should bear fruit to God. (Rom. 7:1–4, our emphasis)

[Do you not know, brothers and sisters—for I am speaking to those who know the law—that the law is binding on a person only during that person's lifetime?

Thus a married woman is bound by the law to her husband as long as he lives; but if her husband dies, she is discharged from the law concerning the husband.

Accordingly, she will be called an adulteress if she lives with another man while her husband is alive. But if her husband dies, she is free from that law, and if she marries another man, she is not an adulteress.

In the same way, my friends, you have died to the law through the body of Christ, so that you may belong to another, to him who has been raised from the dead in order that we may bear fruit for God. (NRSV)]

The term "the law" is a common Pauline code phrase for the law attributed to Moses. Four of the five usages in this text are in that sense, and the fifth is a play on words reflecting that usage ("the law of her husband"). If further confirmation is needed, note the comment "I speak to those who know the law." All Paul's readers knew the *gospel* "law," so he must have had a *different* law in mind. The law that only part of them knew was, of course, that of the Pentateuch.

Now, then, the Law of Moses called the remarried woman an adulteress—so says Paul quite explicitly. This could mean one of two things: The fact that she was remarried automatically *made* her an adulteress or the fact that she was remarried *inferred* that she was an adulteress, for only sexual "uncleanness" could justify divorce. Either approach (or any other that one might eventually arrive at) requires one to face the fact that *moral taint was associated with divorce under the Mosaic legislation.* How could this be true if divorce could properly be for any and all causes?

In contrast, this remark does make sense if we take "uncleanness" as equivalent to Jesus' "sexual immorality." The fact that the woman was divorced and remarried reasonably proved that she was an adulteress since sexual "uncleanness" was required before such a divorce and remarriage occurred. Or, if one takes the text to refer to a woman who was divorced for a reason *other than* sexual immorality/uncleanness and that she is an adulteress *because* of that scripturally unauthorized remarriage, Jesus' words once again are faithfully echoed—for Jesus himself warned that in such a case adultery would occur via the remarriage (Mt. 5:32).

The approach we have taken is one that flies in the face of a mountain of tradition and assumption as to the meaning of the Lord. In spite of this, a close reading of Jesus' words indicates that it was, indeed, his intent to advocate a divorce doctrine strictly in accord with the Torah. To do otherwise would have placed him in defiance of the very Mosaic legal code he had earlier proclaimed would remain authoritative "till all is fulfilled." One may attempt to prove that Deuteronomy 24 is incompatible with Matthew 5:32, but that does not affect the fact that Jesus was *intending* to faithfully and correctly interpret that law. Might it not be that our exegesis of Deuteronomy 24 is faulty and *his* is the correct one?

The Controversy over the Genuineness of the Exception Clause

Before ending our discussion, it would be appropriate to give attention to the approach that denies the genuineness of the exception clause and uses that absence to create an incompatibility between Jesus' teaching and that of Deuteronomy. Of course this is not an issue of textual criticism—based strictly on manuscript evidence, the presence of the exception clause in the existing text is sound and beyond challenge. Hence this approach begins with the *assumption* that Jesus refused to authorize any and all divorce, moves from that to the conclusion that Matthew or an anonymous contributor to the gospel account added the exception clause,[26] and then moves to the conclusion that Jesus' doctrine of divorce was irreparably irreconcilable with that of the Pentateuch.

We have contended—and, we believe, demonstrated—that we must begin with the opposite end of this chain of reasoning: that Jesus intended to be fully, completely, and unquestionably in total harmony with the true intent and implications of the Law of Moses. Hence, in order for Jesus to have been consistent with the Torah, he must have provided for some type of divorce-permitting situation. This is a vital example of how, if one begins with a different set of premises, one will often come to a very different set of conclusions.

If we are anywhere near right in the central thesis of this book, we must start from the diametrically opposing premise of so many scholars: that Jesus intended to be fully compatible with the teaching of the Pentateuch. If so, there *had* to be occasions when the equivalent of the "uncleanness" of Deuteronomy 24 was mentioned by him.

How then can both "absolutist" and "non-absolutist"

texts be genuine? In both Mark 10:2–12 and the concise summary of his thoughts in Luke 16:18, Jesus criticizes divorce—period. The introduction of such "absolute" statements of his doctrine as evidence of the nongenuineness of the "except for immorality" clause overlooks the very nature of an exception clause: It is an exception. The general rule is *no divorce;* the exception tells *when divorce is right and proper.* The "absolutist" statements of Jesus' convictions are useful because they remind us of the underlying *opposition* to divorce found in the antithesis, an emphasis that can easily be overlooked in all the discussions of when and where the exception clause may apply.[27]

Finally, the exception clause can be *effectively* removed without *literally* striking it from the text. Those who take this approach do so by *redefining* the nature of "sexual immorality" in such a way that it applies to such a tiny group of people that it has little real-life application. If it applies (virtually) to no one, how can it be a real exception?

One such minimalization strategy makes the expression describe improperly close marriages among related kinspeople and assumes that it was designed to deal with a problem that could arise among converts among the Gentiles. First of all, one wonders how often it did arise. Secondly, if Jesus was intending conformity with the teachings of Deuteronomy, such an application was not the original point of the teaching. It was addressed to those who already knew and recognized those kinship-marriage limitations. Furthermore, Deuteronomy implicitly accepts the validity of the first marriage; it only prohibits *going back* to that mate. That original marriage was accepted as valid and moral in God's sight. Hence by stating his "exception," Jesus had in mind the *same* type of misconduct named in Deuteronomy and that was clearly *not* a matter of kinship marriages.

NOTES

[1]Robert A. Guelich, *The Sermon on the Mount: A Foundation for Understanding* (Waco, Tex.: Word, 1982), 198.

[2]Grounds for such an appeal included "duly established impotence; refusal to carry out matrimonial duties properly; habitual cruelty; a repulsive and incurable disease, such as leprosy; a change of trade and the adoption of a disgusting kind of work by the husband, such as the collection of dogs' dung for tanners; or the decision to leave Palestine and live far away" (Daniel-Rops, 136).

[3]Michael Hilton with Gordian Marshall, *The Gospels & Rabbinic Judaism: A Study Guide* (Hoboken, N.J.: KTAV, 1988), 126.

[4]Mishnah Gittin 9.10, as quoted by Hilton and Marshall, 126.

[5]Mishnah Gittin 9.10, as quoted by Hilton and Marshall, 126.

[6]Cf. Jacob Neusner, *The Pharisees: Rabbinic Perspectives* (Leiden, Netherlands: E. J. Brill, 1973; reprint, Hoboken, N.J.: KTAV, 1985), 282–84. Neusner recounts the reports of the Hillelites concerning this earlier period that speak of how the Shammaites were willing to use physical force to gain majority support and suppress the supporters of Hillel.

[7]*Ant.* iv. 253, as quoted by Vermes, *World of Judaism,* 70.

[8]*Vita,* 426, as quoted by Vermes, *World of Judaism,* 70.

[9]As quoted by Martin McNamara, *Palestinian Judaism and the New Testament* (Wilmington, Del.: Michael Glazier, 1983), 145. Also quoted by James H. Charlesworth in *Jesus Within Judaism: New Light from Exciting Archaeological Discoveries* (New York: Doubleday, 1988), 72, and in "Jesus, Early Jewish Literature, and Archaeology," in his *Jesus' Jewishness: Exploring the Place of Jesus Within Early Judaism*

(New York: American Interfaith Institute/Crossroad, 1991), 185. Neil S. Fujita (*A Crack in the Jar: What Ancient Jewish Documents Tell Us About the New Testament* [New York: Paulist, 1986], 130), quotes part of the text.

[10]Cf. McNamara, *Palestinian Judaism,* 145–46. Charlesworth speaks far more forcefully of the certainty of the general application of this particular demand in *Jesus Within Judaism,* 72, and in his "Jesus," 185.

[11]Column 4, referring to Genesis 1:27 for support of the prohibitionary argument as Jesus did in Matthew 19, as quoted by Murphy, 334.

[12]To say some of the individuals were, in effect, polygamous does not change this fact. Under the Pentateuch an individual was permitted to be a polygamist, yet there remained a provision for divorce in spite of that, just as applicable to him as to anyone else.

[13]Zimmermann argues that the words "causes her to commit adultery" represents a mistranslation of the Aramaic: "[T]he translator misread as the preposition *lah* instead of *leh;* the translation should not read, 'he makes her an adulteress' but 'makes *himself* an adulterer' "(*The Aramaic Origin of the Four Gospels,* 176). He does this, however, on the assumption that branding *her* remarriage as adulterous does not make good sense and that therefore a mistake in translation must have occurred. This leaves the remainder of the verse untouched: By branding her new partner as adulterous does that not leave her as *still* adulterous? Why then postulate a translation mistake?

[14] Matura, 110.

[15]Ben Witherington III, *The Christology of Jesus* (Minneapolis: Fortress, 1990), 60.

[16]Stanley B. Marrow, *The Words of Jesus in Our Gospels: A Catholic Response to Fundamentalism* (New York: Paulist, 1979), 11.

[17]Daniel J. Harrington, *God's People in Christ: New Testament Perspectives on the Church and Judaism* (Philadelphia: Fortress, 1980), 98.

[18]Newman and Stine, 141.

[19]Others who take this anti-Torah interpretation include Goulder, 261, 290–91, and William G. Thompson, *Matthew's Story: Good News for Uncertain Times* (New York: Paulist, 1989), 69. In addition this approach is implicitly presented by Powell, 83.

[20]*Jesus and the Law in the Synoptic Tradition* (Cambridge, UK: Cambridge University Press, 1975), 193.

[21]W. D. Davies, 104.

[22]Ibid., 103.

[23]Although it is common to contend that the "reason" for divorce given in the exception clause is different from that given in Deuteronomy 24:1–4, others believe "[t]he exceptive clause...corresponds well to the Hebrew of the Mosaic text concerning divorce..." (Bruce Chilton, *Profiles of a Rabbi: Synoptic Opportunities in Reading About Jesus* [Atlanta: Scholars Press, 1989], 63. Chilton goes on to suggest that that *still* leaves unresolved the question of the nature of the "indecency" mentioned in both places. Cf. a similar observation on the meaning of the exception clause in Matthew 19:9 (p. 64). For a denial of the equivalency, see John P. Meier, *Law and History,* 143-44. For a concisive, brief evaluation of the pros and cons, see Hilton and Marshall, 133–34.

[24]W. D. Davies, 104; John W. Wenham, *Christ and the Bible* (London: Tyndale Press, 1972), 34.

[25]Others have used it to prove that Jesus was only interpreting Moses in the exception clauses of Matthew 5:32 and 19:9 and that his new gospel system banned all divorce. This at least maintains the integrity of the New Testament writers against the accusation that they "added" the exception clauses in order to soften Jesus's teaching and make it more adaptable to actual human needs. Even so, it fails to note the true significance of the term "the law" as used in Romans 7.

[26]The motive is usually given as an effort to make the teaching of Jesus more humane or accomplishable among the early disciples. One of the very few scholars to root the alleged alteration in the need for consistency to meet the standard of the

Torah (rather than the purported needs of the early church) is Merkel, 141–42.

[27]Even the absolutist passage in Mark 10:11 provides a contrast with popular attitudes of Jesus' day. As John Marsh comments, "In that society a woman could commit adultery against her husband, but he could not commit adultery against her, but only against another married man. So Jesus was being quite revolutionary when He stated, 'Whoever divorces his wife and marries another commits adultery against her.' He broke new ground in asserting the reciprocal relationships of man and woman in marriage" (John Marsh, *Jesus in His Lifetime* [London: Sidgwick & Jackson, 1981], 135). Here also Jesus is rebuking contemporary views and not necessarily those of the Torah itself. Just as the modern Christian male can "bend" the teaching of scripture in self-serving directions, the ancient Jewish male could as well.

9

Oaths and Swearing
(Matthew 5:33-37)

We have saved for our concluding chapters the two contrastive teachings of Jesus that are most difficult to easily fit into our scenario that Jesus' *exclusive* intention was to reaffirm the teaching of the Pentateuchical law code. Yet even if our analysis should falter on either of these final two themes, the fact would remain that the other four antitheses clearly *do* fall into the category of reinforcing, rather than contradicting, what the Old Testament had taught.

At first glance, Jesus' teaching on swearing certainly seems to be approaching the subject from a radically different and contradictory direction from that of the Torah:

> Again you have heard that it was said to those of old, "You shall not swear falsely,[1] but shall perform your oaths to the Lord."
>
> But I say to you, do not swear at all: neither by heaven, for it is God's throne;

Nor by the earth, for it is His footstool; nor by Jerusalem, for it is the city of the great King.

Nor shall you swear by your head, because you cannot make one hair white or black.

But let your "Yes" be "Yes," and your "No," "No." For whatever is more than these is from the evil one (Mt. 5:33–37).

[Again, you have heard that it was said to those of ancient times, "You shall not swear falsely, but carry out the vows you have made to the Lord."

But I say to you, Do not swear at all, either by heaven, for it is the throne of God,

Or by the earth, for it is his footstool, or by Jerusalem, for it is the city of the great King.

And do not swear by your head, for you cannot make one hair white or black.

Let your word be "Yes, Yes" or "No, No"; anything more than this comes from the evil one. (NRSV)]

The first half of the "it was said" certainly represents Old Testament doctrine: You shall not swear *falsely.* That Testament stressed, "You shall not swear by My name falsely, nor shall you profane the name of your God: I am the Lord" (Lv. 19:12). In other words, one needed to take seriously what was being sworn to. It was not a polite and pious way to dignify a self-interested lie. Nor was it proper to promise something in God's name unless one fully intended to fulfill whatever was being pledged. In either case, the falsity of the oath carried divine censure.

The second half of the "It was said" can either be considered as one point or subdivided into two. For our purpose of analysis the latter approach may be best. First come the words, "[you] shall perform your oaths." Once again we see the stress on performance; they were to be carried out, implemented, executed. Not doing so surely came under the condemnation of "tak[ing] the name of the Lord your God in vain, for the Lord will not hold him guiltless who takes His name in vain" (Ex. 20:7; Dt. 5:11); "…he shall not break his word; he shall do according to all that proceeds out of his mouth" (Nm. 30:2b); "…you shall not delay to pay it; for the Lord your God will surely require it of you, and it would be a sin to you" (Dt. 23:21b). Perhaps this had become a major problem in the days of the writer of Ecclesiastes, for we find him pleading, "When you make a vow, do not delay to pay it; for He has no pleasure in fools. Pay what you have vowed. It is better not to vow than to vow and not pay" (5:4–5).

The concluding words, "to the Lord," stress that all oaths should be to the *right recipient,* to the true God of Israel rather than to some competing deity of the ancient world. As Deuteronomy 6:13 expresses it, "You shall fear the Lord your God and serve Him, and take oaths in His name." A similar thought is echoed a few chapters later: "You shall fear the Lord your God; you shall serve Him, and to Him you shall hold fast, and take oaths in His name" (Dt. 10:20).

Frederick D. Brunner cautiously asserts what others might state with less restraint, "This command of Jesus not to swear at all seems to be a full-blooded antithesis to the many Old Testament commandments to swear.…"[2] William G. Thompson concurs, "The law also prohibits false oaths, but Jesus forbids *all* oath taking" (our emphasis).[3] In a similar vein, Augustine Stock maintains that "[h]ere again an abrogation of part of the Mosaic law in the interest of promulgating more stringent injunctions seems likely."[4] But is this *really the case?*

Oaths versus Vows and the Nature and Purposes of Oaths

William Barclay rightly notes that the "commandment has nothing to do with swearing in the sense of using bad language; it condemns the man who swears that something is true, or who makes some promise, in the name of God, and who has taken the oath falsely."[5] The texts that would condemn vulgarity and obscenity would be found in other places, such as Ephesians 4:29 and Colossians 3:8.

The teaching Jesus gives in Matthew 5 is aimed at two overlapping phenomena, "oaths" (in the strict sense) and "vows" (which, in usage, came to be a near synonym). Stephen Westerholm discusses the similarity and the differences between the two:

> An oath attests the truth of a statement of fact or intention by means of a conditional curse, operative if the facts are falsely represented or the declared intention not carried out...It should be noted that vows at times overlap with oaths, and that the terminology is not always kept distinct.
>
> Theoretically, the difference is clear enough: an oath attests the truth of a statement by means of a conditional curse; with a vow, something is either to be reserved for sacred use or at least treated by those named in the vow as though it were so reserved. Still, a person's intentions may be solemnly affirmed by means of *either* an oath *or* a vow. Already in the Old Testament the terms are combined in such cases (Numbers 30:3 [English, 2]; Psalms 132:2). And, in fact, only the formula used distinguishes the two: "May anything belonging to you which I might eat be *korban*" is a vow; "By my oath! I will not eat anything belonging to you!" expresses the same resolution in the form of an oath. It is thus not

surprising if, in popular speech, what were exact formula
were not always observed, terms of oaths and vows were
sometimes used interchangeably.[6]

Hence, from the practical standpoint, since both
would invoke the name of God, the passages permitting
either would be relevant in the current context.

Above and beyond the occurrence of unexpected
events that make it impossible to fulfill them, every society seems to have means to rationalize a needless violation of one's promises, no matter how solemnly they
have been given. In the society of Jesus' Palestine, one
means of doing so was to make technical distinctions
based, not on the apparent *intent* of one's words, but on
minor differences in how one *expressed* those intentions.
In spite of the anti-oath-taking *official* stance of many
religious leaders then and later (see the next section), in
actual *practice* it was common to provide not only
implicit but explicit justification for such shady dealing.
Jesus tore into this fallacious way of reasoning in
Matthew 23:16–23:

> Woe to you, blind guides, who say, "Whoever swears by
> the temple, it is nothing; but whoever swears by the gold
> of the temple, he is obliged to perform it." Fools and
> blind! For which is greater, the gold or the temple that
> sanctifies the gold?
>
> And, "Whoever swears by the altar, it is nothing; but
> whoever swears by the *gift that is on it,* he is obliged to
> perform it." Fools and blind! For which is greater, the gift
> or the altar that sanctifies the gift?
>
> Therefore he who swears by the altar, swears by it and
> by all things on it. He who swears by the temple, swears
> by it and by Him who dwells in it. And he who swears by
> heaven, swears by the throne of God and by Him who sits
> on it.

[Woe to you, blind guides, who say, "Whoever swears by the sanctuary is bound by nothing, but whoever swears by the gold of the sanctuary is bound by the oath." You blind fools! For which is greater, the gold or the sanctuary that has made the gold sacred?

And you say, "Whoever swears by the altar is bound by nothing, but whoever swears by the gift that is on the altar is bound by the oath." How blind you are! For which is greater, the gift or the altar that makes the gift sacred?

So whoever swears by the altar, swears by it and by everything on it; and whoever swears by the sanctuary, swears by it and by the one who dwells in it. (NRSV)]

If one felt justified in welching on one's solemn word by such distinctions, how much greater must have been the self-justification found in the fact that the name of God was not *explicitly* used in any of these cases! One was supposed to fulfill the pledges one made in *God's* name; the active excuse maker would have found the fact that God's name is found in *none* of these formal pledges an irresistible "explanation" for his nonperformance.

Yet, as Jesus pointed out in the Matthew 23 text above, the verbal substitutes used in his society still retained an *implicit* invocation of the divine name. The same is true of the substitutes mentioned in Matthew 5:33–37. John R. W. Stott brings this out when he observes, "If you vow by 'heaven,' it is God's throne; if by 'earth' it is His footstool; if by 'Jerusalem' it is His city, 'The city of the great King.'" Even the criticism of swearing by one's body carries a similar implication for "it is God's creation and under God's control. You cannot even change the natural color of a single hair, black in youth and white in old age."[7]

The Anti-Oath-Taking Strain in Rabbinic Thought

That Jesus would discourage oath taking is consistent with a major strain of rabbinical thought. (Whether it was consistent with the Pentateuch itself has to be considered as a separate question.) Samuel T. Lachs insists that the rabbis, though discouraging oath taking "did not as a matter of law prohibit it," in contrast with the Essenes, who did so.[8] That may be true for some, but others he quotes seem far more absolutist in their attitude. One insisted, "Right or wrong, do not involve yourself in an oath."[9] Another asserted, "For I swear to you my children, but I will not swear by a single oath neither by heaven or by earth nor by anything made by God."[10]

Philo (a first century Jewish philosopher-theologian living in Egypt) wrote, "The good man's word…should be an oath, firm, unswerving, utterly free from falsehood, securely planted in truth."[11] He also declared,

> That being which is the most beautiful, and the most beneficial to human life, and suitable to rational nature, swears not itself, because truth on every point is so innate within him that his bare words are accounted as oaths. Next to not swearing at all, the second best course is to keep one's oath; for by the mere fact of swearing the swearer raises the suspicion of his not being trustworthy.[12]

Oath taking was rampant, not just among Jews, but among pagans as well. Speaking of the Gentiles in his native Alexandria, Philo wrote, "As it is, so highly impious are they that on any chance matter the most tremendous titles are on their lips and they do not blush to use name after name, one piled upon another, thinking that the continual repetition of a string of oaths will secure them their object."[13]

A close student of oath rendering among the Jews quotes this statement and immediately adds, "Exactly the same can be said of the populace of Palestine. The people swore and adjured on every occasion; they affirmed their statements by an oath in business affairs, in formulas of courtesy when they invited their friends, accepted invitations or rejected them, and in support of stories which strained credulity."[14] He notes that even the rabbis themselves "often swore" but that, in spite of this, they repeatedly criticized promiscuous swearing, swearing "when there is no urgent need for it."[15]

When we shift outside the boundaries of rabbinic opinion, we also find the strongest reservations about oath taking. Josephus tells us how the Essenes "show their love of God...by abstinence from oaths, by veracity..."[16] "Everything they say is more certain than an oath....Indeed swearing is rejected by them as being more evil than perjury. For anyone who does not merit belief without calling on God is already condemned."[17] Assuming the Essenes to be the group occupying the Qumran site (and that still seems the best interpretation), then there was a limitation upon this generalization: They were permitted one oath and one oath only—that at the time of their formal admission into the community.[18] Likewise the Dasmcus Document imposes a considerable limitation upon oaths taken in the Essenic group in Syria. In their case, the only oath permitted was that taken before a court.[19]

Josephus refers to two cases where major elements of the first-century religious leadership rebelled against oaths. In the first part of Herod the Great's reign, the Essenes and two of the schools of Pharisees declined to swear an oath of loyalty to their new ruler. Later, there was a general refusal of Pharisees to undertake an oath to

Caesar. Retribution was inflicted via a fine upon them.[20] More speculative is whether this represented a political opposition (due to the specific individuals to receive the loyalty oath) or whether this represented a *philosophical* hostility to oaths in general.[21] If the latter, Jesus' teaching would have reverberated in a familiar manner.

More hotly contested is the question of whether a double *yes* or a double *no* (such as Jesus urged) constituted an oath. Rabbinical evidence has been introduced to vindicate this belief, but it has been challenged on several grounds, including the late date from which it is documented.[22]

In addition to rabbinical evidence, in the pseudepigraphic 2 Enoch 49:1 a double *yes* and a double *no* are themselves oaths: "I swear to you, my children, but I swear not by an oath neither by heaven nor by earth, nor by any other creature which God created. The Lord said: 'There is no oath in me, nor injustice, but truth.' If there is no truth in men, let them swear by the words 'yea, yea' or 'nay, nay.'"[23] The problem with this source is that the quotation comes from the A recension of the text (which is often regarded as less reliable than the B recension), and the B recension lacks it entirely.[24]

Another strain of rabbinic thought seemingly considered a single *yes* or *no* to be equivalent to an oath—which would implicitly rule out the need for explicit oaths.[25] For example, we read of Rabbi Eleazar asserting, "No is an oath and yes is an oath."[26] The restraint-equals-abolishment approach ultimately won out. Orthodox Jews walk in this tradition when they insist on affirmations of truthfulness rather than swearing.[27] For our purposes, the antiquity of the custom does not matter. That there were repeated efforts to curb the practice and prevalence of swearing is clear. The only question is the degree to which there was a more or less *formalized* effort along the lines of what Jesus himself advocated. What is of significance in the current part of our discussion is that by reining in the practice of oaths, Jesus is taking a course many rabbis would have agreed with, however much most violated that admonition in practice.

Old Testament Texts Critical of Swearing: Targeting False Swearing Only?

An oath solemnized a statement, but it did not guarantee its truthfulness. The man who would callously answer "no" to the question of whether he had assaulted a passing traveler the previous night would be just as likely to add an impressive and lengthy invocation of the Almighty to reinforce that lie.

Zechariah speaks of God warning such individuals: "'I will send out the curse,' says the LORD of hosts. 'It shall enter the house of the thief and the house of *the one who swears falsely by My name.* It shall remain in the midst of his house and consume it, with his timber and stones'" (Zec. 5:4, our emphasis). It is probable that both the thief and the false swearer in this text are the same. Note how the verse refers to the singular "his house" rather than the plural *"their* houses." Even if the verse simply means that the individual who would commit one infamy would just as willingly commit the other, what is important in the present context is the same: the recognition that just as swearing seemed inevitable in Zechariah's society, so did the phenomenon of *false* swearing.

Leviticus 19 speaks in a similar vein, and the listeners are warned not to yield to the temptation to disguise theft behind a solemn oath: "You shall not steal, nor deal falsely, nor lie to one another. And you shall not swear by My name falsely, nor shall you profane the name of your God: I am the LORD. You shall not cheat your neighbor, nor rob him." (v. 11–13). By opposing unrestricted swearing, Jesus was forcing his disciples to control their own honesty (or lack thereof) rather than allowing them to hide their guilt behind a mountain of rhetoric.

In light of the way swearing could be and *was* abused, one can easily grasp why the conscientious Jew might have had considerable scruples about using oaths, especially on any frequent basis. The Old Testament itself contains at least one passage that at least initially seems to condemn swearing *without* specifying false and lying oaths. In Hosea 4:2 we read, "By *swearing* and lying, killing and stealing and committing adultery, they break all restraint, with bloodshed after bloodshed. Therefore the land will mourn; and everyone who dwells there will waste away...." The idea may be that of a lying oath (note the blatant evils it is bracketed with). On the other hand, the text doesn't actually say such, and one could equally well read it as a condemnation at least of *prolifigate* swearing, swearing that became so common and ordinary that it became taken-for-granted rhetoric even when one had committed a gross act toward one's neighbor.

In other words, the *inhibiting* intent of oaths had been removed. If the intent of guaranteeing truth telling had been effectively stripped away by societal misuse, would it be righteousness or sin to continue using them? And if the latter, would not some type of *generalized* or *blanket* condemnation of oaths—similar to the teaching of Jesus—be the likely result and the intent of Hosea? This process of reasoning may well explain the apparent existence of non-oath-takers in the following passage.

Ecclesiastes 9:2 and the Existence of Nonswearers

In Ecclesiastes 9:2 we read,

> Everything occurs alike to all: One event happens to the righteous and the wicked; to the good, the clean, and the unclean; to him who sacrifices and him who does not sacrifice. As is the good, so the sinner, and he who takes an oath as he who fears an oath.

The New American Standard Bible renders the closing words as "the one who is *afraid* to swear" and provides a marginal note, "Literally, fears an oath." The New Revised Standard Version makes the contrast one between "those who swear" and "those who shun an oath." Do we find in this Old Testament passage a reference to a type of individual who, out of conscientious objection (perhaps on the grounds outlined above) refused taking *all* oaths—or so nearly declined them all that the result was virtually the same? If so, we find here an Old Testament precedent for the kind of blanket no-oath-taking generalization that Jesus makes in Matthew 5.

Although this discussion will take a disproportionate amount of space, we believe it to be fully justified because the relevance of this text has often been overlooked as a possible Old Testament basis or foreshadowing of Matthew 5:34. (Indeed, in my research I recall finding no reference to the passage among those directly discussing the Antitheses; the only ones who noticed the similarity were the few referred to below, who were all Ecclesiastes commentators.)

So far as oath taking goes, only two categories are mentioned: those who take them and those who don't. Hence there are two interpretive options available in handling the text.

1. *The nonswearer occupies the superior moral position.* Those who take this approach see in "the one who fears an oath" not an absolute abstainer, but one who, though only using it seriously and when absolutely called for, avoids the *abuse* of swearing that so easily occurred. In other words, they are comparatively (at least), abstainers from oaths.

Otto Zockler considers the first individual, the oath taker, to be "the frivolous swearer" while the second individual is "he that considers an oath sacred."[28] Charles H. Wright uses very similar language, describing the first man as "the profane swearer" and "the one who reverenc[es] the solemn oath."[29]

Franz Delitzsch finds in the oath maker a case of "wanton swearing, a calling upon God when it is not necessary, and, it may be, even to confirm an untruth....Compare Matthew [5:]34."[30] Christian O. Ginsburg sees a reference to "careless swearing, the habit of using an oath at every declaration" and also urges the reader to "compare Matthew [5]:34."[31]

One argument in favor of the swearer being the morally lacking of the two is that of the order of reference found earlier in the verse. George A. Barton argues, "The analogy of the series, in which the bad character uniformly comes first, compels us to take this of profane swearing which was prohibited (Exodus 20:7; cf. Matthew 5:34), and not with Plumptre, of that judicial swearing which was commended."[32] Perhaps an argument of this kind can be based on other texts from Ecclesiastes, but it seems impossible to do so in the present text. The "righteous" are mentioned before "the wicked" and the "good, the clean" are mentioned before the "unclean." Surely this is not uniformly listing the "bad character" first!

Ralph Wardlaw grounds his argument on the words used by the author: "'Swearing,' here being opposed to 'fearing an oath,' must, of course, mean swearing lightly and falsely; and 'fearing an oath' is taking it with solemnity, and keeping it with fidelity under a deep impression of the evil of profaning the great and dreadful name to which the appeal is made."[33] Moses Stuart implies a similar interpretation.[34]

If this be the intent, wouldn't it have made more sense to speak of "those who swear frivolously and those who swear seriously"? To speak in terms of "one who *fears* an oath" seemingly implies considerably more: one who has either totally given up swearing or one who has so *dramatically reduced* his oath taking that they are so uncommon as to represent a *virtual abandonment* of the practice. Perhaps we are being a shade too harsh. In a society given to profligate and empty swearing, would not swearing only serious oaths result in just such a virtual termination of oath making?

2. *The swearer occupies the superior moral position.* Unlike the first view, this approach is incompatible with Jesus' rooting his antithesis in the current text. If the swearer represented the moral ideal and the "one who fears an oath" an individual of lesser character, then Jesus would have been rooting his doctrine in the values of the spiritually dubious rather than in the values of the morally committed. Even if we were to decide that Jesus based his prohibition on other texts, there would still remain the oddity of his endorsing an approach condemned by Ecclesiastes as morally inferior.

E. H. Plumptre concedes that "as commonly interpreted" in his day, the meaning of the verse was that the swearer is "the man who swears falsely" (or such like) and that the abstainer is the one who "looks on its obligation with a solemn awe or whose communication is Yea, yea, Nay, nay, and who shrinks in reverential awe from any formal use of the Divine Name."[35] In other words—though he himself rejects the approach—it was common to interpret the passage in his day as Old Testament precedent for Jesus' yea, yea/nay, nay antithesis.

In contrast, Plumptre believed that the oath taker is the faithful truth teller, whereas the fearer of oaths is one "whose 'coward conscience' makes him shrink from the oath of compurgation on the part of an accused person (compare Aristotle, *Rhetoric,* 1.27), or of testimony."[36] Although it is certainly credible that *some* would be inhibited from oath making because of a guilty conscience, the *prevalent* problem throughout the two testaments seems to be blatant false oaths executed by hardened consciences. The contrast of Ecclesiastes would far more probably be between two common phenomena (such as prolifigate oath taking and non-oath-taking or between reckless and serious oath making) than between a common phenomena (oath giving) and an uncommon phenomena, an individual whose guilt kept him from making the oath.

Although dissenting from this alternative, A. Lukwyn Williams concisely sums up three arguments in its favor:

> (1) This is in accordance with [the text's] previous order, in which the better precedes. (2) It was a duty to swear on proper occasions (Exodus 22:11). (3) Swearing, both in verb and substantive is seldom mentioned in a bad sense, without the addition of "falsely." In this case "he that feareth" an oath would be the man who knows his cause is unjust and will not take the oath in a court of law.[37]

Once again an approach is suggested that would have us interpret the text as alluding to a surely uncommon phenomenon, a guilty conscience making an individual reluctant to testify to a lie. The very fervor with which false swearing is repeatedly denounced in the Torah and the Prophets argues that human nature then was like today—that an individual unscrupulous enough to inflict a major and conscious injustice on another is not likely to hesitate to provide a lying tongue to enable him to hold on to his ill-gotten gains.

The first argument (good being listed before the bad) has more than a little validity, for we read of "the righteous and the wicked." Then we read of "the good, the clean, and the unclean," and the first two are clearly morally approved. Yet the very fact that two morally accepted categories are given together makes one question any rigid alternation of good/bad in this Ecclesiastes text. It demonstrates that the author is quite capable of putting two virtuous categories together. The third grouping concerns "he who sacrifices and him who does not sacrifice." Here we would assume the sacrificing category to be superior to the nonsacrificers. On the other hand, would not the purpose behind the sacrifice determine that question? (In other words, it could very well vary from case to case.) That leaves us with the final grouping of swearers versus nonswearers that is the subject of our discussion.

The duty to swear is alluded to, but the circumstance in Exodus 22:11 is a narrowly defined one, not one of common everyday occurrence. Yet we know that the "propriety" of swearing had been broadened into a justification for it on any and virtually all occasions. Once again, would not the individual who reduced his use of oaths to the bare minimum be well described as the one who "fears an oath"?

The third argument is the most significant because, as Williams notes, precedent can be found in Zechariah 5.[38] In verse 4 one reads of the false swearer, and in verse 3 he is described as one who fears an oath. In actual translation, however, it is not so rendered; typically, we do not find "who does not swear" but "one that sweareth" in the KJV, or in more recent versions, "perjurer," as in the NKJV. Hence, at the most, the idea would be perjury *by silence,* by not swearing to what one does to be the truth. And that certainly would not fit the contrast intended in Ecclesiastes text.

Furthermore, as normally translated, the Zechariah text can be introduced as evidence that swearing had become so abused that it had become synonymous with false swearing. As already observed, this would be the natural human degeneration of the practice: What else could the individual who engages in indiscriminate and unrestrained swearing ultimately be but a false swearer since he is in the habit of covering everything he does with an immediate and automatic oath? He is going to have to back his lies with an oath because everything else he says is backed by an oath. In such a situation, is oath taking morally desirable, even under a system that provided for such? Even if we take Zechariah to have in mind false swearing by silence (v. 3) and false swearing by overt falsehood (v. 4), this would remain the case. If there is skepticism here of those who (allegedly) did not swear, there is certainly skepticism of those who do (v. 4) as well. Hence the whole system had become suspect, however desirable oath taking was in the abstract.

Michael Eaton concedes that "the majority interpretation" makes the text refer to "profane or rash swearing," but he dissents from this approach on the grounds (analyzed above) that "the good characteristic comes first." He takes the reference to be to one who "shuns" any public commitment to "loyalty to the covenant" between God and Israel. Oddly enough, he makes passing reference to the expression "fear[ing] an oath" in 1 Samuel 14:26 as meaning "to honor" an oath, which would seemingly provide evidence that the *non*swearer occupies the superior moral view. Be that as it may, because the expression can have a positive connotation as well, he prefers the rendering "he who shuns an oath."[39] But isn't this making the translation fit what one *thinks* the text means rather than allowing the translation to *create* the interpretation?

The balance of evidence seems in favor of the nonswearer occupying the superior moral position. In all fairness, however, it should be noted that this is irrelevant to the main argument of the Ecclesiastes penman. His concern is not that one is superior to another, but that regardless of where the moral superiority lies, a similar physical fate ultimately occurs to all.

Even so, as a *secondary* point our text bears witness to the existence of individuals who avoided both insincere oaths *and* sacrifices (note the text's reference to "him who sacrifices and him who does not sacrifice").[40] They were *minimalists,* not out of any desire to do the *least* that was acceptable to God, but out of a passion to do only that which was acceptable to Yahweh. They refused to fall into the kind of ritualistic religious practice in which form and image takes the place of sincerity, dedication, and integrity. The gap between such individuals and Jesus is narrowed even further when we recognize that Jesus did not intend to forbid *all* oaths (we speak of judicial oaths in particular). Indeed, when we reach this point, can we meaningfully speak of there being any difference at all? Do not the thought of Ecclesiastes 9:2 and Jesus' teaching overlap, merge, and represent the same strain of thought?

Reconciling Scenarios: Jesus Is Not Talking about Judicial Oaths

It is ironic that the contemporary discussion about the application of Jesus' teaching on nonretaliation always seems to revolve around the question of "whether a Christian can kill in war" rather than about the Christian response to the stresses of everyday life, which is the real subject under discussion. Likewise the current passage is often used as if the subject of *judicial* oaths were under discussion. (Did any culture ever have individuals swear *judicial* oaths by their hair?) The very *type* of oaths Jesus lists shows that he is concerned with the common, garden variety of oaths that were so abundant in his society.

Indeed, we have positive evidence that both Jesus and early Christians emphatically did not interpret Jesus' words as applicable to judicial/legal type oaths. So Jesus *had* to have had something else in mind or his doctrine would have contradicted his practice.

For example, Jesus was put under judicial oath by the high priest: "I adjure You by the living God that you tell us if You are the Christ, the Son of God" (Mt. 26:63). Whether the words "I swear" were in his response or not he was still making a statement *under oath* when he responded, "It is as you said" (v. 64).

We also find judicial-type oaths used to affirm the genuineness of what is being said in the apostolic epistles. We read Paul affirming, "I call God as my witness"

(2 Cor. 1:23). Likewise in both Romans 1:9 and Philippians 1:8, he refers to the fact that "God is my witness." In Galatians 1:20 Paul swears to the truthfulness of his words when he writes, "Before God, I do not lie." In Hebrews 6:16 the writer accepts the propriety of such oaths: "For men indeed swear by the greater, and an oath for confirmation is for them an end of all dispute."

Obligatory Swearing Was the Exception and Not the Rule: Any Limitation of Oaths to Those Limited Circumstances Represented a Virtual Rejection of the Practice of Swearing

Oath making in the Old Testament can be divided into three categories:

1. *Legal/judicial-type oaths were obligatory.* The Torah provided for oaths in certain specified cases. For example, when property left in the charge of someone else had been injured or disappeared, the trustee was to swear it was through no fault of his own (Ex. 22:10–13). This was to be the resort in cases of challenged ownership of a possession (Lv. 6:2–6, especially v. 3). In light of the example of both Jesus and Paul, the antithesis was never intended to apply to such cases.

2. *Most other oaths that were authorized were not obligatory.*

Note the permissive nature of the wording in Numbers 30:2: *"If* a man vows a vow to the Lord, or swears an oath to bind himself by some agreement, he shall do according to all that proceeds out of his mouth." (Also note how vows and oaths are presented as closely related or overlapping phenomena.) What was *not* required, was an individual to make the vow in the first place. You were to swear by the Lord *if* you swore at all, but there was no obligation to commit oneself to an oath to begin with.

Of an oath that took the form of a promise to the Lord we read, "When you make a vow to the Lord your God, you shall not delay to pay it; for the Lord your God will surely require it of you, and it would be a sin to you." Then the text promptly adds, "But if you abstain from vowing, it shall not be a sin to you" (Dt. 23:21–22).

If Jesus intended his antithesis to cover the category of "permitted" rather than "obligatory" oaths, he was still not revoking some demand of the Torah. Under the Torah it was within your choice as a free man or woman to vow or not to vow. Jesus would simply be affirming that his disciples *are to exercise that liberty the Old Testament already provided.*

Did a Jew sin by refusing to get a divorce, though it was authorized by Moses? Of course not. Nor did a Jew do anything contrary to the demand of the old covenant by not exercising its permission to make voluntary oaths.

3. *Finally, there was the totally unauthorized use of vows and oaths as empty words to impress the hearer and reinforce one's public image.* As studied at the beginning of this chapter, we know that promiscuous oath making was pervasive in the society of the first century. Furthermore, the types of oath Jesus condemns in Matthew 5 are the type we would expect in such cases. The explicit name of God is missing in each case, allowing an individual to *technically* avoid taking the name of the Lord in vain while lying his head off. *Implicitly* there was an appeal to God in such verbal substitutions, as Jesus pointed out in Matthew 23:16–21, but because it was not openly *verbalized* there was a legalistic way out of conscious guilt.

For Jesus to have accepted only those oaths *required* by

the Law—and, possibly, the broader category *permitted* by the Law—would have been fully in keeping with the letter and spirit of the Torah and the Prophets. It was reprobate humanity that insisted upon extending the oath concept to every trivial matter, however insignificant and self-serving. The Old Testament never required an individual to be a party to such foolishness. Indeed, one might well argue that if oaths were to be taken as seriously as the God of Israel wanted them to be, then they had to be abstained from in this common and debased form. Once again, Jesus' antithesis is walking in the steps of Moses.

God's Name Is Conspicuously Absent from the List of Condemned Oaths

In the antithesis of Matthew 5, we find four types of oaths condemned: (a) by heaven; (b) by earth; (c) by Jerusalem; (d) by one's head.

In Matthew 23:16–22 we find a variety of oaths mentioned: (a) by the temple; (b) by the gold of the temple; (c) by the altar; (d) by the gift on the altar.

It is these types of oaths that Jesus insists must be abstained from. Rather than swear such oaths, one must be content with an emphatic *yes* or *no:* "Whatever is more than these is from the evil one" (Mt. 5:37) because it tempts one to engage in the making of subtle distinctions between binding and nonbinding oaths of the kind rebuked in Matthew 23.

What is not mentioned is that it was wrong to swear explicitly in God's name. *Nowhere in either text is that subject mentioned.*[41] Indeed, for Jesus to have done so would have been for him to put his doctrine and his practice in open conflict. Again we are forced to the conclusion that Jesus is targeting insincere, frivolous, vain, hypocritical, and deceitful oath taking—the type prevalent in his day and age. The *serious* believer in the kind of oaths permitted or required by the Torah would have had no trouble accepting the generalization found in the antithesis. It would have simply echoed his own practice. Why then should we find some fundamental contradiction between the two covenants?

The Teaching of James

A close kin to this antithesis is found in the book of James:

> My brethren, take the prophets, who spoke in the name of the Lord, as an example of suffering and patience. Indeed, we count them blessed who endure. You have heard of the perseverance of Job and seen the end intended by the Lord—that the Lord is very compassionate and merciful. But above all, my brethren, do not swear, either by heaven or by earth or with any oath. But let your "Yes" be "Yes," and your "No," "No," lest you fall into judgment. Is anyone among you *suffering?* Let him pray. Is anyone cheerful? Let him sing psalms. Is anyone among you *sick?* Let him call for the elders of the church…(Jas. 5:10–14, our emphasis).

> [As an example of suffering and patience, beloved, take the prophets who spoke in the name of the Lord. Indeed we call blessed those who showed endurance. You have heard of the endurance of Job, and you have seen the purpose of the Lord, how the Lord is compassionate and merciful. Above all, my beloved, do not swear, either by heaven or by earth or by any other oath, but let your "Yes" be yes and your "No" be no, so that you may not fall under condemnation. Are any among you suffering? They should pray. Are any cheerful? They should sing

songs of praise. Are any among you sick? They should
call for the elders of the church.... (NRSV)]

It is common to find commentators who take this as a
complete ban on all oath making. James' attitude is
described by such phrases as "unqualified prohibition,"[42]
"absolute prohibition,"[43] and "the total rejection of
oaths."[44] There is a clear verbal similarity to the antithesis we have been studying. This has been rooted in both
a direct reliance on the Matthew text[45] and, alternatively, on both Matthew and James using similar or
identical earlier sources.[46]

In spite of this tendency toward absolutist interpretation, the *same* limitations on James' meaning are appropriate as upon that of the antithesis. If James has in
mind the general principle of indiscriminate oath making, then it is as a means to an end. It is not so much a
question of which oaths are right—if any—but of
impressing upon his readers the need for "unquestion-
able truthfulness."[47] If *that* is present, oaths become an
irrelevancy. The *purpose* behind oaths (trustworthy testimony) is fully achieved without even the need for an
oath to be taken.

The context, however, introduces an additional factor
that may well require a different point being in the
author's mind. Note the emphasis on endurance, perseverance, suffering, and sickness in the text. It would be
a reasonable deduction that James was fearful that the
natural concern with their physical well-being would
lead his readers to use reckless and excessive oaths—
perhaps even vulgar ones as well—out of frustration and
desperation. Although the terms *swearing* and *oaths* are
normally not used in this sense in the biblical texts, this
context of stress, difficulty, and oppression represents a

context when such a usage would be highly appropriate. As James Moffatt notes, "In excitement or irritation there was a temptation to curse and swear violently and profanely."[48] Or as Spiros Zodhiates observes, "When one is sorrowful and dejected, it is very natural that there should be a sigh, a complaint against God, and the possible use of the name of God unworthily."[49] Rather than to do such, it was better not to swear at all.

Or one could find in this an admonition not to make reckless promises to God out of our despair—promises that one may mean at the moment but which will be difficult or impossible to carry out in the future. The old adage that there are "no atheists in foxholes" is germane. Likewise the proverbial stories of individuals who, under grave danger, make the most solemn pledges of moral reform—only to abandon them after the crisis has passed. Rather than make empty promises (even well-intentioned ones), it is better not to make such promises at all.

NOTES

[1]There is a certain ambiguity in the Old Testament text being quoted. Newman and Stine comment in their translator's handbook on Matthew:

"Swear falsely" translates a Greek verb which may mean either "break an oath" or "commit perjury." This is its only occurrence in the New Testament, and both meanings are possible for the context. A related noun form is used in 1 Timothy 1:10 (Today's English Version, "Those who...give false testimony"). Translations are divided rather sharply on the meaning. Today's English Version, New English Bible, New Jerusalem Bible have "break promise (or, oath)"; while others go in the direction of "to perjure" (for example, Moffatt, Phillips, "forswear"; New American Bible, "take a false oath"; Revised Standard Version, American Translation, German Common Language Version 1st edition, "swear falsely"). Anchor Bible has "make vows rashly." As one may expect, New Testament scholars are also divided on their interpretation of this verb, though several commentators note that the meaning "break an oath" goes better with the last clause of the verse. (p. 143)

[2]Brunner, 199.

[3]Thompson, 69.

[4]Stock, 88. Others who see a contradiction with the Mosaic Law include Harrington, *God's People in Christ,* 98; John P. Meier, *Matthew / New Testament Message,* 53; and Obach and Kirk, 66–67.

[5]Barclay, 158.

[6]Westerholm, 104–5. For an in-depth study of vows in particular, see Tony W. Cartledge, *Vows in the Hewbrew Bible and the Ancient Near East* (Sheffield, UK: JSOT, 1992).

[7]Stott, 101.

[8]Lachs, 102.

[9]Ibid., 101.

[10]Ibid.

[11]*Spec. Leg.* ii. 2, as quoted by Vermes, *Jesus the Jew,* 35.

[12]*On the Ten Commandments* (c. 17), as quoted by Marriott, 156. Lachs (101) renders the opening words even more pointedly, "To swear not at all is the best course and most profitable to life…"

[13]*De spec. leg.,* ii. 8, as quoted by Saul Lieberman, *Greek in Jewish Palestine: Studies in the Life and Manners of Jewish Palestine in the II-IV Centuries C.E.* (New York: Jewish Theological Seminary of America, 1942), 116.

[14]Lieberman, 116. An early twentieth century example of how oath-taking was engaged in by merchants and shoppers who spoke Aramaic is provided by George M. Lamsa, who was raised in such a culture:

Each merchant has his own prices and quotes them to
each customer as he pleases. The customer is afraid of
being cheated and has his own idea of the price....When
the price cannot be settled by bargaining, merchants and
their customers generally take oaths by temples and
holy names in proof of their sincerity. They take an oath
saying, "By God's name and his holy angels, this pair of
shoes cost me six dollars but you can have it for three
dollars." When such oaths are ineffective then they
resort to swearing. Thus, "If I lie to you I am the son of a
dog or an ass, the shoes cost me three dollars but I will
let you have them for a dollar and a half." To all of this
the suspecting customer replies, "By my only son's head,
I will not pay you more than a dollar." If this fails the
merchant is apt to spit in the face of the customer.
(*Gospel Light,* 39–40)

[15]Lieberman. 115.

[16]*Omnis probus,* 84, as quoted by Vermes, *Jesus the Jew,* 35.

[17]*War,* ii 135, as quoted by Vermes, *Jesus the Jew,* 35.

[18]Richard Kugelman, *James and Jude* (Wilmington, Del.:
Michael Glazier, 1980), 63.

[19]Ibid.

[20]The two cases are found in *Antiquities* 15.368 and 17.42,
as cited by Powell, 84.

[21]Powell, 84.

[22]Banks (195-96) argues that it is an inaccurate reading of
the evidence to take it to mean that a double affirmation/
denial constitutes an oath. He contends that the key evidence
cited from the Talmud (b. Shab. 36a) is "extremely late (c. A.D.
350)." Furthermore, "wherever else the expression occurs in
the rabbinic sources it is always in a non-formulaic sense, and
repetition is a common semitic usage to emphasize the character of what is being said."

[23]As quoted by Stephenson H. Brooks, *Matthew's Community: The Evidence of His Special Sayings Material* (Sheffield,
UK: JSOT Press, 1987), 136.

[24]Brooks, 136. Banks (196) is convinced that this was "probably a later interpolation, since only one manuscript tradition contains it." James H. Charlesworth (*Jesus Within Judaism,* x), who has himself edited 2 Enoch for publication in English, is inclined to deny that the fuller form has been "expanded by a Christian scribe."

[25]For citations, see Lapide, 73.

[26]Sheb 36a, as quoted by Lapide, 73; also quoted by Klausner, 385.

[27]Lapide, 73.

[28]Otto Zockler, *Ecclesiastes or Koheleth,* trans. William Wells (New York: Charles Scribner & Company, 1870), 124.

[29]Charles H. Wright, *The Book of Koheleth* (London: Holder and Stoughton, 1853), 406.

[30]Franz Delitzsch, *Biblical Commentary on the Song of Songs and Ecclesiastes,* trans. M. G. Easton (Edinburgh: T. & T. Clark, 1877), 357.

[31]Christian O. Ginsburg, *Coheleth: Commonly Called the Book of Ecclesiastes* (London: Longman, Green, and Roberts, 1861), 411.

[32]George A. Barton, *A Critical and Exegetical Commentary on the Book of Ecclesiastes* in the *International Critical Commentary* series (New York: Charles Scribner's Sons, 1908), 159.

[33]Robert Wardlow, *Lectures: Expository and Practical on the Book of Ecclesiastes* (Philadelphia: Wm. S. Rentoul, 1868), 296–97.

[34]Moses Stuart, *Commentary on Ecclesiastes,* ed. and rev. by R. D. C. Robbins (Boston: Draper and Halliday, 1862; 1880 printing), 287.

[35]E. N. Plumptre, *Ecclesiastes,* in the Cambridge Bible for Schools and Colleges series (Cambridge, UK: Cambridge University Press, 1890), 184.

[36]Ibid., 185.

[37]A. Lukwyn Williams, *Ecclesiastes,* in the Cambridge Bible for Schools and College series (Cambridge, UK: Cambridge University Press, 1922), 185. Williams is undecided

between two alternatives, "either, he that respecteth an oath when taken, or…he that feareth to take an unnecessary oath…" (103). The second requires a contrast between lavish and minimal oath making, which would edge one very close to the general principle of de facto total abstinence. The first approach also implies an individual who drastically holds down oath making, for such an individual *because of the very seriousness of the occasion* would want to make sure that only the absolutely truthful was sworn to.

[38]Williams, 103.

[39]Michael Eaton, *Ecclesiastes: An Introduction and Commentary,* in the Tyndale Old Testament Commentary series (Downer's Grove, Ill.: InterVarsity Press, 1983), 125.

[40]R. N. Whybray (*Ecclesiastes,* in the New Century Bible Commentary series [Grand Rapids: Eerdmans, 1989], 141) deduces that "there were evidently differences of opinion in Qoheleth's time about the propriety of taking oaths, as there were on the question of offering sacrifice" but declines to make any commitment as to which side was upholding the Torah tradition and which was defying it.

[41]One could respond by noting that Jews considered God's name too holy to be used. This applied only to that of his proper name, "Yahweh," substitute terms such as Lord being acceptable. Of course one might wonder whether *any* oath was acceptable in such circumstances: If oaths were to be in the name of God and one could not use his *true* name, Yahweh, were the oaths *true* oaths? In such an environment, one might find additional incentive to limit the degree of oath taking to the maximum permitted by the Law itself.

[42]Sophie Laws, *A Commentary on the Epistle of James* (San Francisco: Harper & Row, 1980), 222; cf. 224.

[43]Martin Dibelius, *James,* rev. Heinrich Greeven, trans. Helmut Koester (Philadelphia: Fortress, 1976), 248.

[44]Peter H. Davids, *The Epistle of James: A Commentary on the Greek Text* (Grand Rapids: Eerdmans, 1982), 189. Others who speak of an absolute prohibition include Paul A. Cedar, *James, 1, 2 Peter, Jude* (Waco, Tex: Word, 1984), 97; Ralph P.

Martin, *James* (Waco, Tex: Word, 1988), 204; and G. Leslie Mitton, *The Epistle of James* (London: Marshall, Morgan & Scott, 1966), 192.

[45]Cedar, 97, and A. T. Robertson, *Practical and Social Aspects of Christianity: The Wisdom of James* (New York: George H. Doran Company, 1915), 248. It is implied by E. H. Plumptre, *The General Epistle of St. James* (Cambridge, UK: Cambridge University Press, 1878; 1895 printing), 102, and R. V. Tasker, *The General Epistle of James: An Introduction and Commentary* (London: Tyndale Press, 1956), 124.

[46]Simon J. Kistemaker, *Exposition of the Epistle of James and the Epistles of John* (Grand Rapids: Baker, 1986), 172; Laws, 223; Gerald H. Rendall, *The Epistle of St. James and Judaic Christianity* (Cambridge, UK: Cambridge University Press, 1878; 1895 printing), 67–68.

[47]Timothy B. Cargal, *Restoring the Diaspora: Discursive Structure and Purpose in the Epistle of James* (Atlanta: Scholars Press, 1993), 189–90.

[48]James Moffatt, *The General Epistles James, Peter, and Judas* (New York: Harper and Brothers, 1962), 75.

[49]Spiros Zodhiates, *The Patience of Hope: An Exposition of James 4:13–5:20* (Chattanooga, Tenn.: AMG Publishers, 1981; 1985 printing), 109. Also interpreting the text as profane swearing is Robertson, 249.

10

Loaning, Compulsion, and Unfair Law Courts (Matthew 5:38-42)

In Matthew 5:38–42 Jesus provides a discussion of the believer's proper attitude toward retaliating with violence:

You have heard that it was said, "An eye for an eye and a tooth for a tooth."

But I tell you not to resist an evil person. But whoever slaps you on your right cheek, turn the other to him also.

If anyone wants to sue you and take away your tunic, let him have your cloak also.

And whoever compels you to go one mile, go with him two.

Give to him who asks you, and from him who wants to borrow from you do not turn away.

[You have heard that it was said, "An eye for an eye and a tooth for a tooth."

But I say to you, Do not resist an evildoer. But if anyone strikes you on the right cheek, turn the other also;

And if anyone wants to sue you and take your coat, give your cloak as well;

And if anyone forces you to go one mile, go also the second mile.

Give to everyone who begs from you, and do not refuse anyone who wants to borrow from you. (NRSV)]

Is Jesus' admonition in conflict with Old Testament teaching? Perhaps more than in any of the other antitheses, it is commonly held that this is the case. The Jewish scholar C. G. Montefiore wrote between the two World Wars concerning how these verses raised the most vehement objections from those of his own religious background:

The Jewish critic usually objects to these verses and to their doctrine. In many passages of the Sermon [on the Mount] he is at pains to adduce Rabbinic parallels, and to argue that the teaching of Jesus is on all-fours with the teaching of the Rabbis. Here, however, he usually takes the other line. Here he assumes a contrast, and because there is a contrast, the new teaching of Jesus is unsatisfactory or bad.[1]

C. Milo Connick is especially candid when he writes, "If the saying about divorce does not annul the Old Testament injunction, it considerably restricts it; and the teaching on retaliation *actually overthrows the Old Testament teaching* on 'an eye for an eye'" (our emphasis).[2]

That Jesus may have departed from the rabbinical consensus is, in itself, not overly shocking; we read in the New Testament of his repeated conflicts with the Pharisees and Sadducees. (Perhaps it is more startling, from our perspective of maximizing the differences because of such confrontations, to discover how often he was in *agreement* with them.) Indeed, if there had not been a

number of points on which they were in vehement conflict, there would have been no reason for their profound
hostility toward him, which ultimately lead to his death.

The vital question is (once again) not the Lord's agreement or dissent from the rabbinical approach of his day,
but its conformity with the teaching of the Torah itself,
upon which the rabbis claimed to base their own doctrine. Connick and others see a profound and unbridge-
able gap even when the subject is approached from this
needed direction.

But is that necessarily so? Could it be that we have
assumed what Jesus is advocating and built a contradiction—when he was actually teaching with a very different
point or points in mind? In answering our question, we
need to recognize that there are four aspects to the
instruction found in this antithesis: (a) turning the other
cheek (v. 39); (b) lawsuits (v. 40): (c) legally required work
imposed by the authorities [in this particular case, by an
occupation army] (v. 41); and (d) giving to those request-
ing assistance (v. 42). If we can show the Old Testament
basis of *any* of these, then we have laid the groundwork
for a reconsideration of the anti-Old Testament interpretation of the entirety. Indeed, the more cases of precedent
we can discover in the Torah and the Prophets, the
greater the probability that the *entire* contrast is intended
to establish the true teaching of Moses and the seers of
old. To do this most convincingly, we need to start at the
last of Jesus' assertions and then work our way backward.

The Command to "Give" Reinforces Old Testament Teaching

If this were the only one of Christ's four comparisons
in this antithesis, the theory that Jesus is controverting

the demands of the Mosaic Law would never have prospered. The idea of benevolence to *all* the needy of one's nation is repeatedly stressed in the Old Testament. This aid could come in one of two forms:

1. *The first kind of aid was a non-interest principal-only loan.* In Exodus 22:25 it is said, "If you lend money to any of My people who are poor among you, you shall not be like a moneylender to him; you shall not charge interest." The *if* here could be taken as permissive authority in such cases, leaving the decision whether to help within the sphere of one's private choice. In Leviticus 25:35–37 it is made plain that what is optional is not the loan itself but the fact that one who has the resources to lend may or may not come face to face with such a needy individual. If one does, then the obligation to lend is an *absolute* obligation:

> If one of your brethren becomes poor, and falls into poverty among you, then you shall help him, like a stranger or a sojourner, that he may live with you. Take no usury or interest from him; but fear your God, that your brother may live with you. You shall not lend him money for usury, nor lend him your food at a profit. I am the LORD your God, who brought you out of the land of Egypt, to give you the land of Canaan and to be your God.

> [If any of your kin fall into difficulty and become dependent on you, you shall support them; they shall live with you as though resident aliens. Do not take interest in advance or otherwise make a profit from them, but fear your God; let them live with you. You shall not lend them your money at interest taken in advance, or provide them food at a profit. I am the Lord your God, who brought you out of the land of Egypt, to give you the land of Canaan, to be your God. (NRSV)]

"That he may live with you" conveys the idea that without assistance, he may have no choice but to pull up stakes and move elsewhere. With support, however, he may be able to bridge the crisis period and remain with you in your community. With such assistance he may be able to better himself to the point where he can get back on his feet and not feel compelled to move on to some foreign shore in his effort to keep his (economic) head above water.

The Torah warns against refusing to meet this obligation because the legal deadline was close at hand when all debts would be wiped clean from the books:

> If there is among you a poor man of your brethren, within any of the gates in your land which the LORD your God is giving you, you shall not harden your heart nor shut your hand from your poor brother, but you shall open your hand wide to him and willingly *lend him sufficient for his need, whatever he needs.* Beware lest there be a wicked thought in your heart, saying, "The seventh year, the year of release, is at hand," and your eye be evil against your poor brother and you give him nothing, and he cry out to the LORD against you, and it become sin among you. You shall surely give to him, and your heart should not be grieved when you give to him, because for this thing the LORD your God will bless you in all your works, and in all to which you put your hand. For the poor will never cease from the land; therefore I command you, saying, "You shall open your hand wide to your brother, to your poor and your needy, in your land." (Dt. 15:7–11, our emphasis).

> [If there is among you anyone in need, a member of your community in any of your towns within the land that the Lord your God is giving you, do not be hardhearted or tight-fisted toward your needy neighbor. You should rather open your hand, willingly lending enough to meet the need, whatever it may be. Be careful that you do not entertain a mean thought, thinking, "The seventh year,

the year of remission, is near," and therefore view your needy neighbor with hostility and give nothing; your neighbor might cry to the Lord against you, and you would incur guilt. Give liberally and be ungrudging when you do so, for on this account the Lord your God will bless you in all your work and in all that you undertake. Since there will never cease to be some in need on the earth, I therefore command you, "Open your hand to the poor and needy neighbor in your land." (NRSV)]

Note how this passage goes beyond the outward act—and how often we think of the Old Testament as only concerned with externals—and demands that attention be paid to the inner attitude. One must not be "grieved" when called upon to help. We are reminded of Paul's plea that the contribution for the needy brethren of his day be given not "grudgingly or of necessity; for God loves a cheerful giver" (2 Cor. 9:7). Nor were they permitted the delusion that somehow poverty would one day vanish. True, it might diminish (God be praised!) but even so, "the poor will never cease from the land" (Dt. 15:11), a truism Jesus recognized (Mt. 26:11).

2. *The second kind of aid that could be given to the poor was what we today would call "charity" or "benevolence."* Since the Old Testament uses the term "lend" to apply to it, we might call this a *nonobligatory repayment loan.* In other words, one was not necessarily expected to pay it back to the lender. Alternatively, we could look upon it as a "loan" to be ultimately passed on or "loaned" to others. It was given to one when it was desperately needed; so when one's fortunes are restored, one does not forget about it, but passes it along to others who are now in need. It is, if you will, a *perpetual* loan—one not to be repaid, but to be bestowed just as generously and ungrudgingly as it was received.

Hence we read of individuals lending who are promised *other* rewards than dollars-and-cents reimbursement. The psalmist alludes to the faithful person as one who "is ever merciful, and *lends;* and his descendants are blessed" (Ps. 37:26). Here the repayment is promised to his descendants rather than to the giver himself. Verse 27 shows that the humanitarianism must be accompanied by a good moral character if it is to please God; charity by itself can not buy divine acceptance. Later in the same book one's character is again linked with one's charity: "A good man deals graciously and *lends;* he will guide his affairs with discretion" (Ps. 112:5).

The proverbist urges that the poor receive "mercy" (Prv. 14:31). He stresses that the giver will receive reimbursement from the Lord rather than from the recipient: "He who has pity on the poor *lends to the LORD,* and He will pay back what he has given" (Prv. 19:17). The charitable individual will be acting in a way to assure his own well-being, "He who gives to the poor will not lack, but he who hides his eyes will have many curses" (Prv. 28:27). In urging liberality in giving, Paul uses an argument similar to that found in the first half of this verse: "For I do not mean that others should be eased and you burdened; but by an equality, that now at this time your abundance may supply their lack, that their abundance also may supply your lack—that there be equality. As it is written, 'He who gathered much had nothing left over, and he who gathered little had no lack'" (2 Cor. 8:13–15).

Since Jesus in Matthew 5:42 is speaking in the context of an individual that one has cause to be angry with (cf. v. 41–42), his point would be that *in spite of personal grievance, you need to assist those who stand in need.* "Give to everyone who asks of you" is the wording found in Luke 6:30: and in verses 32–33 the adversarial relationship is clearly brought out: "But if you love those who love you, what credit is that to you? For even sinners love those who love them. And if you do good to those who do good to you, what credit is that to you? For even sinners do the same." In this context the various Old Testament references on love of the neighbor—*including "enemy" neighbors*—is once again highly relevant.

Jesus did not demand—nor did the Torah—some kind of naive, sentimental affection toward the enemy. In contrast, both demand practical, down-to-earth, constructive helpfulness *in spite of the breach* that separates persons. Hence we find Jesus affirming what the Old Testament taught on at least one of the four contrasts in this final antithesis.

Yet the very fact that the teaching matches that of the Law and the Prophets provides our first and quite clear-cut evidence that what Jesus is targeting—is *contrasting* his teaching with—is not the text of the Mosaic Law itself, but what others had done with it: its abuse and misuse. An individual *could* argue that it would be wrong to give charity to a punished felon and quote the Old Testament text given in Matthew 5:38 as proof. To do such would be to ignore other teachings of the Mosaic Law. Jesus refuses to let them get away with it: The Torah demanded both punishment (when it was due) and benevolence (when it was needed). There was a time and place for both.

Accepting Legally Constituted Authority: The Old Testament Basis for Involuntary Service

The third of Jesus' contrasts in this antithesis is "Whoever compels you to go one mile, go with him two"

(Mt.5:41). This is normally interpreted (correctly we believe,) as referring to the Roman government and its army recruiting involuntary local labor for either transporting goods or for other needed purposes. The right of officialdom to demand such service went all the way back to the Persian Empire.[3] According to Walter Wink, "Most cases of impressment involved the need of the postal service for animals and the need of soldiers for civilians to help carry their packs. The situation in Matthew is clearly the latter. It is not a matter of requisitioning animals but people themselves."[4]

Since the pack of a Roman soldier weighed anywhere from sixty pounds to around eighty-five, this was a considerable burden to bear—literally.[5] Entire villages were known to disappear into the countryside when a major Roman force was on the move—to keep from having to carry their packs and weapons.[6]

The imperial right could be easily abused. In A.D. 49 an Egyptian inscription records that henceforth soldiers were not to exercise their power to requisition involuntary transport without specific written authorization from the prefect.[7] An Egyptian decree dating from between 133 and 137 refers to how soldiers had so abused their right to requisition assistance "that the military is associated with arrogance and injustice."[8] Theoretically there were penalties for compelling civilians to carry goods or materials more than a mile, but how much they were actually enforced probably hinged on the attitude of the centurion toward the offending soldier and the local population.[9]

In some cases the "mile" might be a literal one, in other cases simply an assigned task involving a slightly lesser or greater distance. In the latter category we read how, when the weakened Jesus was unable to carry his cross all the way to Golgotha, the Romans "found a man of Cyrene, Simon by name. Him they compelled to bear His cross" (Mt. 27:32). He was picked at random as readily available and strong enough in body; he was simply "coming out of the country and passing by" when the Romans drafted him to carry the cross (Mk. 15:21).

In yielding to such an impressment, one was *obeying the demands of legally constituted authority—and the Old Testament enjoined just such obedience.* To prove that one was expected to obey the king and his delegates seems almost an exercise in futility. The idea of authority over others is inherent in the very concept of "king." God recognized that one day the people would wish to install a king (Dt. 17:14–20), but in doing so they thought only of the advantages they believed the king could give them rather than the disadvantages, including the rejection of God's explicit and direct kingship over them. In the days of Samuel's wicked and corrupt sons, the people demanded a king to "judge" the nation (1 Sm. 8:4–6). Samuel warned them of the negative side of kingship, of how the king had the inherent right to order them and their offspring into the government service where and when he chose:

> Samuel told all the words of the Lord to the people who asked him for a king. And he said, "This will be the behavior of the king who will reign over you:
> *He will take your sons* and appoint them for his own chariots and to be his horsemen, and some will run before his chariots.
> He will appoint captains over his thousands and captains over his fifties, *will set some* to plow his ground and reap his harvest, and some to make his weapons of war and equipment for his chariots.
> *And he will take your daughters* to be perfumers, cooks, and bakers.

And he will take the best of your fields, your vineyards, and your olive groves, and give them to his servants.

He will take a tenth of your grain and vintage, and *give it* to his officers and servants.

And *he will take your menservants and your maidservants* and your finest young men and your donkeys, *and put them to work.*

He will take a tenth of your sheep. *And you will be his servants.* (1 Sm. 8:10–17, our emphasis)

[So Samuel reported all the words of the Lord to the people who were asking him for a king. He said, "These will be the ways of the king who will reign over you:

He will take your sons and appoint them to his chariots and to be his horsemen, and to run before his chariots; and he will appoint for himself commanders of thousands and commanders of fifties, and some to plow his ground and reap his harvest, and to make his implements of war and the equipment of his chariots. *He will take your daughters* to be perfumers and cooks and bakers.

He will take the best of your fields and vineyards and olive orchards and give them to his courtiers.

He will take your male and female slaves, and the best of your cattle and donkeys, and *put them to his work.*

He will take one-tenth of your flocks, *and you shall be his slaves.* (NRSV)]

Note that the king had the authority to "put them to work" at whatever he desired. They would be "his servants" and no longer have the degree of freedom they enjoyed previously.

True, having a prestigious king might well increase their stature in the eyes of the surrounding world, but they would pay a price in involuntary labor and taxation for it. Note that Samuel takes it for granted that *any* monarchy will do this and that—at its extreme—it would become burdensome (cf. v. 18). When the Roman government and army demanded that one provide free short-term assistance (to "go a mile") they were exercising the very power that Samuel warned would be exercised in any earthly regal system. The people had accepted the principle of earthly royal power and suffered the "down" side of it, both from the excesses of their own rulers and from that of foreign conquerors as well.

In addition to recognizing the right of government to impressed, involuntary labor, the Old Testament recognized both the *principle* of governmental authority in general and the propriety of punishment for violating its demands. Both of these also provided Old Testament precedent for providing one's physical labor in cases such as Jesus mentions.

One of the passages that makes explicit the expectation of obedience to government is found in Ecclesiastes 8:2: "I counsel you, 'Keep the king's commandment for the sake of your oath to God.'" First Chronicles 29:23–24 links together earthly rulership and the obligation to obey: "Then Solomon sat on the throne of the LORD as king instead of David his father, and prospered; and *all Israel obeyed him.* All the leaders and the mighty men, and also all the sons of King David, submitted themselves to King Solomon."

More common is reference to the *implicit* threat of punishment for any disobedience: "The wrath of a king is like the roaring of a lion; whoever provokes him to anger sins against his own life" (Prv. 20:2); "He who keeps his command will experience nothing harmful" (Eccl. 8:5). Paul develops this theme in Romans 13:1–7, especially verse 3: "For rulers are not a terror to good works, but to evil. Do you want to be unafraid of the authority? Do what is good, and you will have praise from the same." Rulers exist, Peter argues, not just to punish, but also "for the praise of those who do good" (1 Pt. 2:13–14).

Because the king has this potential for retribution, caution must be taken in how one approaches him; railing attack cannot be substituted for reasonable argument: "Where the word of a king is, there is power; and who may say to him, 'What are you doing?'... A wise man's heart discerns both time and judgment" (Eccl. 8:4, 5b). Hence they were to control what they said about the rulership, even when under provocation: "You shall not revile God, nor curse a ruler of your people" (Ex. 22:28). This was interpreted by Paul to include the religious-secular leadership provided by the Sanhedrin (Acts 23:1–5; in verse 5 Paul quotes the Exodus text). The "cursing" of Exodus 22 was taken to include far more than the narrower definition of vulgarity that we might be inclined to read into it. It included "speak[ing] evil" (i.e., accusing improperly, unjustly, without a backing fact) (Acts 23:5) as well as "revil[ing]" them (v. 4). Leaders were to be treated with respect, not only out of fear of retribution, but because they *deserved* such treatment.

We find in the passages we have surveyed clear evidence that the Torah and the Prophets demanded obedience to legally constituted authority and even make explicit reference to the impressment of civilian labor into government service (which is what Jesus has under discussion). There is the implication that this authority would not always be exercised with due restraint and fairness. But both Jesus and the old covenant are as one concerning the need to obey that legitimate authority even in times of provocation.

Hence we find for the second time that Jesus is *not* contrasting his supposedly "new" teaching with that of the Old Testament; rather he is reaffirming the old covenant. The contrast must be, therefore, with the glosses added by tradition that permitted an individual to escape these obligations. What form this took we can only conjecture. In the present context, one feasible possibility is that they were thinking that the Romans were worthy of punishment for the injustices they inflicted (cf. verse 38 which speaks of the punishment due criminals). How then could anyone demand that an individual bestow willing service to them even when impressed into temporary service? Of course Samuel had warned that kings would do just that. Just as the Israelite kings would ultimately answer to God for any criminal conduct of theirs, so would the Romans. In neither case did this free the individual of yielding that service that kings—by right—were reasonably entitled to. On this Jesus and the Old Testament spoke with one voice, however much personal resentment might cry out for a different approach.

Accepting the Power of the Courts: The Old Testament Basis for Surrendering One's Possessions

Having discovered the last two of Jesus' "contrastive" declarations to be in full conformity to the Jewish law, let us retreat backward one step further and examine the second illustration of difference provided by him: "If anyone wants to sue you and take away your tunic, let him have your cloak also" (Mt. 5:40).

The reference to "sue you" shows that Jesus is referring to the results of a *judicial decision.* The context of "reacting to provocation" would suggest that it is not a "friendly" law suit initiated without animosity because of the legal necessity to bring about the resolution of a dispute. Nor is just the question of liability at issue. Unlike the case of reconciliation called for in Matthew 5:23–24, which implies "you" are in the wrong, here there is not the slightest hint of such. The idea is that one has an *enemy* out to do one in, and he has found a "legal" way to accomplish his goal.

Rather than defy the unjust court decision, one is to be willing to sacrifice even more than the verdict demands, thereby showing one's own good will and, perhaps, also providing a symbolic rebuke of the court's injustice and the foe's chicanery. The latter may be inferred from the fact that one could not legally demand the surrender of one's outer garment (cloak) even when given as temporary security for a loan (Dt. 24:10–13; cf. v. 17; Ex. 22:26–27). To give it up—or to express the willingness to do so—would exhibit one's conviction that such an injustice had been done that one might as well go the whole course and openly violate the intent of the law just as they have done covertly under the pretext of law.

Although Jesus' admonition to do *more* than the court has decreed is definitely a step beyond Old Testament requirements, certainly the Old Testament *did* permit such to occur. (What court in any *age* would object?) Hence what Jesus demands is fully consistent with—though not required by—the existing Mosaic legislation. How then can one speak of a "contradiction" between Jesus' admonition and the Jewish law?

This is the *minimum* assertion that can be made. The consistency can be even *greater emphasized* if we ground our remarks in the authority of the courts under the Old Testament and the moral obligation to obey them. Jesus' embracing the rule of law—of the right of courts to make decisions (even mistaken ones) concerning us—embraces (rather than rejects) the teaching of the Mosaic system.

The authority of courts is intimately related to the right of kings to rule, for it is the ruler who stands behind the courts to back up their authority and who is often individually responsible for their appointment.

The king personally, of course, possessed the right to judge controversial issues. The famous case brought to Solomon of the two women who both claimed to be mother of the same child is surely one of the best illustrations (1 Kgs. 3:16–27). Indeed the case established Solomon's judicial ability in the sight of all the people: "And all Israel heard of the judgment which the king had rendered; and they feared the king, for they saw that the wisdom of God was in him to administer justice" (v. 28).

Just before this incident we read of how God offered Solomon his choice of divine blessings (1 Kgs. 3:4–15). Solomon's request is often summed up in the words "he sought wisdom." That is true as far as it goes, but he specifically sought wisdom in his *judicial and governing capacities:* "Therefore give to Your servant an understanding heart to judge Your people, that I may discern between good and evil. For who is about to judge this great people of yours?" (v. 9).

David himself had personally heard controversies from among the citizens (2 Sm. 15:2). Solomon seems to have gone even further by establishing a "hall" to be used by the king for hearing such cases (1 Kgs. 7:7).

One man could not bear the burden alone. Every community was to have its own judges: "You shall appoint judges and officers in *all* your towns, which the Lord your God gives you, according to your tribes, and they shall judge the people with just judgment" (Dt. 16:18). When the people came back from captivity "magistrates and judges" were appointed by Ezra to "judge all the people" who followed Jehovah's law (Ezra 7:25–26).

Verse 26 is of special interest because it points out that both the Mosaic Law and the king's own law were to be applied in such hearings.

Judges were to be men of integrity and were to be non-biased in regard to every individual who came before them, regardless of who they were or their national origin (Dt. 1:16-17). They were to scrupulously avoid compromising the fairness of their decisions by taking bribes (Dt. 16:19). Yet try as they should, some controversies would seemingly defy all efforts at either establishing the facts or providing a just and equitable verdict. In such cases, an appeal(s) procedure was provided for under which the case would be submitted to a panel of Levites and priests, whose decision would be final (Dt. 17:8–13).

Judges were human. Perverted justice based on bribery or favoritism undoubtedly occurred then as it does today (cf. 1 Sm. 8:3). In some cases successful deception and misrepresentation convinced the court, and the judiciary became a tool to inflict injustice. Jesus was not blind to such dangers. Pure old-fashioned hatred might so blind witnesses that they would testify against an individual out of spite and secure a totally unjust judgment. In such cases of abuse, the courts remained authoritative—wrong, but authoritative.

Just as their decisions had legal force under the Torah, Jesus gave them legal force under his teaching. That did not mean one was to pretend they were right or just—only that one was to pay the fine demanded. The protest against the injustice was not to take the form of cursing the court or defying it, but of giving even *more* than was demanded. Essentially what we are dealing with is *persecution*—not necessarily persecution because of one's religious faith (though that might well be the root of the problem), but quite possibly because someone else has cultivated an unreasoning and irrational hatred for a neighbor.

In taking this approach, Jesus is doing nothing more than the Old Testament demanded: accepting the jurisdiction and power of the relevant courts. If Jesus enjoins more than the Torah required (by paying a greater penalty than demanded), he is certainly doing nothing *inconsistent* with the Torah. As a symbolic protest against injustice, it would have made just as much sense in the days of Solomon as in the days of Jesus.

So far we have discussed the text without stressing the element of *justified mockery* that may well be intended. Since giving *both* tunic *and* cloak would mean that a person would be stark naked, the idea would seem to be "If you want to be so vindictive as this, fine. I can't stop you. Take everything!" Whether the person *literally* handed over all his clothes or only expressed the *intention* of doing so, the irony, the absurdity, of the situation would be apparent to all.[10] An Old Testament adage would spring to mind: "Answer a fool according to his folly, lest he be wise in his own eyes" (Prv. 26:5). Such an individual would be walking in the footsteps of the proverbist. (Though the preceding verse of the proverbist also warns that such a response is surely situational; other situations would call for ignoring him.) The actuality or threat of nudity also created guilt for the one unwilling to compromise to settle the controversy, who would naturally reap the blame for creating the absurd situation.[11]

Whether we stress the element of apparent irony or not, we still find that in at least *three* of the contrasts in the final antithesis, Jesus aligns himself with the teaching of the Old Testament. Should this not require us to approach the final contrast concerning an eye for an eye with an open mind rather than to assume that he must be contradicting existing teaching?

NOTES

[1]Montefiore, 50.

[2]Connick, 248.

[3]Borg, 131; Gardner, 109; Lunny, 118; Luz, *Matthew 1–7,* 326; Newman and Stine, 150.

[4]Walter Wink, "Neither Passivity Nor Violence: Jesus' Third Way (Matthew 5:38–42)," in *The Love of Enemy and Nonretaliation in the New Testament,* ed. Willard M. Swartley (Louisville, Ky: Westminster/John Knox, 1992), 108.

[5]Ibid., 109.

[6]Ibid., 109–10.

[7]Ibid., 109.

[8]As quoted in Ibid., 109.

[9]For a good discussion of the point, cf. Ibid., 110.

[10]On the theme of irony being intended, see Jonsson, 100. Richard A. Horsley, "Ethics and Exegesis: 'Love Your Enemies' and the Doctrine of Nonviolence," in *The Love of Enemy and Nonretaliation in the New Testament,* ed. Willard M. Swartley (Louisville, Ky: Westminster/John Knox Press, 1992), 87, sees the offer/action as producing a "ridiculous situation" but does not develop the theme of irony that could be deduced from such a recognition.

[11]Cf. Wink, 107–8. This was especially true in a Jewish society where blame was placed far more on the viewer of nudity than on the naked individual, an attitude going at least as far back as Genesis 9:20–27. Cf. Walter Wink (107) on this text, and his comments in footnote 18, pp. 119–20.

11

Nonviolence (Matthew 5:38-42, continued)

Having examined other areas of the fifth antithesis, let us turn our attention to how the text deals with the much contested issues of violence and nonviolence: Jesus' attitude toward "an eye for an eye." As previously noted, Jesus' teaching is commonly considered a blatant contradiction of the explicit teaching of the Pentateuch.[1] On the other hand, since what we have studied so far reveals Jesus teaching in accordance with the Torah, we would naturally expect him to be doing so here as well. Nevertheless, the "spin" put on the expressions Jesus uses have become so firmly rooted that we need to carefully reexamine them to make sure that he was using the terms the way later interpreters have used them.

"An Eye for an Eye" Was an Edict of Restraint— Not Overretaliation

Before we turn to the final contrast, it is both appropriate and fair to consider just what the Old Testament had under consideration in the text that Jesus cites, "You have heard that it was said, 'An eye for an eye and a tooth for a tooth.'" The principle was universally held throughout the ancient world in the time before Jesus, both in popular thought and in official legal codes.[2] Whatever may be the correct understanding of those nonbiblical systems, the teaching of the Torah on the subject has been subject to fantastic exaggeration. By some it has been treated as a virtual carte blanche for private retaliation. More restrained individuals are inclined to look upon it with horror as somehow terrible and barbaric.

But was it really such? It is vital to remember that this provision of the Old Testament was given *not to justify private revenge, but to sanction—and limit—the degree of judicial punishment:* "But if any lasting harm follows, then you shall give life for life, eye for eye, tooth for tooth, hand for hand, foot for foot, burn for burn, wound for wound, stripe for stripe" (Ex. 21:23–25). "If a man causes disfigurement of his neighbor, as he has done, so shall it be done to him—fracture for fracture, eye for eye, tooth for tooth; as he has caused disfigurement of a man, so shall it be done to him" (Lv. 24:19–20).

To help protect against lying accusations, an unsupported charge was inadequate to obtain retribution; one's testimony had to be backed up by that of two or three additional witnesses (Dt. 19:15–20). And if it were determined that one had brought an unjust accusation, then the perjurer was to receive the identical punishment he had attempted to inflict on the innocent: "Your eye shall not pity; but life shall be for life, eye for eye, tooth for tooth, hand for hand, foot for foot (Dt. 19:21).

People have always tended toward excess reactions when their own welfare is threatened. "Massive retaliation" was not a doctrine of war invented due to the creation of atomic weapons; it is a mind-set that has tempted every injured person who has the opportunity to do worse to someone who has angered them.[3] The Mosaic Law put a restraint on such human vindictiveness. Not only did the matter have to be judged before a court, but the punishment was limited to *no greater than* the physical injury actually received.

Nor should the *permanence* of the injuries be understated. The regulation did not govern some superficial or temporary aggravation (such as a black eye or bruise or even broken bones); rather the texts cover cases of *permanent* disfigurement (Lv. 24:19), cases in which "lasting harm" occurs (Ex. 21:23). Hence the category of application was strictly regulated and limited—far more so than has commonly been imagined from the phrase itself, "an eye for an eye and a tooth for a tooth."

Robert L. Cate has suggested that we need to remember that "in the world in which Israel lived, vengeance was the rule of the day. Here they were being told that they could exact *nothing more than* justice."[4] Rather than loosing the chains of rage, it reined in how far retaliation could be carried out. We may mock it if we wish, but there remain societies in this world today when this would *still* be a major step forward.

Was this rule of thumb actually being *enforced* in the first century? The point, not surprisingly, has been argued both ways. There are three indications that it continued to be practiced.

The least persuasive evidence is so weak that it actually represents *inferential* evidence that the practice had been (or was being) effectively abandoned: Only one rabbi in the Talmud explicitly embraced the doctrine of stern retribution.[5] This was Rabbi Eliezer ben Hyrcanus who (about A.D. 90) spoke of how "eye for eye [means] actual eye for eye."[6]

A second evidence comes from the doctrine of the Boethuseans, a faction of the Sadducees, who embraced this approach to justice.[7] Since this was the view of a sub-sect of a sect, it would seemingly be an odd choice to single out for rebuke in Matthew 5 where Jesus seems intent on topics of *broad* application.[8] Furthermore, as Daube notes, "There is no sign of His singling out Sadducean doctrines anywhere in the Sermon on the Mount."[9]

The third evidence comes from Josephus. He refers to the fact that the injured party had the option (not the necessity) of accepting a monetary reimbursement: "He that maimeth a man shall undergo the like, being deprived of that limb whereof he deprived the other, unless indeed the maimed man be willing to accept money; for the law empowers the victim himself to assess the damage that has befallen him and make this concession, unless he would show himself too severe."[10] Hence even Josephus did not believe there to be any kind of *absolute* demand for such retribution. Also note that Josephus places the ultimate determination in the hands of the individual who was injured. In contrast, the Pharisees placed it in the hands of the tribunal handling the case.[11]

This evidence is far from strong. The positive eye for eye teaching of a single rabbi, the advocacy by a sub-sect of the Sadducees rather than their broad consensus, and the indication by Josephus that it remained an *option* rather than a necessity.

Turning to the other side of the matter, there is considerably stronger evidence that the practice had been generally abandoned. (Indeed, when the positive arguments are as limited as those we have examined, that very weakness is an argument for the opposite viewpoint.) The first comes from the Talmud:

> Not a single instance of the practice of retaliation is mentioned in the [later Jewish] sources. Both Mishnah and Mekhilta reject any literal interpretation of 'Eye for eye' and lay down that the wrongdoer has to pay damages. It might perhaps be objected that these works, though containing old materials, were not completed till the end of the 2nd century (Mishnah) or even later (Mekhilta). But this argument loses much of its weight when we remember that the system of damages of Mishnah and Mekhilta is of so elaborate and subtle a nature...that we must allow *a long time for its growth.* In other words, talion must have been ousted by a pecuniary settlement *long before* the detailed provisions concerning the latter which we find in Mishnah and Mekhilta were established.[12]

The same author then points out that the very wording Jesus uses in his antithesis make no sense if eye for eye equivalent retaliation were still being carried out:

> Supposing for a moment 'Eye for eye' had then meant actual talion for mutilation and Jesus had intended to attack this principle, would the case of a slap in the face not have been an excessively weak illustration...? Would it not have been absolutely necessary to give a far more *serious* example? Would He not have said something to the effect: But whosoever tears out one of thine eyes, forgive him and do not require that one of his be torn out?...Which shows that He was not combating talion in the case of mutilation.[13]

Although our analysis of Jesus' intent in regard to turning the other cheek does not require the acceptance of the scenario that equivalency in retribution had been (or was being) replaced by monetary damages, this does appear to be the best reading of the evidence. However, was this a justifiable shift in regard to the proper form of judicial punishment? Part of our difficulty in answering this is that the Pentateuch and later books of the Old Testament do not provide examples of its being carried out, nor do we have evidence from nonbiblical sources of the first century or earlier.[14] Although J. Dwight Pentecost does not have this issue specifically in mind, he provides the provocative suggestion that the Old Testament teaching on punishment was permissive rather than obligatory, that it set *limits* rather than *imposing a standard, irreducible punishment:* "No person was *required* by the Law to react in like manner toward an offender."[15] Or as E. P. Sanders words the matter, it "limits retaliation, it does not require it."[16] John W. Wenham goes so far as to argue that the most natural reading of Exodus 21:18–36 is that of a preference for material reimbursement rather than physical retribution.[17]

Even if we limit ourselves to the more modest generalizations of the first two of these commentators, the substitution of less punitive measures—at least as an option—would have been within the injured party's right as well as passing by it entirely if he so desired. But if he chose physical retribution, it had to be the exact same thing he had suffered and *nothing* in excess of that. For the current purpose it does not matter whether this is valid, but it certainly makes a great deal of sense.

Turning the Other Cheek: A Misunderstanding of the Underlying Aramaic?

The original Aramaic that Jesus used might have produced an alternative wording for the teaching: "It is possible that 'the other' is a misunderstanding of 'back' in Aramaic and that the idea is that, when insulted by a slap on the cheek, you should simply turn away and not retaliate."[18] Assuming that such was the original Aramaic (and it is not documentable beyond a hypothetical reconstruction), the hypothesis of misunderstanding is not necessary; to turn the other cheek produces the same result as walking away from the insult. One does not aggravate it, inflame it, escalate the level of hostilities. As Bruce Chilton and J. I. H. McDonald wisely interpret the text, "The strategy of turning the other cheek (5:39) is a refusal to trade insults or blows, or to inflame the situation; it is to create a new situation by refusing to assent to the logic of violence."[19] On the *conceptual* level the same idea is conveyed either way. The scenario of mistranslation or misunderstanding is totally unneeded.

"Turning the Other Cheek" Must be Interpreted Primarily in Terms of Its Judicial Setting

The Old Testament text cited to begin Jesus' antithesis ("an eye for an eye and a tooth for a tooth," v. 38) concerns action decreed by a judicial body. Furthermore, the unjust suing in verse 40 also involves a judicial decision. *Hence the most natural way to interpret Jesus' doctrine of restraint in the intervening verse is as the reaction to the judicial abuse that one is receiving.* Taken this way, verse 39 refers to a situation in which the judicial system has been misused to inflict injustice on another. Undeserved punishment is the result instead of the sought for vindication or acquittal. In such a case Jesus urges, "I tell you not to resist an evil person. But whoever slaps you on your right cheek, turn the other to him also" (v. 39).

The temptation is to rail at the court; one is tempted not only to protest, but to lapse into vile language at the injustice. Jesus' disciple is to resist the temptation. The words of Jude 9 come to mind: "Yet Michael the archangel, in contending with the devil, when he disputed about the body of Moses, dared not bring against him a reviling accusation, but said, 'The Lord rebuke you!'"

Peter ties together the ideas of patiently enduring unjust abuse and controlling one's tongue even under grave and extreme provocation. In fact, it is in regard to a judicial contest—the trial of Jesus—that he writes,

> For what credit is it if, when you are *beaten for your faults,* you take it *patiently?* But when you do good *and suffer for it,* if you take it patiently, this is commendable before God. For to this you were called, because Christ also suffered for us, leaving us an example, that you should follow His steps: "Who committed no sin, nor was guile found in His mouth"; who, when he was reviled, *did not revile in return;* when He suffered, *He did not threaten,* but committed Himself to Him who judges righteously. (1 Pt. 2:20–23, our emphasis)

> [If you endure when you are *beaten for doing wrong,* what credit is that? But if you *endure* when you do right *and suffer for it,* you have God's approval. For to this you have been called, because Christ also suffered for you, leaving you an example, so that you should follow in his steps. "He committed no sin, and no deceit was found in his mouth." When he was abused, he *did not return abuse;* when he suffered he *did not threaten;* but he entrusted himself to the one who judges justly. (NRSV)]

The temptation is to physically strike back at the accuser or to violently resist the implementation of the court's punishment. Instead, one is to acquiesce: "Whoever

slaps you on your right cheek, turn the other to him also."
It doesn't mean it will feel good, but it is what is proper. No
greater condemnation of a court of law can be given than
to endure even more than what the court has unjustly
demanded. James describes those who refuse to use violence to escape injustice: "You [the rich] have condemned,
you have murdered the just; he does not resist you" (5:6,
our emphasis). *Condemn* in the sense of "criticism" doesn't
fit well here; why would the rich find pleasure in criticizing the poor? But *condemn* in the sense of "making or caus-
ing a judicial condemnation" is something else again.[20]
How often in history have the rich used their wealth to
prosecute "lesser" individuals who obstruct their goals!
How often have they produced the judicial "murder" of the
innocent man! This use of *condemn* is in conformity with
the meaning of the Greek word so rendered.[21] Yet rather
than physically rebel, this "just" man "does not resist you."
As Jesus enjoined, he turned the other cheek.

Yet another reaction to unjust conviction is possible.
The temptation is to flee, to run, to avoid the judgment—and understandably. Instead, the individual is to
stoically endure it: "Whoever slaps you on your right
cheek, turn the other to him also." Endure whatever
injustice the power brokers inflict, confident in the heart
that one is being unjustly treated.

Although this would be true of unjust accusations in
general, it would be even more true of enduring unjust
libel due to one's discipleship and of having to answer
before a court of law for one's faith. "Let none of you suffer
as a murderer, a thief, an evildoer, or as a busybody in
other people's matters," Peter pleads (1 Pt. 4:15). With the
possible exception of the "busybody," all the sins suggest
facing trial before a judicial body. Hence it is within that
context that he adds, "Yet if anyone suffers as a Christian,

let him not be ashamed, but let him glorify God in this matter" (verse 16). Instead of fleeing the judicial punishment, one is to endure it, to turn the other cheek if you will: First you have been smitten by unfair and unjust charges; now you endure the second blow of punishment because of those initial malicious accusations.

Just such perseverance under adversity was manifested by Jesus. Jesus was struck by "one of the officers" of the Sanhedrin (Jn. 18:22). We read that he challenged the audience where the justice was in treating him this way (v. 23). We do not read that he literally turned the other cheek, but we do find that he calmly accepted the additional insults that were inflicted upon him both physically and verbally. He certainly acted the role of turning the other cheek whether it was literally done or not.

Indeed, when one perseveres under such outrage without losing one's dignity and loyalty to God, what better term is there than "turning the other cheek"? Furthermore, Peter's remarks in 1 Peter 2:20–23 (quoted above) cite Jesus as an example of enduring (rather than fleeing) physical punishment when one is suffering because of loyalty to God. His instruction to "turn the other cheek" is a plea that his followers patiently endure such *judicial persecution* in a similar manner.

The idea that a duly ordained court was due at least a minimum of respect even when it malfunctioned and abused its power was a reasonable deduction from the Old Testament itself. Paul was tried before the Sanhedrin in Acts 23 and was rebuked for calling the high priest who presided over it a "whitewashed wall" for his "command[ing] me to be struck contrary to the law" (v. 3). Paul could only appeal to his lack of recognizing that the man who had ordered it was the high priest (v. 4). So far as the Old Testament went, even in such cases the official was to be treated with respect, and Paul even quotes the Old Testament text that demanded it (v. 5). So when Jesus demanded that one submit to an unjust judicial act, he was doing no more than what the Law had always demanded.

The Old Testament prophets were considered as prime examples of "suffering and patience" for what they endured by government decree (Jas. 5:10). Of the heroes of faith in Hebrews 11, we read of those who received judicial style punishments, of how "Still others had trial of mockings and scourgings, yes, and of chains and imprisonment" (v. 36). These are the types of actions we most naturally connect with court decisions. Whether these punishments were delivered in formal court-type situations or by rulers as de facto judges matters little since the consequences were the same and the outward form the only difference. By their restraint and refusal to strike out, these Old Testament heroes can rightly be described as turning the other cheek in the face of judicial and quasi-judicial oppression. The concept is clearly present even though the verbal terminology of Jesus is lacking.

Since Jesus was not repudiating the authority of earthly courts, what kind of twist in popular exegesis produced his teaching that one should nonviolently yield to judicial persecution? It has to be speculation, of course, but it would hardly be unexpected if many felt that *an unjust court decision could be properly resisted by any means (verbal or physical) that one had available.* If the Torah taught an eye for an eye, why couldn't the same principle be used to justify retaliation in kind against unjust judicial decisions? Crude justice, in a sense, but once begun, where would one stop? Could any punishment be meted out to anyone without a resulting chain of assaults and counterassaults? What would begin as an understandable outrage against the misuse of judicial power would end up undermining the capacity of any court to make even the most innocent decision. Jesus refused to go along with such violent revolutionary techniques and repudiated them. But as we have seen, the right attitude toward the courts under the Old Testament law similarly demanded a policy of caution and restraint rather than resistance and violence.

A Secondary Application: Restraint Under Provocation in Everyday Life

The principle Jesus deals with would also have a natural application to conflict with others *outside* a judicial setting. In our judgment, this is a *secondary* lesson from Jesus' words because the nonviolence admonition comes in between two verses dealing with explicit *judicial* action. Yet a case can reasonably be made that the everyday application is Jesus' main point. After all, while one seldom has to go to a court appearance, time and again obnoxious and troublesome neighbors and acquaintances plague one's life.

Furthermore, one can easily imagine a popular gloss that would make Jesus' criticism one targeted at everyday life: Many could have easily deduced from the *judicial* rule of an eye for an eye a simultaneous guideline for everyday conduct. Since it is right for the court to do it, surely it must be proper for "me" to use the same standard. Why wait to go through all the legal rigmarole? After all, the same *result* is to occur as what I'm about to do. It's no great secret that multitudes of people today are quite willing to act this way in retaliation for real or perceived wrongs.

Of course, there are three things wrong with this frame of mind: (1) It substitutes private (and perhaps unjustified) anger for the impartial decision of noninvolved individuals; (2) the retaliation almost always ends up being *more* than the offense received; (3) it represents a never-intended deduction from the Torah law of the judiciary. What was intended to restrain and eliminate private retaliation becomes the "authority" for inflicting it! No wonder Jesus could contrast his own teaching with such a misuse of the Mosaic Law!

Instead of private revenge, Jesus demands restraint (turning the other cheek). After all, that's what the courts are for—to settle such matters. Jesus does not prohibit *judicial* retribution; he prohibits the *individual from doing it himself.* Since the Old Testament courts were set up "for this very reason," it follows that the Old Testament itself intended to prohibit this kind of private retaliation.

Although the verbal formulation of self-restraint used by Jesus (turning the other cheek) is not found in the Old Testament, that covenant unquestionably implores the kind of self-control and holding back of retaliation demanded by the Lord. Proverbs 24:29 implored," Do not say, 'I will do to him just as he had done to me; I will render to the man according to his work.'" (Do we not see here a kind of "reverse" Golden Rule: *not* doing to others what they've done to us?) In context (v. 28) the idea is not to strike back through perjury, but if one is to avoid using the judicial process to get back at someone who deserves it (though not for the particular act he is currently being charged with) would the writer have been thrilled at the individual's taking the law into his own hands and striking out in entirely private vengeance?

The saying in Proverbs 20:22 is laid down as a blanket statement without any type of limitation: "Do not say, 'I will recompense evil'; wait for the LORD and He will save you." Private settling of scores is rejected. When Jesus says turn the other cheek, he is calling a halt to any attempt to getting revenge *by not letting it get started in the first place;* therefore, his teaching is quite consistent with the Jewish law. Furthermore, all the old covenant passages that we have examined concerning love of neighbors—even one's obnoxious neighbor—posed additional inhibitions against indiscriminate retaliation.

All this is very reasonable, but I suspect that it still misses the point a bit. Jesus' point is self-control under provocation, but the kind of provocation is not the extreme kind often assumed to be under discussion. Jesus is not talking about self-defense. He does not say, "If someone takes a baseball bat and swings it at you...." Nor does he say, "If someone takes a knife and comes at you to kill you...." These acts threaten your life and physical existence. What He *does* say is, "whoever *slaps* you on your right cheek...." That is not life-threatening; rather, it is *insulting.* It is a blow not to our life, but to our pride. What Jesus is talking about is *enduring the "petty insults and pains" of life without physically striking back.*

Hence, when one takes this text and attempts to make Jesus lay down some ironclad rule of *pacifism,* one is missing the point entirely. Whether to serve as a soldier is an important ethical decision but not one that this text directly discusses. Even if one makes the "wrong" decision, one will only be serving for a few years. In vivid contrast, how one is to treat one's fellow man, when unjustly provoked, involves a principle that affects every day of one's life. Indeed, by expropriating the text to a subject not under discussion, one avoids the painful application of the passage to the area where it *does* belong, to how one handles conflicts with one's neighbors and acquaintances. Jesus says to endure them with restraint and self-control—the same principle taught by the Torah and the Prophets.

Much of the reason that a contradiction is assumed between turning the other cheek and the Old Testament lies in the misunderstanding that Jesus is enjoining rigid nonviolence, while the Old Testament quite clearly referred to cases of war being authorized by God. A pacifist interpretation would make sense if the Torah or prophetic text being analyzed dealt with war; but the passage quite obviously deals with the completely different subject of the *judicial system* and the punishments it was to carry out. In that context, a declaration of wartime pacifism would make absolutely no sense at all.

Nonviolence/Restraint as Implied Criticism of Zealot-Type Movements

Whatever our conclusions concerning whether Jesus' demand for restraint required an absolute pacifism (and hence was contradictory to the Old Testament), there can be no question that his pivotal emphasis on restraint and the avoidance of violence represented a repudiation of the central attitudes of the Zealot-type movements that repeatedly sprang up in the land. But this represents an indirect consequence of his teaching, rather than its central purpose or thrust.

Armed revolutionary militants existed in several forms in Roman-occupied Palestine of the first century. Josephus refers to two rebel bands (those of John of Gischala and those of Simon bar Giora), to the Sicarii (who assassinated individual Romans), to the Zealots proper, and to an ongoing Idumaean anti-Roman movement. Of course additional groups with similar agendas may well have existed. Collectively they are commonly lumped together as Zealots, but their actual degree of ideological unity is purely speculative.[22] Sean P. Kealy says it well: "[Jesus'] criticism of much of the Pharisaic legislation and behavior would have been quite offensive to many Zealots. In particular Jesus' radical approach with regard to the renunciation of violence would have been considered crazy by a Zealot."[23] Hence Jesus' teaching on this matter would have offended a militant minority of Jews in their interpretation of the Torah, not to mention a much wider band of sympathizers. But again, this was the result, not the central purpose, of Jesus' teaching. And even here, this indirect teaching touches far more on revolution than on war in its broader sense.

Jesus' Terminology Indicates That Insult Rather Than Physical Assault Is Under Discussion

The idea that physical assault is under discussion probably arises in large part from the impact of the KJV rendering of Matthew 5:39: "Whosoever shall *smite* thee on thy right cheek, turn to him the other also." Smiting suggests grievous physical assault—even assault and battery. Many translations update this rendering slightly. For example, the New Revised Standard Bible, renders it, "If anyone *strikes* you on the right cheek, turn the other also." Yet other translations, such as the one we are using, render the term as "slap," which implies insult rather than assault. Which is correct?

The text itself provides us with strong inferential evidence that the latter is under consideration. Jesus specifying the *right* cheek as the one involved (5:39) is of special significance in interpreting the thought Jesus has in mind. Most people are right-handed. It is awkward and difficult to hit a person on the right cheek with one's own right hand. The only *natural* action which would produce this is a back-handed slap; a punch would hit the left cheek rather than the right one, which Jesus specifies.[24] Furthermore, there was a religious bias against the use of the left hand, at least among the Qumran Sect in the first century. To even make a gesture with that hand resulted in ten days of penance. This may reflect a broader societal bias as well.[25]

We can even make a reasonable guess as to the type of individual who would be most in danger of receiving such treatment. The Talmud indicates that hitting one's social equal earned a substantial fine, but that there were no such fines when the recipient was a mere bondman.[26] Hence to be on the receiving end of such treatment indicated that one was socially and financially less significant or important than the one inflicting the blow: "A backhand slap was the usual way of admonishing inferiors. Masters backhanded slaves; husbands, wives; parents, children; men, women; Romans, Jews. We have here a set of unequal relations, in each of which retaliation would be suicidal."[27]

The same writer effectively argues the positive psychology for the powerless that lies behind this type of reaction to non-lifethreatening insults: "[T]his action robs the oppressor of the power to humiliate. The person who turns the other cheek is saying in effect, 'Try again. Your first blow failed to achieve its intended effect. I deny you the power to humiliate me…You cannot demean me.'"[28] Regardless of whether we follow this train of reasoning to this ultimate conclusion, the beginning points are clearly valid: The very terminology

Jesus uses requires insults to be under consideration rather than grave bodily threats.

Job 16:10 as Precedent for Nonretaliation

Although what we have said so far has been presented in terms of texts that do not have a verbal similarity with Jesus' instruction in Matthew 5:39, there are two neglected Old Testament passages that provide examples of individuals specifically being described as acting the way Jesus taught, as well as an Isaian text that may be intended to provide an example of the Messiah acting in just such a manner.

The first case is found in Job 16:10. In that verse we discover that during his afflictions Job endured physical insults without retaliation: "They gap at me with their mouth, *they strike me reproachfully on the cheek.* They gather together against me" (our emphasis). [Cf. NRSV: "They have gaped at me with their mouths; they have struck me insolently on the cheek; they mass themselves together against me."] Note the implication that he was repeatedly mistreated in this way and did not use violence to stop it. Do not the words of this text—and the practice of Job described—represent a precedent for the kind of conduct Jesus demanded?

Although some commentators caught the parallel with Lamentations 3:30 (which we will study next), none of those surveyed detected the parallel with Jesus' injunction, and no one who discussed the meaning of Jesus' antithesis called attention to the Job text. The Job commentators, however, did stress the humiliating and insulting nature of the suffering Job had to endure. "The gestures described are those of contempt and destructive hatred," notes A. B. Davidson.[29] What they were doing represented "an insulting action (cf. Lamentations 3:30)," comments Rabbi Victor E. Reichart.[30] It was "an act of human derision," David J. A. Clines rightly notes.[31] H. H. Rowley suggests that, from a practical standpoint, the idea being described translated into "insulting me."[32]

Edgar C. S. Gibson provides several citations to prove that " '[g]aping with the mouth' and 'smiting upon the cheek' are common terms for insult and scorn. Cf. Micah 5:1 (Hebrews 4:14); 1 Kings 22:24; Psalms 22:13."[33] E. Delitzch reminds his readers that "[s]miting on the cheeks is in itself an insult (Lamentation 3:30)" and points out that "insulting words...accompany the act."[34]

S. Nowell-Roston sums up the contempt being described in the verse: "The people of his village surrounded him, gaping upon him open-mouthed with curiosity and contempt, smiting him upon the cheek revilingly, united in opprobrium and hostility."[35] John E. Hartley stresses that the treatment was especially humiliating for a man of Job's background, "Job's sorrow is multiplied as the masses revile him with gesture and insulting blows...They slap Job's cheeks contemptuously and reproach him with taunts and insulting gestures. The lower the status of the mockers, the more insulting are their jeers against a nobleman."[36] Norman A. Habel wonders whether the smiting "may...imply ritual gestures of disgrace"—socially ordained forms to show public contempt and rejection.[37]

The one commentator who finds an event in Christ's life to mention selects Jesus' treatment during his pseudo-trial rather than the antithesis. E. Dhorme writes that the Hebrew "denotes both the jaw (40:26) and the cheeks. To smite the cheeks, to give a slap on the face is the supreme outrage (Micah 4:14: Psalms 3:8;

Lamentations 3:30). Cf. the passion scene with the high priest immediately after the false witnesses have just given their evidence (Matthew 27:67–68)."[38]

Is Job an Israelite, however, thereby providing Jewish precedent? Commentators normally refer to Job as either a non-Israelite[39] or as a real or mythical individual who lived in the pre-Mosaic patriarchal age;[40] that is, at a time when the Jew-Gentile division was either nonexistent or essentially irrelevant. The fact that the book found a place in the Jewish canon certainly argues that it contained lessons considered morally beneficial to those living under the Old Testament system. In other words, Job's restraint was considered as fully compatible with the Mosaic Law; therefore, Jesus' teaching about enduring insults was similarly compatible. The fact that the idea of nonretaliation for private insults was considered acceptable and proper is further strengthened if, as many claim, the book was not written until the days of Solomon or later. Certainly at that late date, no one was likely to pen a book (and certainly not for a book to be accepted as religiously authoritative) if its contents were in clear defiance of the demands of the Torah.[41]

Lamentations 3:28–30 as
Precedent for Nonretaliation

In Lamentations 3:28–30 we read of other individuals being urged to act in a way similar to Job: "Let him sit alone and keep silent, because God has laid it on him; let him put his mouth in the dust—there may yet be hope. *Let him give his cheek to the one who strikes him,* and be full of reproach" (our emphasis). [Cf. the reading of the NRSV: "To give one's cheek to the smiter, and be filled with insults."] The individual is described in more detail in the preceding verses, "The Lord is good to those who wait for Him, to the soul who seeks Him. It is good that one should hope and wait quietly for the salvation of the Lord. It is good for a man to bear the yoke in his youth" (verses 25–27).

It is this *innocent* individual who is urged "to give his cheek to the one who strikes him." "God has laid it on him" (v. 28), not because he is guilty of any transgression, it would seem, but because of his need to "bear the yoke in his youth" and his need to learn in "hope and wait quietly for the salvation of the Lord." In other words, the difficulties are part of divine providence building up his ability to morally and spiritually persevere. (Compare the doctrine of divine chastening for spiritual strengthening found in Hebrews 12:3–13, which the writer of Hebrews erects, in part, on old Testament texts.)

"Let him give his cheek to the one who strikes" is not verbally identical with "turn the other [cheek] to him also," but is not the *idea* the same? Both represent restraint under provocation and the development of one's self-control. When done in youth (the case of the Lamentations text), it sets a pattern for self-control in later life.

Few have thought to correlate these verses with Matthew 5:39. Perhaps it is simply one of those passages we tend to "read without seeing" because we are so confident that Jesus was giving thoroughly *new* teaching in regard to nonretaliation that we pass over, without thought, similar sentiments found in the prior covenant. Of ten more or less randomly chosen commentaries that we will examine (the only standard for citation being that they had something useful to say about the text), only one (with one possible addition) makes an explicit tie-in between these two scriptural statements;

and only two additional ones suggest that the reader should compare this with the teaching of Jesus. None of these remarks are presented in such a way as to force the similarity to the center of one's attention. The New Testament commentators touching on this antithesis fail to ponder the significance of Lamentations 3:28–30— and rarely if ever even recognize its existence.

Norman C. Habel sums up the theme of verses 28 to 30 by saying that the author "is aware that ideally a man should swallow insults without retaliating."[42] Edward R. Daglish sees the verses as an appeal "to the suffering Exilic community to be patient in its trials and hopeful of a blessed outcome."[43] R. K. Harrison believes that the assumption is that "[s]uch burdens can best be borne in youth when a man has the requisite vigor, and when his personality needs to be disciplined more than would be the case in his more mature years."[44] Iaian Provan argues that the probable "point is that one should not even respond to those fellow human beings who rain down upon one physical and verbal abuse. Complete passivity is required in the face of suffering."[45]

Norman K. Gottwald notes that "[i]n this text there is an extinction or suppression of all pride and personal feeling, the stilling of every angry protest. Why this indifference, this almost Stoic forbearance and self-effacement? Because the suffering originates with the Lord and is ultimately an expression of His goodness, the sufferer must wait upon his action (3:25–27)."[46] That does not mean that the foe has been sentimentally transformed into someone virtuous, but that "the present pain could be endured."[47]

A. C. Gaebelein provides no exposition of the meaning of the phrase to its initial readers, but stresses the theme of divine comfort found in the broader context and that the "godly of all ages" suffer in a similar fashion. He suggests that there is a foreshadowing here of "the afflictions of the Afflicted One," (i.e., Jesus).[48] Robert Davidson points to the Old Testament development of this suffering theme, "Verse 30 is echoed in the picture of the Servant of the Lord in Isaiah 50:4–9 as one who, through the acceptance of suffering, fulfilled his God-given mission."[49]

C. W. Eduard Naegelsbach effectively presents the evolution of the prophet's argument: "If the three propositions, verses 28–30, be compared one with another, a certain gradation will be perceived. For sitting alone and silent is comparatively easy. To put the mouth in the dust and yet to hope, is more difficult. But the hardest of all, without question, is to present the cheek to the smiter and patiently accept the full measure of disgrace that is to come upon us."[50]

A. W. Steane comments that the reference to the face in the dust is "the Eastern way of expressing absolute submission."[51] In verse 30 "we have the climax, the exhortation of verse 29 being more difficult to obey than that in the first of the group, and this is the most difficult of all."[52] He recognizes at least some kind of relevance to the antithesis by adding, "Compare Matthew v. 39."[53]

R. Payne Smith provides a strong suggestion of a conceptual tie-in by commenting on verse 30 that "the harder task is imposed of bearing contumely with meekness, Matthew v. 39, and being content to be filled full, literally, saturated with reproach, not shrinking even from the last dregs of the cup."[54]

The only writer who pointedly ties the two texts together is one found in the expository section of the Naegelsbach commentary. There an individual by the name of Foster (no first name provided) asks whether one can take these two passages together and insist on the absolute nonviolence advocated by some. He argues that this is an improper use of these texts because "[a] distinction must be made between public and private, and lawful and unlawful revenge."[55]

We have quoted these writers because they reinforce the emphasis in Lamentations on nonretaliation. They compel us to give prolonged thought to the meaning of the text rather than merely the momentary attention that allows the full significance of the text to escape us. Clearly the idea behind Jesus' "new" antithesis and that behind this quite ancient Lamentations passage *are identical.* Even the wording itself is sufficiently close to compel us to dismiss any scenario of mere coincidence. Hence we seem forced to conclude that Jesus did not originate some new doctrine in his teaching on nonretaliation, but was faithfully presenting an approach voiced by the sages recorded in the Old Testament: an *ignored* and perhaps even *intentionally forgotten* doctrine (so far as general recognition), but their doctrine nonetheless.

Hence—in the Lord's seemingly most radical departure from the Old Testament—he is actually upholding the prophetic doctrine of Israel. The antithesis was targeted at the *distortions* and *misrepresentations* of existing scriptural teaching rather than at its overthrow or reversal.

Isaiah 50:6 as Possible Precedent for Nonretaliation

In Isaiah 50:6 the Messiah is pictured in terms of avoiding striking out at his foes: "I gave My back to those who struck Me, *and My cheeks to those who plucked out the beard;* I did not hide My face from shame and spitting." The NRSV similarly speaks of "those who pulled out the beard." M. D. Goulder provides this rendering of the Septuagint version of verses 6 and 7: "I gave my back to the whips, *my cheeks to the blows:* I turned not my face from the shame of spitting.… For he is near who justifies me: who is he that goes to law with me? Let him oppose me together."[56] He concludes, "The verbal links are too strong to be accidental: the 'but I say to you' section is a midrashic expansion of Isaiah."[57]

Although Goulder assumes that the "expansion" is done by Matthew rather than by Jesus himself, the Isaiah text is certainly one that would have come to mind to the Greek-speaking Jew of the first century. It would be viewed as further Old Testament precedent for Jesus' teaching of restraint: If the Messiah was to exercise restraint, and if the disciple is to emulate the life-pattern of Jesus (a basic New Testament assumption), then it would naturally follow that *the Christian is to similarly avoid yielding to a violent response to provocation.*

Until the discovery of the Dead Sea Scrolls, our manuscripts of the Hebrew Testament came from long after the first century. Now there is very limited, but early, Hebrew language evidence for the Septuagint "variant": an Isaiah scroll from the Dead Sea containing the reading "cheek."[58] If this was a common reading of the Hebrew at the time of Jesus, the case is measurably strengthened that—in part—he had this messianic text in mind when he delivered the Sermon on the Mount.

Most commentators have missed the significance of the Isaiah text as precedent for Jesus' teaching. Although various commentators have effectively stressed the humiliation and insult involved in having one's beard plucked (in the text as we currently have it), eighteen out of twenty surveyed pass over both the

Greek textual alternative and the passage itself as being the possible partial root of Jesus' teaching.[59]

The sole source to mention the Septuagint reading was the great nineteenth-century commentator Albert Barnes: "The LXX renders this, 'I gave my cheeks to buffeting'; that is, to being smitten with the open hand, which was literally fulfilled in the case of the Redeemer (Matthew 26:67; Mark 14:65)."[60]

George A. F. Knight seems to have the *idea* in his mind, though he stops short of making an explicitly textual reference to the Sermon on the Mount: "The most telling insult that the East could perpetrate on one whom the average man sought to insult and so to render inferior, or to put him in his place, was to pluck the hairs from his beard (cf. Nehemiah 13:25). But the Servant *had now learned to turn the other cheek*" (our emphasis).[61]

*   *   *

Hence there are two prophetic texts that advocate nonretaliatory conduct and that could easily have been in Jesus' mind when he spoke his antithesis. Furthermore, the nature of restraint expected in the Messiah may also have caused him to advocate similar restraint among those who would be his followers. Not only is Jesus' doctrine in conformity with the Old Testament, but also at least two of these texts provide more than adequate precedent. His teaching was not a repudiation of the teaching of the prophets of old; it was, rather, a firm demand that it be followed.

NOTES

[1]For example, Goulder, 20; and Meier, *Matthew,* 54.

The argument that Jesus was rejecting Old Testament teaching does not necessarily have to be made in a way that downgrades the significance of the Torah. For example, one can (quite accurately) argue that the eye for an eye teaching was actually "a humane advance on the earlier unrestricted blood-feuds in retaliation for unintended injuries" while contending that Jesus carried the demand for peacefulness even further (Audrey, 118). Others who point out the progressive aspect of the eye for an eye principle include W. F. Albright and C. S. Mann, *Matthew,* in the Anchor Bible series (Garden City, N.Y.: Doubleday, 1971), 171; and Frederick Neumann, *The Binding Truth: A Selective Homilectical Commentary on the New Testament, Vol. 1: The Proper Self-Concern: The Gospel According to Matthew* (Allison Park, Pa: Pickwick Publications, 1983), 60.

[2]Dorothy Jean Weaver, "Transforming Nonresistance: From *Lex Talionis* to 'Do Not Resist the Evil One,'" in *The Love of Enemy and Nonretaliation in the New Testament,* ed. Willard M. Swartley (Louisville, Ky: Westminster/John Knox, 1992), 36.

[3]Properly speaking, "massive retaliation" was seen as retaliation for a nuclear attack, especially a *major* nuclear assault, rather than retribution for the use of conventional weaponery. In private individuals, massive retaliation represents the attitude that I am so important that the individual hurting me deserves overwhelmingly greater pain and anguish than he has inflicted. In the field of nuclear strategy, massive retaliation maintained at least some balance between action and reaction (some crude idea of equity); the mind-set of individuals in striking out at their enemies rarely retains any such limitations except practicality and the fear of punishment by the law.

[4]Robert L. Cate, *Old Testament Roots for New Testament Faith* (Nashville: Broadman, 1982), 43.

[5]David Daube, *The New Testament and Rabbinic Judaism* (London: University of London/Athlone Press, 1956), 255.

[6]*b. B. Qam.* 84a, as quoted by Betz, 279.

[7]Ibid.

[8]Hans D. Betz's assertion that the Sadduccees (i.e., the group as a whole) took this approach (279) would partly neutralize this argument, but it would still face the difficulty Daube raises.

[9]Daube, 255.

[10]*Antiquities* iv, as quoted by Betz, 279; cf. Daube, 256, and Vermes, *Jesus the Jew,* 36. Banks (199) uses this Josephus passage to prove that "the *principle* of retribution itself still remained a basic tenet in rabbinic teaching" while conceding the existence of evidence that it was on the way out so far as actual practice went.

[11]Betz, 279.

[12]Daube, 255.

[13]Ibid., 256–67.

[14]Wenham, 35.

[15]J. Dwight Pentecost, *The Words and Works of Jesus Christ: A Study of the Life of Christ* (Grand Rapids: Zondervan, 1981), 180.

[16]E. P. Sanders, *The Historical Figure of Jesus* (London: Allen Lane/Penguin Press, 1993), 211. Sanders speaks of the general Old Testament teaching on the subject rather than explicitly citing the Exodus text.

[17]Wenham, 35. The Palestinian Targum interpreted the demand of Exodus 21 in explicitly financial terms: "The value of an eye for an eye; the value of a tooth for a tooth; the value of a hand for a hand; the value of a foot for a foot," etc. (as quoted by Vermes, *Jesus the Jew,* 36).

[18]Harrington, *Matthew,* 88.

[19]Bruce Chilton and J. I. H. McDonald, *Jesus and the Ethics of the Kingdom* (Grand Rapids: Eerdmans, 1987), 104.

[20]Extrajudicial direct punishment of the poor by the well-to-do would also fit. We are assuming that in most such cases, even the wealthiest *abuser* of law would prefer to act under the

guise of law in his unlawful conduct, for reasons of public image if nothing else.

[21]See "Condemn," *Vine's Expository Dictionary of New Testament Words,* 1:222.

[22] See Sean P. Kealy, *Jesus and Politics* (Collegeville, Minn.: Liturgical Press, 1990), 35–38.

[23]Ibid., 68.

[24]Wink (104–5) challenges his readers to play-act this out and see for themselves.

[25]Cf. ibid., 104.

[26]Ibid., 105.

[27]Ibid.

[28]Ibid.

[29]A. B. Davidson, *Book of Job* in the Cambridge Bible for Schools and Colleges (Cambridge, UK: Cambridge University Press, 1891), 121.

[30]Victor E. Reichart, *Job: With Hebrew Text and English Translation* (Hindhead, Surrey, [UK]: Soncino Press, 1946), 82.

[31]David J. A. Clines, *Job 1–20* in the Word Biblical Commentary series (Dallas: Word Books, 1989), 383.

[32]H. H. Rowley, *Job* in the New Century Bible commentary series (Greenwood, S.C.: Attic Press, 1976), 119.

[33]Edgar C. S. Gibson, *Book of Job* in Westminster Commentaries series, rev. ed. (London: Methuen, 1905), 82.

[34]E. Delitzch, *Biblical Commentary on the Book of Job,* 2nd ed., rev. trans. Francis Bolton (Edinburgh: T. & T. Clark, 1881), 284.

[35]S. Nowell-Roston, *The Challenge of Calamity: A Study in the Book of Job* (London: T-T-S/Lutterworth, 1939), 103.

[36]John E. Hartley, *Book of Job* in the New International Commentary on the Old Testament series (Grand Rapids: Eerdmans, 1988), 260–61.

[37]Norman A. Habel, *The Book of Job: A Commentary* (Philadelphia: Westminster, 1985), 272.

[38]E. Dhorme, *Commentary on the Book of Job,* trans. Harold Knight (New York: Nelson, 1967), 235.

[39]Dhorme, xv.

[40]Clines, lvii; Davidson, iv; Gibson, xix-xx; Hartley, 16; Nowell-Roston, 2; Rowley, 23.

[41]Clines (lvii) sums up the evidence for the commonly asserted time gap between the time when the events of the book are pictured as happening and the time when the volume was actually written:

> There can be little doubt that the author of the book was an Israelite. It is true that Job's homeland is depicted as Northern Arabia or possibly Edom, and in most of the book Job himself does not know God by the Israelite name Yawheh. Nor does the book refer to any of the distinctive historical traditions of the Hebrew people. But these facts only mean that the author has succeeded well in disguising his own age and background in his creation of the character of his hero.

Three observations immediately come to mind: (1) Would a fiction-writing author go to the trouble of making the past so much different from his own day and age? Especially in the ancient world, would not the more normal assumption of a writer have been, "what is, always has been this way"? (2) Could he avoid obvious anachronisms this well? Would it really be within his capacity to backdate his narrative so successfully? (3) Since the dilemma of righteousness going unrewarded has always been an obvious fact of earthly life, why would there have been any perceived reason to date the supposedly fictional tale in such a distant era?

The issue is further complicated by the question of whether (and to what extent) there were non-Jewish worshippers of Yahweh. Since the Law attributed to Moses was designed with the Jewish people in mind, we would not expect such an outsider to be following the detailed provisions of that code. On the other hand, an Israelite who learned or observed the story of such a Yahweh-fearing non-Israelite would surely see in the fall and vindication of that individual a useful lesson for the worshippers of the same God back in Palestine. All such theorizing is speculative by its very nature for there is no "hard" data in Job as to the actual date the story is supposed to take place nor are their textual claims of who (and under what circumstances) it was committed to writing.

[42]Norman C. Habel, *Jeremiah / Lamentations* in the Concordia Commentary series (St. Louis: Concordia, 1968), 407.

[43]Edward R. Daglish, *Jeremiah / Lamentations* in the *Layman's Bible Book Commentary* series (Nashville, Tenn.: Broadman Press, 1983), 158.

[44]R. K. Harrison, *Jeremiah and Lamentations: An Introduction and Commentary* in the *Tyndale Old Testament Commentary* series (London: Tyndale Press, 1973), 226.

[45]Iaian Provan, *Lamentations* in the New Century Bible Commentary series (Grand Rapids: Eerdmans, 1991), 96.

[46]Norman K. Gottwald, *Studies in the Book of Lamentations* (London: SCM Press, Ltd., 1954), 105.

[47]Ibid., 105–6.

[48]A. C. Gaebelein, *Proverbs-Ezekiel* in the Annotated Bible series (New York: Publication Office "Our Hope," 1921), 259–60.

[49]Robert Davidson, *Jeremiah and Lamentations* in the Daily Study Bible series (Philadelphia: Westminster, 1985), 158.

[50]C. W. Eduard Naegelsbach, *The Book of Lamentations* in the Lange Commentary series, trans. enl. and ed. Samuel Ralph Asbury (New York: Charles Scribner's Sons, 1870), 118.

[51]A. W. Steane, *The Book of the Prophet Jeremiah Together with the Lamentations* in the Cambridge Bible for Schools series (Cambridge: Cambridge University Press, 1881), 378.

[52]Ibid., 379.

[53]Ibid.

[54]R. Payne Smith, *"Lamentations"* in *Isaiah-Jeremiah-Lamentations* in The [Anglican] Bible Commentary series (New York: Charles Scribner's Sons, 1907), 595.

[55]Quoted in Naegelsbach, 143.

[56]M. D. Goulder, 293.

[57]Ibid.

[58]Gundry, 95. The Aramaic targum on Isaiah, however, retains the reference to the beard being plucked. For text of the entire targum, translated into English, see Bruce Chilton, *The Isaiah Targum: Introduction, Translation, Apparatus and Notes* (Wilmington, Del.: Michael Glazier, Inc., 1987). The Isaiah targum is dated to the early centuries A.D. (For a discussion of the dating, see pages xx–xxv of the aforementioned translation.)

[59]Commentaries that pass over the matter include: (1) Bruce C. Birch, *Singing the Lord's Song: Isaiah 40–55,* in the Abingdon Lay Bible Studies series (Nashville: Abingdon, 1981), 118; (2) Richard J. Clifford, *Fair Spoken and Persuading: An Interpretation of Second Isaiah* (New York: Paulist, 1984), 163–164; (3) W. Kay, "Isaiah," in *The Holy Bible...Commentary,* Vol. 5: *Isaiah-Jeremiah-Lamentations,* ed. F. C. Cook (New York: Charles Scribner's Sons, 1902), 259; (4) A. S. Herbert, *The Book of the Prophet Isaiah, Chapters 40–66* (Cambridge: Cambridge University Press, 1975), 96; (5) William Kelly, *An Exposition of the Book of Isaiah,* 4th ed. ([n.p.]: G. Morris, 1897; reprint, Minneapolis: Klock & Klock, 1979), 329; (6) Elmer A. Leslie, *Isaiah* (New York: Abingdon, 1963), 185; (7) Reuben Levy, *Deutero-Isaiah: A Commentary* (London: Oxford University Press, 1925), 238; (8) F. Duane Lindsey, *The Servant Songs: A Study in Isaiah* (Chicago: Moody Press, 1985), 87; (9) Christopher R. North, *The Second Isaiah: Introduction, Translation and Commentary to Chapters XL-LV* (Oxford: Clarendon, 1964), 203; (10) George L. Robinson, *The Book of Isaiah—in Fifteen Studies* (New York: Young Men's Christian Association, 1910), 144–45; (11) Steven Scherrer, *A Commentary on the Book of Isaiah: Isaiah as Sacred Scripture* (Maryknoll, N.Y.: St. Jerome Publications, 1993), 123; (12) John Scullion, *Isaiah 40–66* in the Old Testament Message series (Wilmington, Del.: Michael Glazier, Inc., 1982), 106; (13) Ulrich E. Simon, *A Theology of Salvation: A Commentary on Isaiah 40–55* (London: S.P.C.K., 1953), 173–74; (14) J. Skinner, *The Book of the Prophet Isaiah: Chapters XL–LXVI* in the Cambridge Bible for Schools and Colleges (Cambridge: Cambridge University Press, 1898; rev. 1917), 115; (15) James D. Smart,

History and Theology in Second Isaiah: A Commentary on Isaiah 35, 40–66 (Philadelphia: Westminster, 1965), 172; (16) W. E. Vine, *Isaiah: Prophecies, Promises, Warnings* (Grand Rapids: Zondervan, 1946; reprint, 1968), 152–53; (17) Claus Westermann, *Isaiah 40–66: A Commentary* in The Old Testament Library series (Philadelphia: Westminster, 1969), 230; (18) Owen C. Whitehouse, *Isaiah XL–LXVI* in the New Century Bible series (Oxford: Oxford University Press, [n.d.], 171.

[60]Albert Barnes, *Isaiah* reprint (Grand Rapids: Baker, 1950), 222.

[61]George A. F. Knight, *Deutero-Isaiah: A Theological Commentary on Isaiah 40–55* (New York: Abingdon, 1965), 202.

Bibliography

(The only books listed are those actually cited in notes or text)

Abrahams, I. *Studies in Pharisaism and the Gospels.* First Series. Cambridge: Cambridge University Press, 1917. Reprint, New York: KTAV, 1967.

Albright, W. F., and C. S. Mann. *Matthew.* Vol. 26, *Anchor Bible.* Garden City, N.Y.: Doubleday, 1971.

Alford, Walter. *The Old and New Testament Dispensations Compared.* London: Thomas Hatchard, 1858.

Audrey, Sister. *Jesus Christ in the Synoptic Gospels.* London: SCM Press Ltd., 1972.

Aulen, Gustaf. *Jesus in Contemporary Historical Research.* Translated by Ingalill H. Hjelm. Philadelphia: Fortress Press, 1976.

Balch, David L. "The Greek Political Topos...and Matthew 5:17, 19, and 16:19." In *Social History of the Matthean Community: Cross-Disciplinary Approaches,* edited by David L. Balch, 68–84. Minneapolis: Fortress Press, 1991.

Banks, Robert. *Jesus and the Law in the Synoptic Tradition.* Cambridge: Cambridge University Press, 1975.

Barclay, William. *The Gospel of Matthew.* Rev. ed. Vol. 1, *Daily Study Bible Series.* Philadelphia: Westminster Press, 1975.

Barnes, Albert. *Isaiah.* Reprint: Grand Rapids: Baker Book House, 1950.

Barton, George A. *A Critical and Exegetical Commentary on the Book of Ecclesiastes.* International Critical Commentary. New York: Charles Scribner's Sons, 1908.

Barton, Stephen C. *The Spirituality of the Gospels.* London: SPCK, 1992.

Bassett, Jerry F. *Rethinking Marriage, Divorce & Remarriage.* Eugene, Ore.: Western Printers, 1991.

Betz, Hans D. *The Sermon on the Mount.* Minneapolis: Fortress Press, 1995.

Birch, Bruce C. *Singing the Lord's Song: Isaiah 40–55. Abingdon Lay Bible Studies.* Nashville: Abingdon Press, 1981.

Bishop, Eric F. F. *Jesus of Palestine: The Local Background to the Gospel Documents.* London: Lutterworth Press, 1955.

Black, Matthew. *An Aramaic Approach to the Gospels and Acts.* 3rd. ed. Oxford: Clarendon Press, 1967.

Bligh, John. *The Sermon on the Sermon on the Mount.* Slough, England: St. Paul Press, 1975.

Borg, Marcus J. *Conflict, Holiness & Politics in the Teachings of Jesus.* New York: Edwin Mellen Press, 1984.

Breen, A. E. *A Harmonized Exposition of the Four Gospels,* Vol. 2. Rev. ed. Rochester, N.Y.: John P. Smith Printing Company, 1908.

Broadus, John A. *Commentary on the Gospel of Matthew. American Commentary on the New Testament.* Philadelphia: American Baptist Publication Society, 1886.

Brooks, Stephenson H. *Matthew's Community: The Evidence of His Special Sayings Material.* Sheffield, England: JSOT Press, 1987.

Brown, Raymond E. *John.* Vol. 29, *Anchor Bible.* Garden City, N.Y.: Doubleday & Company, 1966.

Bruce, F. F. *The Hard Sayings of Jesus.* Downers Grove, Ill.: InterVarsity Press, 1983.

Brunner, Frederick D. *The Christbook: A Historical / Theological Commentary, Matthew 1–12.* Waco, Tex.: Word Books, 1987.

Burton, Ernest DeWitt, and Shailer Matthews. *The Life of Christ.* 5th ed. Chicago: University of Chicago Press, 1904.

Cagal, Timothy B. *Restoring the Diaspora: Discursive Structure and Purpose in the Epistle of James.* Atlanta, Ga.: Scholars Press, 1993.

Cartledge, Tony W. *Vows in the Hebrew Bible and the Ancient Near East.* Sheffield, England: JSOT Press, 1992.

Cate, Robert. *Old Testament Roots for New Testament Faith.* Nashville, Tenn.: Broadman Press, 1982.

Cedar, Paul A. *James, 1, 2, Peter, Jude.* In the *Communicator's Commentary.* Waco, Tex.: Word Books, 1984.

Charette, Blaine. *The Theme of Recompense in Matthew's Gospel.* Sheffield, England: JSOT Press, 1992.

Charlesworth, James, "Jesus, Early Jewish Literature, and Archaeology." In *Jesus' Jewishness: Exploring the Place of Jesus within Early Judaism,* edited by James Charlesworth, 177–98. New York: American Interfaith Institute/Crossroad Publishing Company, 1991.

Charlesworth, James, *Jesus within Judaism: New Light from Exciting Archaeological Discoveries.* New York: Doubleday, 1988.

Chilton, Bruce. "Forgiving at and Swearing by the Temple." In *Judaic Approaches to the Gospels,* edited by Bruce Chilton, 111–22. Atlanta, Ga.: Scholars Press, 1994.

Chilton, Bruce. *Profiles of a Rabbi: Synoptic Opportunities in Reading about Jesus.* Atlanta, Ga.: Scholars Press, 1989.

Chilton, Bruce D. *The Isaiah Targum: Introduction, Translation, Apparatus and Notes.* Wilmington, Del.: Michael Glazier, Inc., 1987.

Chilton, Bruce D. *A Galilean Rabbi and His Bible: Jesus' Use of the Interpreted Scripture of His Time.* Wilmington, Del.: Michael Glazier, Inc., 1984.

Chilton, Bruce, and J. I. H. McDonald. *Jesus and the Ethics of the Kingdom.* Grand Rapids: Eerdmans, 1987.

Clifford, Richard J. *Fair Spoken and Persuading: An Interpretation of Second Isaiah.* New York: Paulist Press, 1984.

Clines, David J. *Job 1–20. Word Biblical Commentary.* Dallas: Word Books, 1989.

Connick, C. Milo. *Jesus: The Man, the Mission, and the Message.* 2nd ed. Englewood Cliffs, N.J.: Prentice-Hall, 1974.

Cox, Edwin. *This Elusive Jesus.* London: Marshall's Educational, 1975.

Daglish, Edward R. *Jeremiah / Lamentations. Layman's Bible Book Commentary.* Nashville, Tenn.: Broadman Press, 1983.

Daniel-Rops, Henri. *Daily Life in the Time of Jesus.* Translated by Patrick O'Brian. New York: Hawthorn Books, 1962; paperback edition, N.Y.: American Library, 1964.

Daube, David. *The New Testament and Rabbinic Judaism.* London: University of London/Athlone Press, 1956.

Davids, Peter H. *The Epistle of James: A Commentary on the Greek Text. New International Greek Testament Commentary.* Grand Rapids: Eerdmans, 1982.

Davidson, A. B. *Book of Job. Cambridge Bible for Schools and Colleges.* Cambridge: Cambridge University Press, 1891.

Davidson, Robert. *Jeremiah and Lamentations. Daily Study Bible.* Philadelphia: Westminster Press, 1985.

Davies, Margaret. *Matthew.* Sheffield, England: JSOT Press/Sheffield Academic Press, Ltd., 1993.

Davies, W. D. *The Setting of the Sermon on the Mount.* Cambridge: University of Cambridge Press, 1964; reprint, Atlanta, Ga.: Scholars Press, 1989.

Delitzsch, E. *Biblical Commentary on the Book of Job.* Rev. ed. Translated from the German by Francis Bolton. Edinburgh: T. & T. Clark, 1881.

Delitzsch, Franz. *Commentary on the Song of Songs and Ecclesiastes.* Translated from the German by M. G. Easton. Edinburgh: T. & T. Clark, 1877.

Derrett, J. Duncan. *Law in the New Testament.* London: Darton, Longman & Todd, 1970.

Dhorme, E. *Commentary on the Book of Job.* Translated from the French by Harold Knight. New York: Nelson, 1967.

Dibelius, Martin. *James.* In the *Heremenia—A Critical and*

Historical Commentary on the Bible. Revised by Heinrich Greeven. Translated by Helmut Koester. Philadelphia: Fortress Press, 1976.

Drane, John. *Son of Man: A New Life of Christ.* Grand Rapids: Eerdmans, 1993.

Du Plessis, Paul Johannes. *Teleios: The Idea of Perfection in the New Testament.* South Africa: Litgave J. H. Kov N. V. Kampen, 1979.

Eaton, Michael. *Ecclesiastes: An Introduction and Commentary. Tyndale Old Testament Commentary.* Downer's Grove, Ill.: InterVarsity Press, 1983.

Fitzmyer, Joseph A. *A Christological Catechism: New Testament Answers.* Rev. ed. New York: Paulist Press, 1991.

Fitzmyer, Joseph A. *Luke.* Vol. 28, *Anchor Bible.* Garden City, N.Y.: Doubleday, 1981.

Fitzmyer, Joseph A. "The Languages of Palestine in the First Century A.D." In *A Wandering Aramean: Collected Aramaic Essays,* 29–56. Missoula, Mont.: Scholars Press, 1979.

Fitzmyer, Joseph A. "The Study of the Aramaic Background of the New Testament." *A Wandering Aramean: Collected Aramaic Essays,* 1–28. Missoula, Mont.: Scholars Press, 1979.

France, R. T. *Divine Government: God's Kingship in the Gospel of Mark.* London: SPCK, 1990.

France, R. T. *Matthew: Evangelist and Teacher.* Grand Rapids: Academie Books/Zondervan, 1989.

Freyne, Sean. *Galilee, Jesus and the Gospels: Literary Approaches and Historical Investigations.* Philadelphia: Fortress Press, 1988.

Fujita, Neil S. *A Crack in the Jar: What Ancient Jewish Documents Tell Us About the New Testament.* New York: Paulist Press, 1986.

Gaebelein, A. C. *Proverbs-Ezekiel. Annotated Bible.* New York: Publication Office "Our Hope," 1921.

Gardner, Richard B. *Matthew.* Scottdale, Pa.: Herald Press, 1991.

Gibson, Edgar C. S. *Book of Job. Westminster Commentaries.* Rev. ed. London: Methuen & Company, 1905.

Ginsburg, Christian D. *Coheleth Commonly Called the Book of Ecclesiastes.* London: Longman, Green, Longman, and Roberts, 1861.

Gottwald, Norman K. *Studies in the Book of Lamentations.* London: SCM Press, 1954.

Goulder, M. D. *Midrash and Lection in Matthew.* London: SPCK, 1974.

Green, Michael. *Matthew for Today: Expository Study of Matthew.* Dallas: Word Publishing, 1988.

Guelich, Robert A. *The Sermon on the Mount: A Foundation for Understanding.* Waco, Tex.: Word Books, 1982.

Gundry, Robert H. *Matthew: A Commentary on His Handbook for a Mixed Church Under Persecution.* 2nd ed. Grand Rapids: Eerdmans, 1994.

Habel, Norman A. *The Book of Job: A Commentary.* Philadelphia: Westminster Press, 1985.

Habel, Norman C. *Jeremiah / Lamentations. Concordia Commentary.* St. Louis, Mo: Concordia Publishing House, 1968.

Hagner, Donald A. *The Jewish Reclamation of Jesus.* Grand Rapids: Academie Books/Zondervan, 1984.

Hargeaves, John. *Guide to St. Mark's Gospel.* Rev. ed. London: SPCK, 1995.

Harrington, Daniel J. *God's People in Christ: New Testament Perspectives on the Church and Judaism.* Philadelphia: Fortress Press, 1980.

Harrington, Daniel J. *The Gospel of Matthew.* Collegeville, Min.: A Michael Glazier Book/Liturgical Press, 1991.

Harrington, Daniel J. "The Jewishness of Jesus: Facing Some Problems." In *Jesus' Jewishness: Exploring the Place of Jesus within Early Judaism,* edited by James H. Charlesworth, 123–52. New York: American Interfaith Institute, 1991.

Harrington, Wilfrid. *Mark. New Testament Message: A Biblical-Theological Commentary.* Wilmington, Del.: Michael Glazier, Inc., 1979.

Harrison, R. K. *Jeremiah and Lamentations: An Introduction and Commentary. New International Commentary on the Old Testament.* Grand Rapids: Eerdmans, 1988.

Hartley, John E. *Book of Job. New International Commentary on the Old Testament.* Grand Rapids: Eerdmans, 1988.

Harvey, A. E. *Strenuous Commands: The Ethic of Jesus.* London: SCM Press/Philadelphia: Trinity Press International, 1990.

Herbert, A. S. *The Book of the Prophet Isaiah, Chapters 40–66.* Cambridge: Cambridge University Press, 1975.

Hilton, Michael with Gordian Marshall. *The Gospels & Rabbinic Judaism: A Study Guide.* Hoboken, N.J.: KTAV Publishing House, 1988.

Hobbs, Herschel H. *An Exposition of the Gospel of Matthew.* Grand Rapids: Baker Book House, 1965.

Hooker, Morna D. *The Gospel According to St. Mark. Black's New Testament Commentaries.* London: A & C Black, 1991.

Horsley, Richard A. "Ethics and Exegesis: 'Love Your Enemies' and the Doctrine of Nonviolence." In *The Love of Enemy and Nonretaliation in the New Testament,* edited by Willard M. Swartley, 72–101. Louiville, Ky: Westminster/John Knox Press, 1992.

Howley, H. H. *Job. New Century Bible Commentary.* Greenwood, S.C.: Attic Press, 1976.

Hunter, Archibald M. *A Pattern for Life: An Exposition of the Sermon on the Mount.* Rev. ed. Philadelphia: Westminster Press, 1965.

Johnson, Luke T. *The Gospel of Luke. Sacra Pagina.* Collegeville, Minn.: A Michael Glazier Book/Liturgical Press, 1991.

Jonsson, Jakob. *Humour and Irony in the New Testament.* Leiden: E. J. Brill, 1985.

Kay, W. "Isaiah." In *The Holy Bible...Commentary, Volume V: Isaiah-Jeremiah-Lamentations,* edited by F. C. Cook. New York: Charles Scribner's Sons, 1902.

Kaylor, R. David. *Jesus the Prophet: His Vision of the King-*

dom on Earth. Louisville, Ky.: Westminster/John Knox Press, 1994.

Kealy, Sean P. *Jesus and Politics*. Collegeville, Minn.: The Liturgical Press/A Michael Glazier Book, 1990.

Kelly, William. *An Exposition of the Book of Isaiah*. 4th ed. G. Morrish, 1871; reprint, Minneapolis: Klock & Klock, 1979.

Kilgallen, John J. *A Brief Commentary on the Gospel of Mark*. New York: Paulist Press, 1989.

Kistemaker, Simon J. *Exposition of the Epistle of James and the Epistles of John. New Testament Commentary*. Grand Rapids: Baker Book House, 1986.

Klausner, Joseph. *Jesus of Nazareth: His Life, Times, and Teaching*. Translated from the Hebrew by Herbert Danby. New York: Macmillan Company, 1924; reprint, 1945.

Knight, George A. F. *Deutero-Isaiah: A Theological Commentary on Isaiah 40-55*. New York: Abingdon Press, 1965.

Kugelman, Richard. *James & Jude. New Testament Message: A Biblical-Theological Commentary*. Wilmington, Del.: Michael Glazier, Inc., 1980.

Lachs, Samuel T. *A Rabbinic Commentary on the New Testament: The Gospels of Matthew, Mark, and Luke*. Hoboken, N.J.: KTAV Publishing House, Inc./New York: Anti-Defamation League of B'nai B'rith, 1987.

Lamsa, George M. *Gospel Light: Comments on the Teachings of Jesus from Aramaic and Unchanged Eastern Customs*. Philadelphia: A. J. Holman Company, 1939; reprint, 1985 (one-volume edition).

Lamsa, George M. *Idioms in the Bible Explained and a Key to the Original Gospels*. San Francisco: Harper & Row, 1931.

Lapide, Pinchas. *The Sermon on the Mount: Utopia or Program for Action*. Translated from the German by Arlene Swidler. Maryknoll, N.Y.: Orbis Books, 1986.

Laws, Sophie. *A Commentary on the Epistle of James. Harper's New Testament Commentaries*. San Francisco: Harper & Row, 1980.

Lee, Bernard J. *The Galilean Jewishness of Jesus: Retrieving the Jewish Origins of Christianity.* New York: A Stimulus Book/Paulist Press, 1983.

Leslie, Elmer A. *Isaiah.* New York: Abingdon Press, 1963.

Levine, Etan. *The Aramaic Version of the Bible: Contents and Context.* Berlin: Walter de Gruyter, 1983.

Levy, Reuben. *Deutero-Isaiah: A Commentary.* London: Oxford University Press, 1925.

Lieberman, Saul. *Greek in Jewish Palestine: Studies in the Life and Manners of Jewish Palestine in the II–IV Centuries C.E.* New York: Jewish Theological Seminary of America, 1942.

Lindsey, F. Duane. *The Servant Songs: A Study in Isaiah.* Chicago: Moody Press, 1985.

Lunny, William J. *The Jesus Option.* New York: Paulist Press, 1994.

Luz, Ulrich. *Matthew in History: Interpretation, Influence, and Effects.* Minneapolis: Fortress Press, 1994.

Luz, Ulrich. *Matthew 1-7: A Commentary.* Translated by Wilhelm C. Linss. Minneapolis: Augsburg, 1989.

Mackintosh, Robert. *Christ and the Jewish Law.* London: Hodder and Stoughton, 1886.

Manson, T. W. "The Sayings of Jesus." In *The Mission and Message of Jesus: An Exposition of the Gospels in the Light of Modern Research,* edited by H. D. A. Major, T. W. Manson, and C. J. Wright. London: Macmillan and Company, 1937.

Marriott, Horace. *The Sermon on the Mount.* London: Society for Promoting Christian Knowledge, 1925.

Marrow, Stanley B. *The Words of Jesus in Our Gospels: A Catholic Response to Fundamentalism.* New York: Paulist Press, 1979.

Marsh, John. *Jesus in His Lifetime.* London: Sidgwick & Jackson, 1981.

Martin, Ralph P. *James. Word Biblical Commentary.* Waco, Tex.: Word Books, 1988.

Matura, Thaddee. *Gospel Radicalism: The Hard Sayings of*

Jesus. Translated from the French by Maggi Despot and Paul Lachance. Maryknoll, N.Y.: Orbis Books, 1984.

McNamara, Martin. *Palestinian Judaism and the New Testament.* Wilmington, Del.: Michael Glazier, Inc., 1983.

McNamara, Martin. *Targum and Testament: Aramaic Paraphrases of the Hebrew Bible—A Light on the New Testament.* Grand Rapids: Eerdmans, 1972.

McNeile, Alan Hugh. *The Gospel According to St. Matthew.* London: Macmillan, 1915, 1952.

Meeks, Wayne A. "Breaking Away: Three New Testament Pictures of Christianity's Separation from the Jewish Communities." In *Essential Papers on Judaism and Christianity in Conflict: From Late Antiquity to the Reformation,* edited by Jeremy Cohen, 89–113. New York: New York University Press, 1991.

Meier, John P. *The Vision of Matthew: Christ, Church and Morality in the First Gospel.* New York: Paulist Press, 1979.

Meier, John P. *Law and History in Matthew's Gospel.* Rome: Biblical Institute Press, 1976.

Meier, John P. *Matthew.* Vol. 3, *The New Testament Message Commentary.* Collegeville, Minn.: A Michael Glazier Book/Liturgical Press, 1990.

Meier, John P. "Reflections on Jesus-of-History Research Today." In *Jesus' Jewishness: Exploring the Place of Jesus within Early Judaism,* edited by James H. Charlesworth, 84–107. New York: American Interfaith Institute/Crossroad Publishing Company, 1991.

Menninger, Richard E. *Israel and the Church in the Gospel of Matthew.* New York: Peter Lang, 1994.

Merkel, Helmut, "The Opposition between Jesus and Judaism." In *Jesus and the Politics of His Day,* edited by Ernst Bammel and C. F. D. Moule, 129-144. Cambridge: Cambridge University Press, 1984.

Milton, G. Leslie. *The Epistle of James.* London: Marshall, Morgan & Scott, 1966.

Moffatt, James. *The General Epistles James, Peter, and*

Judas. Moffatt New Testament Commentary. New York: Harper and Brothers, 1962.

Moloney, Francis J. *The Living Voice of the Gospel: The Gospels Today.* New York: Paulist Press, 1986.

Montefiore, C. G. *Rabbinic Literature and Gospel Teachings.* London: Macmillan, 1930.

Murphy, Frederick J. *The Religious World of Jesus: An Introduction to Second Temple Palestinian Judaism.* Nashville: Abingdon Press, 1991.

Myers, Ched. *Binding the Strong Man: A Political Reading of Mark's Story of Jesus.* Maryknoll, N.Y.: Orbis Books, 1988.

Naegelsbach, C. W. Eduard. *The Book of Lamentations. Lange Commentary.* Translated, enlarged, and edited by Samuel Ralph Asbury. New York: Charles Scribner and Company, 1870.

Neumann, Frederick. *The Binding Truth: A Selective Homilectical Commentary on the New Testament; Vol. 1: The Proper Self-Concern: The Gospel According to Matthew.* Allison Park, Pa.: Pickwick Publications, 1983.

Neusner, Jacob. *The Pharisees: Rabbinic Perspectives.* Leiden: E. J. Brill, 1973; reprint, Hoboken, N.J.: KTAV, 1985.

Newman, Barclay W., and Philip C. Stine. *A Handbook on the Gospel of Matthew.* New York: United Bible Societies, 1992.

North, Christopher R. *The Second Isaiah: Introduction, Translation and Commentary to Chapter XL–LV.* Oxford: Clarendon Press, 1964.

Nowell-Roston, S. *The Challenge of Calamity: A Study in the Book of Job.* London: T-T-S/Lutterworth Press, 1939.

Obach, Robert E., and Albert Kirk. *A Commentary on the Gospel of Matthew.* New York: Paulist Press, 1978.

Patte, Daniel. *The Gospel According to Matthew: A Structural Commentary on Matthew's Faith.* Philadelphia: Fortress Press, 1987.

Pentecost, J. Dwight. *The Words and Works of Jesus Christ: A Study of the Life of Christ.* Grand Rapids: Zondervan, 1981.

Piper, John. *"Love Your Enemies:" Jesus' Love Command in*

the Synoptic Gospels and in the Early Christian Paraenesis. Cambridge: Cambridge University Press, 1979.

Plumptre, E. H. *Ecclesiastes. Cambridge Bible for Schools and Colleges.* Cambridge: Cambridge University Press, 1890.

Plumptre, E. H. *The General Epistle of St. James. Cambridge Bible for Schools and Colleges.* Cambridge: Cambridge University Press, 1878; 1895 printing.

Powell, J. Enoch. *The Evolution of the Gospel: A New Translation of the First Gospel with Commentary and Introductory Essay.* New Haven: Yale University Press, 1994.

Provan, Iaian. *Lamentations. New Century Bible Commentary.* Grand Rapids: Eerdmans, 1991.

Rauschenbusch, Walter. *The Social Principles of Jesus.* New York: Association Press, 1911; 1919 printing.

Reichert, Victor E. *Job: With Hebrew Text and English Translation.* Hindhead, Surrey: Soncino Press, 1946.

Reimarus, Hermann Samuel. *The Goal of Jesus and His Disciples.* Translated by George W. Buchanan. Leiden: E. J. Brill, 1970.

Rendall, Gerald H. *The Epistle of St. James and Judaic Christianity.* Cambridge: Cambridge University Press, 1927.

Ridderbos, H. N. *Matthew. Bible Student's Commentary.* Translated from the Dutch by Ray Togtman. Grand Rapids: Regency Reference Library/Zondervan, 1987.

Robertson, A. T. *Practical and Social Aspects of Christianity: The Wisdom of James.* New York: George H. Doran Company, 1915.

Robinson, George L. *The Book of Isaiah—in Fifteen Studies.* New York: Young Men's Christian Association Press, 1910.

Roetzel, Calvin J. *The World That Shaped the New Testament.* Atlanta: John Knox Press, 1985.

Rowley, H. H. *Job. New Century Bible Commentary.* Greenwood, S.C.: Attic Press, 1976.

Saldarini, Anthony J. "The Gospel of Matthew and Jewish-Christian Conflict." In *Social History of the Matthean Community: Cross-Disciplinary Approaches,* edited by David L. Balch, 38–61. Minneapolis: Fortress Press, 1991.

Sanders, E. P. *Jesus and Judaism.* Philadelphia: Fortress Press, 1985.

Sanders, E. P. *Judaism: Practice & Belief, 66 BCE–66 CE.* London: SCM Press, 1992.

Sanders, E. P. *The Historical Figure of Jesus.* London: Allen Lane/Penguin Press, 1993.

Sanders, Jack T. *Schismatics, Sectarians, Dissidents, Deviants: The First One Hundred Years of Jewish-Christian Relations.* Valley Forge, Pa.: Trinity Press International, 1993.

Scherrer, Steven. *A Commentary on the Book of Isaiah: Isaiah as Sacred Scripture.* Maryknoll, N.Y.: St. Jerome Publications, 1993.

Schweizer, Eduard. *Jesus.* Translated by David E. Green. Richmond, Va.: John Knox Press, 1971.

Scullion, John. *Isaiah 40–66. Old Testament Message.* Wilmington, Del.: Michael Glazier, Inc., 1982.

Segal, Alan F. "Matthew's Jewish Voice." In *Social History of the Matthean Community: Cross-Disciplinary Approaches,* edited by David L. Balch, 3–37. Minneapolis: Fortress Press, 1991.

Senior, Donald. *Jesus: A Gospel Portrait.* Rev. ed. New York: Paulist Press, 1992.

Simon, Ulrich E. *A Theology of Salvation: A Commentary on Isaiah 40–55.* London: SPCK, 1953.

Skinner, J. *The Book of the Prophet Isaiah, Chapters XL–LXVI. Cambridge Bible for Schools and Colleges.* Cambridge: Cambridge University Press, 1898; revised, 1917.

Smart, James D. *History and Theology in Second Isaiah: A Commentary on Isaiah 35, 40–66.* Philadelphia: Westminster Press, 1965.

Smith, R. Gregor. "Perfect." In *A Theological Word Book of the Bible,* edited by Alan Richardson. New York: Macmillan Company, 1950; 1964 reprint.

Smith, R. Rayne. "Lamentations." In *Isaiah-Jeremiah-Lamentations. The* [Anglican] *Bible Commentary.* New York: Charles Scribner's Sons, 1907.

Steane, A. W. *The Book of the Prophet Jeremiah Together with the Lamentations. Cambridge Bible for Schools.* Cambridge: Cambridge University Press, 1881.

Stier, Rudolf. *The Words of the Lord Jesus,.* Vol. 1. 4th American ed. Translated by William B. Pope and revised by James Strong and Henry B. Smith. New York: N. Tibbals & Son, 1864.

Stock, Augustine. *The Method and Message of Matthew.* Collegeville, Minn.: A Michael Glazier Book/Liturgical Press, 1994.

Stott, John R. W. *Christian Counter-Culture: The Message of the Sermon on the Mount.* Downers Grove, Ill.: InterVarsity Press, 1978.

Strecker, Georg. *The Sermon on the Mount: An Exegetical Commentary.* Translated from the German by O. C. Dean, Jr. Nashville, Tenn.: Abingdon Press, 1988.

Stuart, Moses. *Commentary on Ecclesiastes.* Edited and revised by R. D. C. Robbins. Boston: Draper and Halliday, 1862; 1880 printing.

Syreeni, Kari. *The Making of the Sermon on the Mount: A Procedural Analysis of Matthew's Redactoral Activity. Part I: Methodology & Compositional Analysis.* Helsinki: Suomalainen Tiedeakatemia, 1987.

Tasker, R. V. G. *The General Epistle of James: An Introduction and Commentary. Tyndale New Testament Commentaries.* London: Tyndale Press, 1956.

Tholuck, D. *Commentary on the Sermon on the Mount.* 4th ed. Translated by R. Lundin Brown. Philadelphia: Smith, English, and Company, 1860.

Thompson, William G. *Matthew's Story: Good News for Uncertain Times.* New York: Paulist Press, 1989.

Vaught, Carl G. *The Sermon on the Mount: A Theological Interpretation.* Albany, N.Y.: State University of New York Press, 1986.

Vermes, Geza. *Jesus and the World of Judaism.* Philadelphia: Fortress Press, 1983.

Vermes, Geza. *The Religion of Jesus the Jew.* Minneapolis: Fortress Press, 1993.

Vine, W. E. *Expository Dictionary of New Testament Words.* Original one-volume edition, London: Oliphant, 1953; U.S. reprint.

Vine, W. E. *Isaiah: Prophecies, Promises, Warnings.* Grand Rapids: Zondervan, 1946; reprint, 1968.

Vos, Howard F. *Mark: A Study Guide Commentary.* Grand Rapids: Zondervan, 1978.

Wardlaw, Ralph. *Lectures: Expository and Practical on the Book of Ecclesiastes.* Philadelphia: Wm. S. Rentoul, 1868.

Weaver, Dorothy Jean. "Transforming Nonresistance: From *Lex Talionis* to 'Do Not Resist the Evil One.'" In *The Love of Enemy and Nonretaliation in the New Testament,* edited by Willard M. Swartley, 32–71. Louisville, Ky: Westminster/ John Knox Press, 1992.

Wells, G. A. *The Historical Evidence for Jesus.* Buffalo, N.Y.: Prometheus Books, 1982.

Wenham, J. W. *Christ and the Bible.* London: Tyndale Press, 1972.

Westermann, Claus. *Isaiah 40–66: A Commentary. The Old Testament Library.* Philadelphia: Westminster Press, 1969.

Westerholm, Stephen. *Jesus and Scribal Authority.* Coniectanea Biblica: New Testament Series Number 10. Doctoral Thesis at Lund University. GWK Gleerup, 1978.

Whitehouse, Owen C. *Isaiah, XL–LXVI. New Century Bible.* Oxford: Oxford University Press, [n. d.].

Whybray, R. N. *Ecclesiastes. New Century Bible Commentary.* Grand Rapids: Eerdmans, 1989.

Wilcox, Max. "The Aramaic Background of the New Testament." In *The Aramaic Bible: Targums in Their Historical Context,* edited by D. R. G. Beattie and M. J. McNamara, 362–378. Sheffield, England: JSOT Press, 1994.

Williams, A. Lukyn. *Ecclesiastes. Cambridge Bible for Schools and Colleges.* Cambridge: Cambridge University Press, 1922.

Wink, Walter. "Neither Passivity Nor Violence: Jesus' Third

Way (Matthew 5:38–42)." In *The Love of Enemy and Nonretaliation in the New Testament,* edited by Willard M. Swartley, 102–25. Louisville, Ky: Westminster/John Knox Press, 1992.

Winter, David. *The Search for the Real Jesus.* Wilton, Conn.: Morehouse-Barlow, 1982.

Witherington, Ben, III. *The Christology of Jesus.* Minneapolis: Fortress Press, 1990.

Wright, Charles H. *The Book of Koheleth.* London: Holder and Stoughton, 1853.

Zeitlin, Irving M. *Jesus and the Judaism of His Time.* Cambridge, England: Polity Press/New York: Basil Blackwell, Inc., 1988.

Zimmermann, Frank. *The Aramaic Origin of the Four Gospels.* New York: KTAV, 1979.

Zockler, Otto. *Ecclesiastes or Koheleth.* Translated by William Wells. New York: Charles Scribner & Co., 1870.

Zodhiates, Spiros. *The Patience of Hope: An Exposition of James 4:13–5:20.* Chattanooga, Tenn.: AMG Publishers, 1981; 1985 printing.

Index

Footnotes are cited when including a discussion of matter related to interpreting the nature and meaning of the Sermon on the Mount.